YOU NEVER FORGET YOUR FIRST

✷ YOU ✷
Never Forget
YOUR
FIRST

A Biography of
GEORGE
WASHINGTON

Alexis Coe

VIKING

VIKING

An imprint of Penguin Random House LLC

penguinrandomhouse.com

ISBN 9780735224100 (hardcover)

ISBN 9780735224124 (ebook)

Printed in the United States of America

1   3   5   7   9   10   8   6   4   2

Book design and manicule illustrations by Daniel Lagin

For Anthony, the only man for the job

Contents

"The greatest man on earth."

—JOHN MARSHALL,
CHIEF JUSTICE OF THE SUPREME COURT (1784)

"All the land knew him and loved him for gallantry
and brave capacity; he carried himself like a prince."

—WOODROW WILSON,
28TH PRESIDENT OF THE UNITED STATES,
GEORGE WASHINGTON (1896)

"I heard that motherfucker had like thirty goddamn dicks."

—BRAD NEELY,
COMIC BOOK ARTIST, YOUTUBE VIDEO (2009)

"Next to Washington, they all look small."

—KING GEORGE
IN LIN-MANUEL MIRANDA'S *HAMILTON* (2015)

GEORGE WASHINGTON
AT A GLANCE

(1732–1799)

JOBS

- Surveyor
- Virginia militia colonel (British Army)
- Member of the Virginia House of Burgesses
- Gentleman farmer
- Commander in chief of the Continental Army
- President of the Constitutional Convention
- First president of the United States
- Land developer

TITLES

- Master
- His Excellency
- General
- Mr. President

GREATEST HITS

- Raised, trained, and led a militia against the greatest superpower in the world
- Refused payment for leading the army
- Gave up power after winning the American Revolution
- First president, and set precedents by adding hallmarks that weren't in the Constitution, like a cabinet and term limits
- Declined to run for a third term
- Paved a road to freedom for his slaves in his will

PETTIEST ACTS

- Took two impoverished girls to court for stealing from his clothes while he swam
- Named a dog Cornwallis after the British general he defeated in the Revolutionary War

RELIGION

- ❂ "Warm Deist"
- ❂ Believed in an afterlife
- ❂ Christian (liberal Anglican/ Episcopalian)
- ❂ Attended services of many denominations
- ❂ Supported freedom of conscience, including for non-Christians
- ❂ Corresponded with leaders and practitioners of various denominations, from Jews to Quakers

FATHER OF

- ❂ No one (biologically)
- ❂ The United States of America
- ❂ Two stepchildren
- ❂ Two step-grandchildren
- ❂ The American Foxhound

LIKES

- ❂ The circus
- ❂ Being home
- ❂ Dancing
- ❂ Dogs
- ❂ Donkeys
- ❂ Mules
- ❂ Exotic animals
- ❂ Fishing
- ❂ Horseback riding
- ❂ Horticulture
- ❂ Hunting
- ❂ Reading books and newspapers
- ❂ Theater

DISLIKES

- ❂ Idle chatter
- ❂ Sitting for portraits
- ❂ Inherited titles
- ❂ Wasted opportunity
- ❂ Procrastination
- ❂ Slapstick humor
- ❂ Political parties

CLOSEST FRIENDS
- John Augustine Washington
- George William Fairfax
- Dr. James Craik
- Martha Washington
- Tobias Lear
- Marquis de Lafayette
- Elizabeth Powel

FRENEMIES
- Thomas Jefferson
- James Madison
- James Monroe
- Edmund Randolph
- Thomas Paine

GREATEST ADVERSARIES
- King George III of England
- Charles Lee
- Horatio Gates
- Thomas Conway

INNOVATED/IMPROVED
- A sixteen-sided barn
- Crop rotation
- North American animals and husbandry

FAVORITE FOOD & DRINK
- Hoecakes swimming in butter and honey
- Any kind of fish
- Tea
- Hot chocolate
- Madeira

FAVORITE WRITERS
- William Shakespeare
- Joseph Addison
- Humphrey Bland
- Henry Fielding
- Tobias Smollett
- Jethro Tull
- Arthur Young

LIES WE BELIEVE ABOUT THE MAN
WHO COULD NOT TELL THEM

	LIE	TRUTH
1	He was an unparalleled military leader.	He lost more battles than he won. See Part II.
2	He had wooden teeth.	It was a lot worse, as you'll see in the Preface.
3	He grew weed.	He grew hemp, which was used for making rope, sail canvas, and thread for clothing, not getting high.
4	He wore a wig.	That would have been a lot easier. He had his hair gathered, fluffed, curled, and, before his reddish-brown hair turned gray, powdered white.
5	He kneeled to pray at Valley Forge.	One of Parson Weems's many tall tales. See the Preface.
6	He skipped a silver dollar all the way across the Potomac River.	Impossible! It's a mile wide.
7	He was a Republican.	He was a Federalist, but so disliked political parties that he did not publicize it.
8	He was the first president to live in the White House.	Washington helped choose the site of the White House, but John Adams was the first president to live there.
9	He's buried beneath the U.S. Capitol.	He's buried at Mount Vernon, his Virginia plantation.
10	He could not tell a lie.	He could, and did—especially during the Revolution in order to mislead the British.

DISEASES SURVIVED

T HE GREATEST THREATS TO WASHINGTON'S LIFE WERE ARMED men and deadly diseases. In the eighteenth century, physicians and healers knew almost nothing about sources of contagion or effective treatments for illness or infection, and they subjected their patients to "remedies" that strike us today as either bogus or barbaric. Even the mildest of diseases could prove fatal, yet Washington managed to survive them time and again. He outlived all the men in his family (many of whom were likely felled by tuberculosis) and was often one of the last ones standing after any outbreak.

AGE	DISEASE	SYMPTOMS	TREATMENTS
15	Black canker (diphtheria)	Chills, fever, bluish skin, foul-smelling discharge, difficulty breathing, and gray coating on the throat	Prayer
17, 21, 30, 39, 52, 66	River fever (malaria)	Fever, sweating, vomiting, diarrhea, bloody stool, and rectal abscesses	Diluted barley water, flax tea, watery gruel; "The Waters," which he obtained after a difficult trip to Warm Springs, Virginia; calomel, an all-purpose purgative made of mercury chlorine (long-term effects included inflammation of the gums and loosening of the teeth); bloodletting to "evacuate the poisonous matter;" Peruvian bark and a cathartic (laxative)

AGE	DISEASE	SYMPTOMS	TREATMENTS
19	Smallpox	Raging fever, unquenchable thirst, excruciating headache and backache, red sores, rash, pustules, and scabs (which left pockmarks and permanent scars on his face)	Cold compresses, laudanum (opium), ointment
19, 35	Consumption (tuberculosis)	According to Washington, a "violent pleurise which has reduced me very low"	Ipecac (an emetic to cause vomiting), rest, and fresh air
23, 33, 35, 39	Bloody flux (dysentery) and consumption	The usual symptoms of each, but the combined effect was so severe that doctors and family feared he would not survive.	Ipecac, bloodletting
44	Cheek erosion from gum abscess	Exactly what it sounds like.	Draining
47	Quinsy (tonsillitis)	Fever, throat pain	Draining
57, 59	Carbuncle	Red, swollen, painful boils under the skin	Draining
58	Pneumonia	Fever, swelling, nausea, vomiting	Bloodletting
67	Epiglottitis (fatal)	Swelling of the throat, fever, difficulty swallowing and breathing	Bloodletting

ALL THE PRESIDENT'S ANIMALS

SWEETLIPS. MADAME MOOSE. TRUE LOVE. FOR A MAN KNOWN FOR his serious (if not grave) disposition, George Washington gave his dogs fairly ridiculous names. But they were just one of many types of animals at Mount Vernon that entertained and fed the family.

BEES

In 1787, Washington noted that three hundred nails were given to indentured English joiner Matthew Baldridge to "make a bee house." The bees were likely an attempt to support his considerable honey habit; he liked his morning hoecakes swimming in it.

BISON

Washington spent years trying to get bison. "I am very anxious to raise a Breed of them," he wrote to his overseer in 1775. He'd seen them on the frontier and asked around, but they weren't common. He finally succeeded in acquiring them later in life, but it's unclear how long the animals survived.

DOGS

Every morning, Washington visited his dogs in their kennel, which had a fresh spring running through it; every evening, he came back to say goodnight. He is known for developing the American Foxhound, which he loved to hunt with, but he also kept terriers, coach dogs, and Newfoundlands. They appear in letters and can be seen in the background of family portraits. In one missive from 1798, a former employee asks Washington to "inform your Lady that our little Slut died in the Straw," which the editors of his paper understand to be "one of a number of hints . . . that Mrs. Washington was particularly fond of dogs."[1]

CATS

The Washingtons were clearly dog people, but cat bones have been found in slave quarters at Mount Vernon, suggesting the animals were kept as pets, most likely for rodent control.

CATTLE

Washington had more than three hundred cattle branded with his initials. Oxen were used on the farms for plowing, and cows provided the family with meat, milk, butter, cheese, and cream.

FOWL	Washington raised chickens, geese, turkeys, and ducks, most of them after Martha and her children arrived at Mount Vernon. They provided eggs, feathers, and meat. Martha had several pet birds, and at least one parrot. Every December, the Washingtons ate turkey in their Yorkshire Christmas pie. There is also evidence that their slaves raised chickens and ducks and hunted wild turkeys.
HOGS	Washington's hogs ran wild, foraging for food until it came time for fattening; in November, Mount Vernon slaves would catch the hogs and pen them until the end of the year. After that, they were served up as bacon, chitterlings, ham, and salted pork.
HORSES	According to Thomas Jefferson, Washington was "the best horseman of the age and the most graceful." He began riding in his youth and continued throughout his time as a surveyor, soldier, farmer, general, and president. He rode two of his favorite horses, Nelson and Blueskin, during the Revolution, and his horse Prescott, who was described as "purely white, and sixteen hands high," during his presidency. Washington also raced horses, including an Arabian stallion named Mongolia.
MULES	The so-called Father of the American Mule began breeding mules— the offspring of a male donkey and a female horse—after he received a stud from the King of Spain in 1785. Within fifteen years, he had a herd of nearly sixty. They plowed fields and pulled wagons.
SHEEP	In the summer of 1794, Washington wrote to a friend in England: "After the Peace of Paris in 1783, and my return to the occupations of a farmer, I paid particular attention to my breed of Sheep (of which I usually kept about seven or eight hundred)."[2] American wool, he declared, was equal to anything found abroad. He bred his sheep in October, welcomed lambs in March, and sheared in May. It isn't clear which breed he raised at Mount Vernon, but he used them for more than wool; his archives tell us they provided manure for his five farms, lanolin for ointment, and meat for dinner.

Timeline

⭐

1732	On February 22, George Washington is born in Westmoreland County, Colony of Virginia, British America.
1739	Likely starts school, around the age of seven.
1743	Father dies. Washington, age eleven, inherits ten enslaved people.
1749	Appointed to his first public office as surveyor of Culpeper County at age seventeen.
1751–1752	Travels to Barbados, his only trip abroad, with half brother Lawrence.
1752	Lawrence dies, and his widow leases Mount Vernon to Washington.
1752–1758	Fights on behalf of the British in the French and Indian War, which he had unwittingly started.
1759	Retires from the military and becomes a gentleman farmer. On January 6, marries Martha Custis, widow of Daniel Parke Custis, and becomes stepfather to Jacky, age four, and Patsy, age two.
1761	Inherits Mount Vernon after Lawrence's widow dies.
1761–1776	Is a member of the Virginia House of Burgesses.
1773	Patsy, age seventeen, dies in Washington's arms.
1774–1775	Virginia delegate to the Continental Congress.
1775	Appointed commander in chief of the Continental Army in the American Revolution.
1783	Formally gives up military commission, much to the surprise of the world.
1787	Heads the Constitutional Convention.
1789	Unanimously elected the first U.S. president. Mary, his mother, dies.
1793	Unanimously reelected to second term as president.
1797	Refuses a third term, setting a two-term precedent. Retires to Mount Vernon.
1799	Dies on December 14 at Mount Vernon at the age of sixty-seven.

Preface

You Never Forget Your First—
But You Do Misremember Him

YEARS INTO WRITING THIS BOOK, I MOVED MY DESK AND REARranged my George Washington books by category, which is when I noticed something curious about my collection of popular biographies: All of them were authored by men.[1]

In the course of my research, I got used to a certain male skew (a lot more on that in the Introduction), but I hadn't realized quite how persistent it was. I thought that perhaps my small library—which did not include the out-of-print books or budget breakers I borrowed from the library—simply didn't represent an accurate sample. When digital sleuthing seemed to confirm the disparity, I dismissed that sample, too, this time for being too large. I wrote to a researcher at Mount Vernon, Washington's historic home, and asked her to confirm my findings, only to send her down the same path. She, in turn, consulted with an editor at the University of Virginia's George Washington papers, and on and on it went, all leading to the same conclusion: No woman has written an adult biography of George Washington in more than forty years, and no woman historian has written one in far longer. (His most recent female biographers, a journalist and a travel writer, contributed two books out of hundreds.[2])

For nearly two and a half centuries, most of the stories Americans have told themselves about their country's past have been about men, by men, for men. Women, like people of color, have typically been relegated to supporting roles. And so when women biographers and historians get a chance to correct the record, they tend to shift the focus away from the leading man, lingering instead on the forgotten people and understudied issues around him—which are actually integral to the understanding of him, too.

In 1997, for instance, Annette Gordon-Reed, a professor of law and history at Harvard, published *Thomas Jefferson and Sally Hemings: An American Controversy*, a groundbreaking investigation that includes a brilliant review of the people who denied that Jefferson fathered children with Hemings, whom he enslaved.[3] By highlighting their prejudices and inaccuracies, Gordon-Reed forever changed the way we talk about Jefferson. In 2017, Erica Dunbar, a professor of history at Rutgers, made a significant contribution to Washington studies with *Never Caught: The Washingtons' Relentless Pursuit of Their Runaway Slave, Ona Judge*. Dunbar brings Judge's courageous story to the forefront and forces us to reconsider Washington's much-lauded reputation as the only Founding Father to emancipate his slaves in his will. These kinds of books somehow manage to cover much of what can be found in the 900-page brick of a presidential biography on your dad's nightstand, only with far more nuance—and in far fewer pages.

In fact, women historians have often reminded us that we don't always know what we think we know. There's a lot more work to be done, and it's not limited to "women's history." We need to question and review *everything*—including presidential biographies—but there's an expectation that women will write books about women; people of color will write about people of color. I was constantly reminded of this when I was asked what I was working on.[4] The conversation often went like this:

"What's your book about?"
"George Washington."

"His marriage?"
"No."

"His wife?"
"No."

"His . . . social life?"
"No. It's a biography. Like a man would write."

The typical Washington biographer grew up on the East Coast, most often in Virginia. He began visiting Mount Vernon and Revolutionary War battlefields as a boy, and now, as a man, he does his research there, among others who look like him. I, on the other hand, grew up in California, which became a state fifty-one years after Washington died and almost eighty years after the American Revolution began. This means that I faintly recall learning about Washington in my textbooks, but was surrounded by the physical relics of another history—Spanish missions, the ghosts of the Gold Rush. I didn't even visit Mount Vernon until I was in graduate school, and I certainly didn't leave thinking, "One day, I'll write a book about George Washington!"

My preoccupation with Washington began years later, with an attempt to read between the lines of his major biographies—particularly Ron Chernow's *Washington: A Life*. At first, I found the male historians' fixation on his manliness entertaining, but the sheer repetition of their narratives needled me. They always presented Washington's half brother as his god, for example, and his mother as his scourge. I began to dig into the primary sources they cited and was, almost immediately, vexed by some of their interpretations and the opportunities they missed. They seemed bound to follow rote protocols, distancing us from a man we really ought to know better. And then we, in turn, end up inadvertently perpetuating so many stereotypes and exaggerations.

Consider, for instance, the old story about Washington's wooden teeth. If you actually think about it, it doesn't really make sense. Wood would be a *terrible* material for dentures. Moisture makes it swell and soften and split. Whatever bits of denture Washington didn't accidentally swallow would fall out of his mouth while he was, say, leading the Continental Army or quelling conflict between Alexander Hamilton and, well, nearly anyone. His breath, moreover, would have been legendarily bad—embarrassing fodder for the gossipy Founding Fathers.

So perhaps it's not surprising that there is not a single letter or diary entry substantiating the wooden teeth. Nor are there instructional materials on wooden-tooth making in early American medical literature, or anything to suggest that Washington was a dental innovator. The wooden teeth are a myth, plain and simple. Some of us accept it, perhaps instinctually, because we haven't been taught to think critically about Washington, our mysterious national father figure. Then again, maybe we'd simply prefer not to know the appalling truth.

There's no doubt that Washington had terrible teeth. He began pouring money into dentists, toothbrushes, medications, and cleaning solutions by the age of twenty-four, when he paid a "Doctr Watson" five shillings to pull a tooth. By the age of fifty-seven, the unanimously elected first president of the United States had but one tooth of his own left and had long been investing in dentures. If you examine the paintings Washington sat for, it's easy to see that each set had a different effect on his bite. (His changing jawline looks particularly awkward on the dollar bill, painted by Gilbert Stuart.) But the dentures' poor aesthetics paled in comparison to the physical discomfort they caused, "forc[ing] the lip out just under the nose." Washington complained throughout his letters and diaries, in which he frequently writes of aching teeth and inflamed gums.

Washington kept some of his dead teeth at Mount Vernon, in hopes they might be reused in dentures. "I am positive I left them there, or in the secret drawer in the locker of the same desk," he wrote to Lund Washington, the distant cousin whom he'd hired to plantation-sit during the Revolutionary War. But those teeth didn't get a second chance, for the same reason they didn't survive in his mouth the first time around. John Greenwood, a dentist he hired to fix his dentures, admonished Washington in one letter, writing that the teeth he had sent were "very black, occasioned either by your soaking them in port wine, or by your drinking it." (If he'd been better acquainted with Washington, he would have known that his patient's drink was Madeira, a fortified wine.) Greenwood would have to rely on other materials, none of which were wood.

At best, we can say that Washington had a poacher's smile. His dentists took chunks of ivory from hippopotamuses, walruses, and elephants, sculpted them down, and affixed them to dentures using brass screws. They filled in any gaps with teeth from less exotic animals, such as cows and horses, or—when the Madeira stains weren't too bad—from Washington himself. But he didn't always have to look quite so far afield. At the age of eleven, he inherited ten slaves from his father, and over the next fifty-six years, he would sometimes rely on them to supply replacement teeth. He paid his slaves for their teeth, but not at fair market value. From his ledger, recorded in his own hand, we see that he offered six pounds and two shillings for at least nine teeth—two-thirds less than Greenwood offered in newspaper advertisements.[5]

So how did we get from a mix of teeth from slaves and animals to wooden teeth? No one is quite sure, which has led me to wonder whether this myth is connected to another even more pervasive one. When Washington was young, the story goes, he got a little too excited about a new hatchet and hacked away at his father's beloved cherry tree. Upon being caught, he supposedly confessed on the spot, proclaiming, "I cannot tell a lie."

Washington's act of arborcide is another fabrication, but this time we know who is responsible for it: Mason L. Weems, a broke itinerant parson bookseller with impeccable timing.[6] Weems decided to write a biography a year before Washington died and promised Philadelphia printer Matthew Carey that *The Life of George Washington*, crammed with the apocryphal stories that we still tell today, would "sell like flax seed."

And Weems was right. Readers got the exclusive stories they hungered for, and they embellished them and passed them on. Slowly, Washington ceased to be a man and became the embodiment of the nation at its best, most noble and public-spirited. The outright fabrications may have stopped, but the mythmaking persists.

Introduction

The Thigh Men of Dad History

ALL OF THE FOUNDING FATHERS HAVE PROBLEMS. THOMAS JEF-
ferson strikes modern audiences as beyond hypocritical, John
Adams as tiresome, and James Madison as downright boring. But
according to Washington's own biographers, he's in real trouble.

Joseph Ellis calls him "the original marble man." Ron Chernow says
he is "composed of too much marble to be quite human." Harlow Giles
Unger says he's "as stonelike as the Mount Rushmore sculpture."[1] What
is to blame for Washington's inhuman stature? Well, for starters, his
renowned self-control.[2] "My countenance never yet betrayed my feelings," Washington once said. That was an exaggeration, but he was discreet enough to land himself, as Richard Brookhiser has lamented, in
"our wallets, but not our hearts." Every biographer humbly endeavors to
break Washington out of his sepulchre—by proceeding in almost the
exact same way as the one who came before him.[3]

First, his biographers stick a portrait of the man Ellis calls America's
"foundingest father" on the cover.[4] Many favor Washington's most iconic
image, his rigid and gloomy face on the one-dollar bill, but most prefer

a painting that shows his whole body, because his thighs drive them *wild*. Brookhiser, examining a portrait from 1792, can't help but notice how "well-developed" they are. Ellis admires how they "allowed him to grip a horse's flanks tightly and hold his seat in the saddle with uncommon ease." For Chernow, Washington's "muscular thighs" were just the beginning. He was a "superb physical specimen, with a magnificent physique . . . powerfully rough-hewn and endowed with matchless strength. When he clenched his jaw, his cheek and jaw muscles seemed to ripple right through his skin."[5]

They pair that visual coffin of a cover with a verbal coffin of a title, often adhering to the same stale format. *George Washington: A Biography. George Washington: A Life. George Washington: A President.* The more adventurous among them might throw in a hyperbolic word or two (Destiny! Power! Genius!) or a phrase borrowed from Washington's time, immediately lost on potential new readers ("His Excellency" or "For Fear of an Elected King"). With titles this stodgy, presidential biographies will always appear as if they are for men of a certain age, intended to be purchased on Presidents' or Father's Day.[6]

The Thigh Men, as I came to think of these kinds of biographers over the years, are a decidedly "size matters" crowd.[7] Chernow's book on Washington, which won the Pulitzer Prize, clocks in at almost a thousand pages, a record among single-volume editions on our first president—in no small part because it takes every opportunity to remind readers that the great general was very, very manly. This seems obvious from a basic review of the facts: Washington survived every disease he contracted (apart from the last one, of course) without much more than a few pockmarks to show for it. He walked away basically unscathed from every battle and skirmish, though some of the horses he rode in on were less fortunate. After a while, it begins to feel as though there's something hinky behind these biographers' repetitive insistence on Washington's conspicuous masculinity—because there is.

A Childless Father

The father of this country was no father. At least, not biologically. When Washington married the widow Martha Custis, he became the guardian to her two children—a son named Jacky, age four, and a daughter named Patsy, age two—whom he appears to have loved and treated as if they were his own. Washington was devastated when Patsy, who had epilepsy, passed away. He was endlessly effortful with Jacky, who often shirked responsibility and made rash decisions. And the older Washington got, the more wards he seemed to inherit. He considered Marquis de Lafayette, for instance, a surrogate son. (The affection was mutual: Lafayette named his own son George Washington and his daughter Virginia.)

In a young, monarchy-weary America, Washington's lack of heirs gave him a distinct political advantage; it comforted people to know that he had no bloodline to preserve, no power-hungry scion to worry about. He didn't avoid the subject of childlessness or wax regretful over it, which suggests it wasn't a source of great tragedy in his life. Yet the Thigh Men are obsessed with it. They spend dozens of pages discussing how it happened and why it doesn't detract from his innate virility—as if that's a preoccupation everyone shares.

In all likelihood, Washington was left sterile from an illness in his youth. Even here, though, the usual culprits just won't do for a man of his towering reputation. "A sexually transmitted disease seems unlikely in Washington's case, given his character and strong sense of moral propriety," John K. Amory, a professor and practicing physician at the

University of Washington School of Medicine, wrote in the scientific journal *Fertility and Sterility*.[8] Chernow agrees that "Washington was noticeably attracted to women, but his steely willpower and stern discipline likely overmastered any fugitive impulses to stray."[9] Amory also argues that Washington was too healthy to suffer from erectile dysfunction (performance anxiety was apparently out of the question), and that watching his siblings multiply, as well as the animals of the farm, left him with a precocious understanding of procreative sex. (To be fair, Washington did become the nation's foremost mule breeder.) Chernow implores readers to look at the *right* parts: Washington's hands were so large that he wore custom-made gloves, and his feet, of course, "were famously huge." Even his writing was "masculine."[10]

After defending Washington, the Thigh Men usually turn their sights on Martha, blaming her for the couple's childlessness. There's little to suggest she endured difficult births during her first marriage, but the very notion that such births can be linked to infertility is enough for them to cast a critical eye in her direction. If anything, the fact that Martha had children at all offers convincing evidence that she remained fertile in her twenties, when she married Washington.

In the end, you begin to wonder why so many pages and articles have been devoted to something that won't help "break" Washington out of that marble mold or decode his legacy. For whatever reason, he didn't have biological children; no one seemed to care too much about it in the eighteenth century, so why should we?

Mary, Mary, Not So Contrary

Chernow's biography of the first president, published in 2010, contains a notably dramatic scene between Washington and his only living parent, Mary Washington. (His father, Augustine, died when he was eleven.)

It occurs in the spring of 1755, when Washington, then in his early twenties and a soldier in the British militia, was due to meet Captain Robert Orme in Alexandria. Washington's departure was delayed, Chernow writes, when his mother appeared at Mount Vernon "like the wrath of God." He had "sparked a family feud" by attempting to recruit John Augustine, his younger brother, to look after Mount Vernon while he was away. That the Washington family was so prone to reality-TV theatrics is surprising, in no small part because it took more than two hundred years for a historian to unearth these sensational details in the archives.

Not quite. "Like Washington's teeth, his life as told here is less than fully rooted in its surroundings," Pulitzer Prize–winning author T. J. Stiles wrote in a *New Statesman* review of Chernow's book. (Stiles added, "Let's be clear: *Washington* is a true achievement. A reader might agree with my criticisms yet thoroughly enjoy the book." For the record, I am that reader.) In this instance, Chernow doesn't cite a newly discovered document, but rather the very same letter from April 2, 1755, that practically all Washington scholars have always cited, in which Washington explains his delay to Captain Orme:[11]

> The arrival of a good deal of Company (among whom is my Mother, alarmed at the report of my intentions to attend to your Fortunes)—prevents me the pleasure of waiting upon you today as I had intended; I therefore beg that you'll be kind enough to make my compliments & excuse, to the Generl . . .[12]

That's it. That's how Washington describes the scene. Chernow's portrayal of Mary arriving "like the wrath of God" is the product of his imagination—and it's not his only foray into creative writing.[13]

For Chernow, the fact that Mary was already twenty-three at the time of her marriage "may say something about her feisty personality or about Augustine's hopeful conviction that he could tame this indomitable woman." But Augustine, Washington's father, left nothing to indicate he harbored such a "a hopeful conviction," nor does Chernow offer a source.[14] He doesn't need to: Everyone knows that, in the absence of evidence to the contrary, a woman is probably a shrew. And shrews, of course, need taming.

A SAMPLING OF RON CHERNOW'S DESCRIPTIONS OF MARY WASHINGTON

shrewish	stubborn	whining	trying
thwarting	unlettered	self-centered	querulous
headstrong	plain	demanding	disciplinarian
unbending	homespun	crude	forbidding
illiterate	strong-willed	coarse	hypocritical
slovenly	self-interested	strangely indifferent	feisty
crusty	difficult	anxious	complainer[15]

For the Thigh Men, Mary's histrionics begin when she declines to enlist her fourteen-year-old son in the navy and continue to the very ends with her griping about elder care.

Like Washington, in fact, Mary has always been a one-dimensional caricature, a prop to be used as others see fit. In the early nineteenth century, when the young nation was obsessed with middle-class values, saintly mothers, and stories about good patriots, there was no greater model than Mary. President Andrew Jackson laid the cornerstone of a monument dedicated to her, and suffragists such as Elizabeth Cady Stanton even used her image in an effort to align themselves with "all that a mother ought to be." But by the late nineteenth century, experts began turning on her. Paul Leicester Ford, an editor of Thomas Jefferson's papers, argued that the popular version of Mary as the patron saint of republican motherhood "partakes of fiction rather than of truth."[16] He depicted her as the tyrant Washington was constantly trying to escape, and accused her of decidedly unladylike tendencies, like smoking a pipe. That narrative was well received, too; America loves a self-made man, particularly one who overcomes the manipulations of a petty woman to seize his great *destiny*.

The further from Mary's actual time period historians are, the more they seem inclined to ignore the prevailing norms and values of her day. In 1929, Shelby Little called Mary "illiterate, untidy, and querulous," even though we know she *was* literate, if not especially well read. She stuck to the Bible and books about it, and her letters reflect that: Her vocabulary was limited, her prose artless. We have no idea what she said to Washington in person, or how she spoke off the page, but if her writing is any indication, she thought mostly in terms of death and survival. Biographers have interpreted this as evidence of an unsupportive and even thwarting disposition. On the occasion of Washington's birthday bicentennial celebrations, Samuel Eliot Morison called her "grasping, querulous, and vulgar" and accused her of "oppos[ing] almost everything he did for public good."[17] By the time Chernow's take emerged, anything Washington tried to accomplish that wasn't in his mother's "immediate service, she attempted to stop."[18] Mary showed "little that savored of maternal warmth," Chernow adds.[19]

WASHINGTON'S SPIRITUAL EDUCATION

Mary lacked a formal education, as did most of the women of her time. There is strong evidence, however, that she was not illiterate, as some biographers have claimed. Some of her letters survive, as do her devotional books, which show her hand throughout. These titles later appear in Washington's personal library, and he often quoted her favorite passages. Her grandson George Lewis fondly remembered spending Sunday evenings listening to her read from the Bible: "[I] gazed with childish wonder and admiration at the rude representations of saints and angels, and the joys of the redeemed, and shuddered at the sight of the skeleton death and devils with horns and hoofs, holding in their claws pitchforks of fire."[20]

The Thigh Men would have done well to review scholarship on early American motherhood with the same amount of interest they had for military history. If they had, they would have considered the average eighteenth-century matriarch, whose primary concerns were keeping her children alive and well and avoiding sin and vice, and who was not sentimental and praising. (As Abigail Adams, born a generation after Mary, once wrote, "I will not say that all my Geese are swans" and "where much is given, much shall be required." [21]) If Mary had boasted, no doubt she would have been called out for it.

As the story goes, George Washington became George Washington in spite of his mother, but in fact he and Mary had an awful lot in common. If you were feeling generous toward Mary, you might even argue that she passed on and cultivated admirable (and sometimes less so) characteristics in her son. They were tall and athletic and moved with notable grace, whether it be on the dance floor or on horseback. They were industrious and anxious, demanding much of those around them.

MARY'S GREATEST SUCCESS

What if historians have actually missed what Mary considered her greatest parental success?

Archeological digs around Ferry Farm, where Washington and his siblings grew up, reveal that Mary may have been working hard to ensure Betty, her only daughter, married well. The family rooms were equipped to entertain, with the cheapest version of items that visiting gentry would expect to see—tea sets, hooks that point to fashionable needlepoint, an engraved spoon. Betty surely had her charms, but matchmaking and courtship were usually family affairs, and Mary clearly managed those well.[22] And if she taught Betty to live the gentry lifestyle, maybe not all of Washington's manners, flattered throughout his life, came from copying (perhaps just to practice penmanship) the *Rules of Civility.*

Heaven help the fool who challenged them on anything to do with money.[23] Washington had a zeal for bookkeeping, a skill it seems Mary taught him early on. And when Washington decided to sue two girls who allegedly stole valuables out of his clothes while he was "washing in the river," it was no doubt at his mother's encouragement. (The sheriff carried one of them "to the Whipping post & Inflict fifteen lashes on her bare back."[24]) Mary was never afraid to stand up for herself in court, where few women were present.

That's not to say that Mary, who was fiercely independent in an era in which female independence was totally unacceptable, didn't have a challenging personality. In Chapter 12, Washington's annoyance with her is palpable on the page, but that's just how he felt on that particular day, in response to a specific situation; on other days, he appears quite patient with his mother. And when there's occasion for sentiment, it's easy to find: In 1789, when Mary died of breast cancer, Washington wrote in a letter to his sister that the loss was "awful, and affecting."[25]

A New Biography

And so begins my addition to a crowded bookshelf. In Part I, I describe how Washington—like his successors Franklin Roosevelt, Bill Clinton, and Barack Obama—was raised by a single mother. As he struggles to find his place in the world, he makes mistakes of global consequence and becomes a colonial celebrity. Life becomes happy and settled once he meets Martha and becomes a father to her children. But as his entrepreneurial ambitions (which largely depend on the hundreds of people he enslaved) are repeatedly thwarted by the British, he begins down the path toward rebellion. In Part II, I explore the war he fought without arms. His diplomatic, propaganda, and espionage campaigns greatly contributed to the improbable American victory. And there's another story, too, about the personal cost of war—to him and his family. In Part III, Washington is pressured out of retirement by Alexander Hamilton, James Madison, and other founders. He wins election to the presidency by a unanimous vote, becoming the country's "first." After eight years of increasing partisanship, near rebellion, and threats from abroad, he's done. In Part IV, he returns, at long last, to Mount Vernon. This stage in his life, though brief, is often celebrated because it's when he decides to free the men, women, and children he enslaved. In fact, though, he passes the buck to Martha, emancipating only one man, outright, upon his death. Until the very end, Washington worries about respect and reputation. He needn't have; the nation hasn't always remembered him clearly, but we've never forgotten our first.

✦ PART I ✦

Reluctant Rebel

CHAPTER 1

His Mother's Son

WHEN IT CAME TO FAMILY, MARY BALL WASHINGTON, GEORGE Washington's mother, was always unlucky. Her father died when she was an infant. By the time she turned twelve, she had buried her stepfather, her half brother, and her mother. Mary's two surviving siblings, although grown and married, did not take her in; instead, she became the legal ward of a neighbor.

Her life immediately got worse. The man who had worked for her late family as an overseer successfully sued her for back wages, and Mary, as a girl in early America, would have little opportunity to recover the financial loss. For her, everything depended on marrying well, just as it had for her mother, who had come to America as an indentured servant.

In 1731, at the age of twenty-three, Mary found a promising match. Augustine Washington, an educated widower fourteen years her senior, was a justice of the peace who owned a small tobacco farm, and an increasing number of slaves.[1]

The details of their twelve-year marriage are scant, but one thing is for sure: It produced six children, whom they raised at Ferry Farm, a modest enterprise outside of Fredericksburg, Virginia.[2] George was their first, followed by Betty, Samuel, John Augustine, and Charles Washington. (Their youngest daughter, Mildred, died at sixteen months old.) They lived in a two-story house that looked out on the Rappahannock River and slave quarters, rough wooden structures that housed about twenty people of African descent.[3] The tobacco-drying sheds, the dairy barn, the smokehouse, and Mary's vegetable and medicinal herb gardens lay beyond.

Mary's husband and stepsons had attended the prestigious Appleby Grammar School in England, and she planned to send her own sons there, too, no doubt with dreams of social advancement in mind. Mary had never left Virginia, but her sons would see the motherland.

And then, in 1743, her husband died. Augustine was buried with his first wife, a sign of things to come for Mary and her five children. His sons from his first marriage, Lawrence, twenty-five, and Augustine, Jr., twenty-three, inherited the bulk of the estate—including Mount Vernon. Lawrence gifted his stepmother a mourning ring, but neither he nor his brother had any legal obligation to her. Mary and her five children were left to manage Ferry Farm on their own. George was never going to Appleby.

Mary, now thirty-five, took up the job of maintaining a property that legally belonged to her eleven-year-old son. Having learned at an early age how it felt to be powerless, she started off decisively, selling off some of the family's best tracts. The corn, flax, wheat, oat, rye, vegetables, and tobacco grown on the remaining land would have to be enough to feed and support her family, the people she enslaved, and her farm animals. With great luck and even better weather, there might be a big enough yield to sell in Great Britain.

Unfortunately for Mary, the years that followed were recorded as dry. She managed to scrape together enough to sell abroad, but that was only half the battle. British merchants had a monopoly on trade, and they couldn't be depended on to deal fairly. Their terms stated that no sale was final until the product reached Great Britain. This allowed them to accuse American farmers, and they often did, of including inferior crops, especially with small operations. When Mary tried to sell her tobacco, she was twice accused—and twice vindicated. By the 1760s, she had decided the enterprise wasn't worth the trouble.

And throughout all this struggle, Mary's efforts, past immediate survival, offered her no long-term guarantees. At the age of twenty-one, Washington would inherit the entirety of Ferry Farm. But that was it. Augustine had made no provisions in his will to educate his younger sons, abroad or at home. Soon, Washington would have to drop out of a local school. He would spend the rest of his life trying to catch up.

Mary could have remarried. It was such a commonplace practice, in fact, that Augustine's will anticipated it. A new husband would have offered her some degree of financial security and, presuming she was lonely, companionship, even love. And Mary was a catch: She had a home, however temporary, and a hearty constitution. But Mary wasn't eager to submit to a new husband's demands. (Perhaps she had learned a lesson from her own mother's second marriage. Tellingly, her eldest son would later come to the defense of remarried widows, against husbands who illegally withheld their wives' property.) Instead, she poured her energy into the farm and her children, especially George and Betty.

Mary remained strategically close to her stepsons. Lawrence, who was ten years her junior, had come back from Appleby with the entitlement and ambition of a colonizer, not of a man born in the colonies. With a commission from King George II, he had served as a captain in the War of Jenkins' Ear, fighting the Spanish in the West Indies.

Lawrence returned the summer after his father died and immediately capitalized on his recent inheritance and glamorous war experience by marrying exceptionally well. Ann Fairfax, daughter of Colonel William Fairfax, lived at Belvoir, the grand estate bordering Lawrence's Mount Vernon. She offered him entry into what was arguably the colony's most powerful family.

Mary made sure that Washington was a frequent visitor at Mount Vernon, and thus also at Belvoir, where he could observe elite masculinity up close. Washington supplemented his fieldwork by studying *Rules of Civility & Decent Behaviour in Company and Conversation,* a sixteenth-century book on etiquette.[4] He likely copied down all 110 lessons merely to work on his penmanship, but what he managed to absorb didn't hurt his reputation among the gentry.

THE ABRIDGED *RULES OF CIVILITY*

NUMBER	RULE
2	When in Company, put not your Hands to any Part of the Body, not usualy Discovered.
7	Put not off your Cloths in the presence of Others, nor go out your Chambers half Drest.
24	Do not laugh too loud or too much at any Publick [Spectacle].
54	Play not the Peacock, looking every where about you, to See if you be well Deck't, if your Shoes fit well if your Stockings sit neatly, and Cloths handsomely.
56	Associate yourself with Men of good Quality if you Esteem your own Reputation; for 'tis better to be alone than in bad Company.

73	Think before you Speak pronounce not imperfectly nor bring ou[t] your Words too hastily but orderly & distinctly.
82	Undertake not what you cannot Perform but be Carefull to keep your Promise.
90	Being Set at meal Scratch not neither Spit Cough or blow your Nose except there's a Necessity for it.
92	Take no Salt or cut Bread with your Knife Greasy.
100	Cleanse not your teeth with the Table Cloth Napkin Fork or Knife but if Others do it let it be done wt. a Pick Tooth.

Washington understood his role. He moved with seeming ease between the sometimes desperate conditions of Ferry Farm and the genteel abundance of Mount Vernon. On one occasion, however, he could not make the two-day ride to visit Lawrence because there wasn't enough corn to feed his horse. According to Washington, the animal was "in very poor order," a startling admission in Virginia, where men who traveled even the shortest distances on foot were understood to be poor. If the animals were hungry, then the future president and his family—and most of all, their slaves—were likely suffering, too.[5]

The masters of Mount Vernon and Belvoir knew that Washington was not one of them, but they recognized that he was a quick study. His eagerness to be helped no doubt flattered their egos, and he became a kind of pet project. They decided that he was in need of travel and adventure, and that the only way to get it was by sea.[6] But since Washington could not pay his own way, they concluded he would have to join the British Royal Navy as a midshipman. They then launched an almost conspiratorial campaign to achieve their goal.

✦ ✦ ✦

Mary Washington was no fool. At first, she seemed open to the idea of Washington's enlistment in the navy, but it didn't take long for her to realize she was being set up. She had learned in her youth to view the world with a critical eye, and in her time running a small farm, that eye had sharpened. Would Washington really find opportunity at sea? Was it better than what he would find at home? And what were the risks to her fourteen-year-old son?

Mary had good reason to believe they were great. Lawrence's own letters home from service had been full of tales of disease, deprivation, and death. His brother-in-law had lost his life in a naval battle with the French. And both had been officers; Washington would be a midshipman, one of the lowest-ranking, subjugated positions on a vessel. (As it happens, her instincts were right. Of the recruits who joined the navy at Washington's age, about a third did not survive their first two years in the navy—and there was little chance of promotion before then.)[7]

It seems Mary tried to discuss these concerns with Lawrence's co-conspirators, but they had no patience for them. Robert Jackson, the executor of her late husband's will, dismissed them as "trifling objections such as fond and unthinking mothers naturally suggest."[8]

Others, however, agreed with her. Joseph Ball, Mary's half brother in England, thought the whole thing was a terrible idea:

I think he had better be put apprentice to a tinker, for a common sailor before the mast has by no means the common liberty of the subject; for they will press him from ship to ship where he has fifty shillings a month, and make him take twenty-three, and cut and slash and use him like a negro, or rather like a dog.[9]

8

And with that, the matter was settled. Whether Mary handed down her decision or she reached it in consultation with her son, we'll never know. But in the aftermath, no one seemed at odds over it. Washington visited Mount Vernon just as often, and Lawrence called on Joseph Ball the next time he went to England. He even brought back presents for Mary.[10]

If Washington had ever truly wanted to become a midshipman, his interest was probably less about the experience than the twenty-three shillings a month he would have earned. The situation at Ferry Farm was increasingly dire. "With much truth I can say, I never felt the want of money so sensibly since I was a boy of 15 years old," he would later write.[11] But his mother wouldn't sacrifice him to the navy, no matter how bad things got.

☆ ☆ ☆

Mary's children stayed at home with her until there was a good reason for them to leave. In 1750, Washington gave away his sister, Betty, age seventeen, to Fielding Lewis, the son of a respectable merchant in town. Like her mother and grandmother, she pushed the boundaries of wifehood in early America: Her mark and signature can be found alongside her husband's on business transactions, from land purchases to tobacco shipments.[12]

Washington, meanwhile, was becoming Mary's business partner more than her child. An appetite for land ran in his father's family, a side he seemed eager to emulate, and so Mary encouraged him to become a surveyor. The job attracted young men precisely because it offered upward mobility; a surveyor might earn a hundred pounds annually, and he was first on the scene, able to buy the choicest properties for himself. The profession suited Washington's personality: He liked the outdoors, he was good at math, and he could use his father's surveying tools. (He later brought some of those tools on his presidential tours of the northern and southern states.)

Lawrence and the Fairfaxes were supportive, too. They hired Washington to look after their western holdings, allowing him to skip a long apprenticeship. They also talked him up among the local gentry. By age seventeen, he was the surveyor of Culpeper County, the youngest ever hired, and by eighteen he had purchased thousands of acres of land in the Shenandoah Valley. Thanks to him, there was finally steady money coming in at Ferry Farm.

CHAPTER 2

"Pleases My Taste"

WHILE WASHINGTON WAS THRIVING, HIS HALF BROTHER WAS failing. Lawrence's misfortunes began in 1749 with a cough so bad that he had to sail to England for medical care. It was tuberculosis, which only worsened during the trip. Nor did his illness improve the following year when he traveled to the spa town of Warm Springs, Virginia, to bathe in its reputedly restorative waters. Facing another long, frigid Virginia winter, during which he would most likely be quarantined from his wife, who had just given birth to a baby girl and had already lost three newborns, Lawrence set his sights on the Caribbean.

He chose to risk hurricane season in the West Indies in hopes that a few warm months of rest and relaxation in Barbados would help. He invited Washington, who had never been outside of Virginia, and together they boarded the *Success*, a small trading ship. For six weeks, Washington distracted himself from the "fickle & Merciless Ocean" by recording the weather and by fishing for barracuda, mahi mahi, and shark.[1] (He rarely caught anything.) Finally, at four o'clock in the morning on November 2, 1751, they arrived in Barbados, a diminutive land mass that had become the economic and political hub of the British Empire.

The nineteen-year-old Washington was immediately taken with the flora and fauna. He sampled avocados, guavas, and pineapples for the first time, writing "[N]one pleases my taste as dos the Pine."[2] But he was most interested in the people—though not the enslaved Africans who were brought there in chains to grow and harvest sugar. "[A] Man of oppulent fortune And infamous Charactar was indicted for committing a rape on his servant Maid," he reported, "and was brought in Guiltless and sav'd by one single Evidence."[3] Washington watched the "not over-zealously beloved" governor in action and dined with the island's elite. They invited him to their "Beefsteak and Tripe Club," where he met judges and admirals and listened to the concerns of wealthy merchants and commodores. It was a far more diverse and worldly set of men than Lawrence knew back home.

Washington hardly mentions Lawrence, then thirty-four, who was usually too weak to leave his quarters. Soon enough, illness came for Washington, too. "Was strongly attacked with the small Pox," he wrote in his diary on November 16, 1751. Although he emerged with some scarring on his face, he also acquired the gift of immunity. Smallpox was rare in the Colonies, and his resistance to the virus would serve him well during the Revolution.

Washington recovered quickly. Lawrence did not. In late December 1751, they parted ways in Barbados. Lawrence boarded a ship for Bermuda, and Washington headed home on the *Industry*. He spent nearly the entire trip seasick and was at one point robbed by a fellow passenger, but he was a changed man. He had survived a great illness and traveled what would ultimately be the farthest distance of his life.

When Washington returned home, he delivered letters from the gentry of Barbados to Robert Dinwiddie, the British governor of Virginia, who welcomed him with a dinner invitation. He seemed to finally feel like a person of distinction, confident enough of his prospects to court one wealthy, unattainable young woman after another. When Elizabeth Fauntleroy rejected him, he wrote to her father, who owned a considerable amount of land, seeking a visit with "Miss Betcy, in hopes of a revocation of the former, cruel sentence and see if I can meet with any alteration in my favor."[4] During a visit to Belvoir, Washington wrote to a friend that he'd flirted with George Fairfax's sister-in-law, Mary Cary. She's "a very agreeable Young Lady," he said, but one who "revives my former Passion for your Low Land Beauty."[5] (The identity of the Low Land Beauty has never been confirmed.) If Miss Betcy's wary father wrote back, Washington did not keep the letter—but it is safe to assume that Fauntleroy, a member of the Richmond elite, was uninterested in a young man of no fortune or great estate.

Lawrence found no more relief in Bermuda than he had in Barbados, or Virginia, or England. Weakened and exhausted, he soon returned to Mount Vernon and wrote his will. He died in July 1752.

Washington was presumably saddened by the loss of his half brother, but his letters on the subject were strictly about estate and inheritance matters. Lawrence had named him executor and an inheritor. He received several parcels of land in Fredericksburg, along with the promise of Mount Vernon, should Lawrence's widow and daughter die. But Ann was a young woman. Her daughter, Sarah, was younger still. And it was not lost on Washington that the men in his family died young. For all he knew, he had a decade left, maybe two.

He wasted neither time nor opportunity, immediately setting his sights on Lawrence's now vacant position in the Virginia militia. Despite having no military experience, he worked his connections and ultimately got the job—along with its annual salary of one hundred pounds. Washington went into his twenty-first birthday with the title of major, a dependable income, a flourishing surveying business, and more land than his father had ever owned. And although he had no diplomatic or foreign-language skills to speak of, Governor Dinwiddie selected him for a mission into the wilds of the Ohio territory. He carried with him an order signed by King George's own hand.

CHAPTER 3

"The World on Fire"

TANACHARISON, THE SENECA CHIEF, KNEW JUST WHAT TO CALL
the twenty-one-year-old upstart who summoned him in 1753. His
Christian name might have been George Washington, but Tanacharison, known to Europeans as the "Half-King," would call him "Conotocarious." In English, it translated to Town Taker, or Devourer of Villages.

Earlier chiefs, in an earlier century, had bestowed the same name on
John Washington, George's great-grandfather. It was a fair comparison:
Both men served in the Virginia militia, and both had lit out for the
frontier to secure the crown's holdings. But while George was allied
with the Indians against the French, John had been sent to confront the
tribes about their alleged crimes against British settlers. His great-
grandfather earned the name of Conotocarious when negotiations with
Susquehannock chiefs turned violent; chaos erupted in the region, and
the chiefs were murdered by white settlers.

Washington was clearly pleased to have inherited the murderous
nickname. Decades later, when he had a legacy to consider and thus
doctored other aspects of his record from this time, he left the episode

relatively unchanged, and Conotocarious untouched. By then, he would have even more in common with John: In 1779, he ordered several Indian villages in western New York be razed to avenge and deter attacks on white settlers along the frontier.[1]

But in 1753, Washington's orders from Dinwiddie, the British governor, urged discretion and caution. First, he was to ask the Indians to escort him and his party—an assistant and four woodsmen—into the frontier. The Half-King, as Washington called him, and three other prominent chiefs signed on. Next, Washington was to determine how many "Forts the French have erected, & where; How they are Garrison'd & appointed, & what is their Distance from each other. . . . what gave Occasion to this Expedition of the French. How they are like to be supported, & what their Pretentions are."[2] If, as Dinwiddie suspected, those French forts were on territory claimed by the British, Washington would demand their immediate withdrawal. If the French refused, he would return with a small contingent of Virginia troops. It was a tricky mission: Although traveling with armed men, he was supposed to stick with diplomacy.

Washington didn't trust the Half-King or his other chiefs. "The Indians are mercenary," he later wrote. "[E]very service of theirs must be purchased; and they are easily offended, being thoroughly sensible of their own importance."[3]

Yet Washington and the chiefs had one thing in common: an enmity toward the French. As he well knew, the Half-King believed they had captured, cooked, and eaten his father. He exploited this the first chance he got. When Christopher Gist, a British colonial frontiersman, arrived at Great Meadows (present-day Pennsylvania) with a message that the French had inquired after the Half-King, Washington greatly exaggerated it. "I did not fail to let the young *Indians* who were in our Camp know, that the *French* wanted to kill the Half King," he wrote in late May 1754. The manipulation "had its desired effect." [4]

In return, Washington received his own bad translation. A runner named Silver Heels delivered him a startling reconnaissance report from the Half-King that said some fifty French soldiers had been spotted no more than fifteen miles away. Unsure of their intentions, Washington felt obliged to make a move.

"I set out with 40 Men before 10, and was from that time till near Sun rise before we reach'd the Indian's Camp, havg Marched in small path, & heavy Rain, and a Night as Dark as it is possible to conceive," he recounted in a letter to Dinwiddie. On the way to rendezvous with the Half-King, his men "were frequently tumbling one over another, and often so lost that 15 or 20 Minutes search would not find the path again."[5] When they finally made it to the Half-King's camp, Washington was met with disappointment. The Half-King had mustered fewer than a dozen warriors, a quarter as many as he'd hoped. Still, those men knew how to track the French, so they had the element of surprise on their side.

It took them until dawn to find the enemy camp. A few groggy French soldiers were lighting fires or heading into the woods to relieve themselves, but of the thirty-five men below, most were still asleep. The Virginians probably fired the first shots as the French scrambled in confusion, taking cover and grabbing their muskets. Their weapons, however, were of little use. It had rained the previous night, and the French hadn't bothered to keep them dry. "I can with truth assure you, I heard Bulletts whistle and believe me there was something charming in the sound," Washington wrote to his brother John Augustine on May 31.[6] The skirmish was over in fifteen minutes.

When the smoke cleared, it revealed ten French bodies, men killed by British guns and Indian tomahawks. "The Indians scalped the Dead, and took away the most Part of their Arms," Washington wrote in his diary. A few got away, and the rest—twenty-one men—were taken prisoner.

Washington had no idea what he'd done. No better evidence of this exists than another letter he sent Dinwiddie after the bloodbath. In a staggering demonstration of priorities, he spent the first *eight* paragraphs of the letter complaining about his pay (it denied him "the pleasure of good Living," he said) before getting to the news of the massacre. Washington noted matter-of-factly that "We killed Mr. *de Jumonville*, the Commander of that Party." (John Shaw, an eyewitness with a flair for the dramatic, claimed that the Half-King had split de Jumonville's skull open with his tomahawk, lifted out his brain, and squished it in his hands, saying, "Thou art not yet dead, my father.") This was a diplomatic nightmare, and so, in a letter to his superiors in London, Dinwiddie passed the buck. "[T]his little Skirmish was by the Half-King & their Indians, we were as auxiliaries to them, as my Orders to the Commander of our Forces [were] to be on the Defensive," he wrote.[7]

The French, however, laid the blame squarely at Washington's feet. De Jumonville would become a martyr—and a persuasive tool for rallying the public against the British. "The Misfortune is, that our People were surprized," they wrote in an official report.

> The *English* had incircled them, and came upon them unseen.... The *Indians* who were present when the Thing was done, say, that Mr. *de Jumonville* was killed by a Musket-Shot in the Head, whilst they were reading the Summons; and that the *English* would afterwards have killed all our Men, had not the *Indians* who were present, by rushing in between them and the *English*, prevented their Design.[8]

The French had dispatched de Jumonville on a diplomatic mission exactly like the kind Dinwiddie had envisioned for Washington: He was there to secure King Louis VI's claim to the land and demand that the Virginians withdraw. De Jumonville was leading an ambassadorial delegation and never had any intention to fight. Had Washington attempted to engage peacefully, the French claimed, de Jumonville would have made that clear. Instead, a letter stating as much was later found on de Jumonville's corpse.

Retaliation was all but guaranteed. Washington immediately began fortifying the aptly named Fort Necessity, a feeble wooden structure that stood exposed in an open field. A month later, on another rainy day, his troops were swiftly overwhelmed by a larger French and Indian force led by none other than de Jumonville's half brother, Louis Coulon de Villiers. Washington agreed to sign Coulon's terms of surrender, but would later claim that the translator omitted key phrases—which is how he ended up admitting to the assassination of de Jumonville.

"The volley fired by a young Virginian in the backwoods of America set the world on fire," British writer Horace Walpole commented at the time. At the age of twenty-two, Washington had committed a political misstep of global consequence. The British and the French were now formally engaged in a battle (known as the French and Indian War) for American land, forcing their allies in Austria, Germany, Prussia, Russia, Spain, and Sweden to take sides. The theater of war quickly spread into far-flung colonial holdings in the Americas, Africa, India, and even the Philippines. If the American Revolution had not taken place, Washington would probably be remembered today as the instigator of humanity's first world war, one that lasted seven years.

Many of Washington's men deserted him on the way home to Virginia, and he would soon do the same to Dinwiddie. When he learned that new colonial regulations would forever limit his rank to captain, he quit in a huff. He intended to return to private life—a decision that lasted all of five months.

☆ ☆ ☆

Washington's disastrous performance on the frontier somehow turned out to be a social climber's dream. Upon his return, he gave Dinwiddie his personal journal, which the governor recognized as a powerful tool for whipping up popular animus against the French; he had it published in newspapers throughout the colonies. It was a hit—a propaganda victory for the cause and a boost to the career of its author. Within months, the British had commissioned a special edition. Few British subjects were willing to leave home for the better part of a year and trudge through a couple thousand miles of wilderness, but almost everyone wanted to read about it from a safe distance.

The diary culminates in a moment of acute misery: On his way back to Dinwiddie, Washington falls off a hastily constructed raft into the ice-clogged, rushing waters of the Allegheny River. He eventually makes his way to a nearby island, where he spends a particularly dismal night. Despite his diminished food supply and his threadbare clothing, the exhausted Washington carries home a letter from the French, who refused to vacate, proving himself loyal to the crown.

But royal recognition didn't pay the bills. Washington dismissed the fifty pounds Dinwiddie paid him—over $11,000 today—as insufficient recompense for risking life and limb. In a letter to his brother Augustine, he wrote, "and what did I get by it? my expenses borne!"[9] He'd basically broken even.

The entire experience had completely failed to live up to the promise of the frontier. Washington was supposed to die a noble death or emerge with great spoils. It was then, after his very first "victory" on behalf of the British, that he learned an important lesson: Colonists looking to make a small fortune off the British military were best off starting out with a large one. He could have made more money had he just stayed home and continued surveying.

And yet, he continued to serve when called upon. When Dinwiddie asked him to train a hundred militia troops with orders to erect a fort in the Ohio country, he agreed—though not without telling Richard Corbin, a Virginian in charge of the government's finances, that he thought himself "worthy of the post of Lieutenant-colonel." Channeling the *Rules of Civility* ("Strive not with your Superiors in argument, but always Submit your Judgement to others with Modesty"), Washington asked Corbin to "mention it at the appointment of officers."[10]

Thanks to his widely read journal, Washington received the commission. He was twenty-two. He began studying whatever books and pamphlets on military strategy he could get his hands on. He pressed the colonial governors of Maryland and Pennsylvania to rise "from the lethargy we have fallen into" and display "the heroick spirit of every free-born Englishman to assert the rights and privileges of our king."[11] But Washington's enthusiasm wasn't contagious, and his recent celebrity lacked real influence. Maryland sent a paltry number of soldiers, and Pennsylvania provided none at all.

Small victories against the British hierarchy were encouraging, but Washington soon had to face reality. Under the British imperial system, even the most enterprising colonist would remain second class. An Englishman who held a lower rank could order him around, and worse, that Englishman made more money than he did.

Everyone knew it, too, which outraged Washington and made recruiting colonists for the British cause a constant challenge. At one point, an official suggested that he supplement his ranks with men from the county jail. Washington privately complained that he'd have better luck trying "to raize the Dead to Life again." In a letter to Dinwiddie, he equated the undervalued work of colonial officers with those held in bondage: "to be slaving dangerously for the shadow of pay, through the woods, rocks, mountains,—I would rather prefer the great toil of a daily laborer, and dig for a maintenance . . . than serve upon such ignoble terms."[12]

At long last, facing the prospect of an undermanned militia, Dinwiddie promised land grants as compensation to new recruits. But even the latter-day Town Taker wasn't satisfied. He needed money now, not just to entice men to join but also to supply them with adequate clothing, shoes, and guns. And this time, he refused to take no for an answer. To accept inferior compensation was to admit that he was inferior to the Dinwiddies and Fairfaxes of the world, an idea he couldn't abide. So he offered to serve the crown on a volunteer basis, without pay, hoping it would send the message that he was their equal. Washington had yet to grasp that any value they saw in merit and loyalty paled beside the importance of birthright.

CHAPTER 4

"Blow Out My Brains"

DINWIDDIE DIDN'T UNDERSTAND HOW TO FLATTER WASHINGTON into another expedition, but British Brigadier General Edward Braddock did. Braddock, sixty, could not offer Washington, twenty-three, the rapid ascent he craved, but he invited him into his "family," an inner circle of military aides.[1] If he could impress Braddock in the Ohios, where the British intended to capture Fort Duquesne and drive out the French once and for all, perhaps Braddock would get Washington a special exemption from the imperial system. (Never mind that that the crown had sent Braddock to the colonies precisely because the Virginians, under Washington, had suffered such a humiliating defeat by the French.) "I am very happy in the Generals Family, being treated with a complaisant Freedom which is quite agreeable to me," he wrote to his mother on May 6, 1755, adding he had "no reason to doubt the satisfaction I hoped for, in making the Campaigne."[2]

But Washington soon found his place wasn't at all "agreeable." Braddock had been schooled in European warfare since the age of fifteen, and he wasn't interested in hearing about how that translated in the colonies. His imperious demands that the royal governors of Massachusetts, Maryland, Pennsylvania, and Virginia fund his fortifications seemed unreasonable, especially to the pacifist Quaker population. And he thoroughly botched a meeting with Indian leaders, even rejecting the help of Moses the Son, a Mohawk who had a copy of Fort Duquesne's layout. Worst of all, he demanded that soldiers build a road as they advanced, which slowed progress and strained supplies.

Washington, who was not half recovered from "a violent illness that had confin'd me to my Bed, and a Waggon, for above 10 Days," tried to reason with Braddock. But the general refused to abandon his narrow-minded theories of war—and soon paid for his pigheadedness on the battlefield.

The British were just ten miles away from Fort Duquesne when the French and their Indian allies, though outnumbered, attacked from the woods. Braddock had four horses shot out from under him and was felled by musket balls through the shoulder and chest, placed on the back of a wagon, and wheeled off the field while his army was still under attack. Within hours, half of his soldiers, including Braddock's second in command and several of his aides-de-camp, were killed or wounded.

Sensing an opportunity, Washington, who rode into battle with a pillow on his saddle, stepped up. He assumed command of the remaining half, rapidly issuing orders from horseback—in the general's ceremonial red sash. "I luckily escapd witht a wound, tho' I had four Bullets through my Coat, and two Horses shot under me," Washington proudly reported back to his mother on July 18, 1755. Of Braddock's fate, he wrote only that "The Genl was wounded; of wch he died 3 Days after."[3]

The French triumphed for a second time, cementing their control of the Ohios. Yet Washington returned from the Battle of the Monongahela even more of a star than before. In newly ordered shirt ruffles and silk stockings, he began making demands of Dinwiddie: He would return to the field only if he was able to choose his own officers (including two aides-de-camp) and received a military chest—that is, real money he could spend on them.[4]

Washington got what he wanted, but he still had to raise an army on his own, a frustrating proposition. The sort of men who were open to recruitment were typically desperate for money. Desertion was constant, and the local townspeople, among whom the war was unpopular, were often willing to shelter fugitives. Those soldiers who made it to the end of their short conscriptions typically didn't stick around.

Supplies were a problem, too. Britain's wartime decrees required that farmers hand over food to the troops, but when Washington demanded his cut, angry mobs threatened to "blow out my brains."[5] He had been given an important task—establishing a firm line of defense along the western border, which had been pushed back since Braddock's defeat—without the resources to do it properly.

CHAPTER 5

The Widow Custis

GREAT LOVE STORIES DON'T OFTEN BEGIN WITH DYSENTERY. BUT had George Washington not contracted the disease during his final year of British military service, he would never have met Martha Dandridge Custis. In the spring of 1758, Washington had traveled to Williamsburg, Virginia, to see a doctor; having received a clean bill of health, he decided to stay for a while and check out the social scene. The legislature was in session, which meant that the colony's capital was abuzz with news, activity, and eligible women. His Majesty's Army was clearly failing to make Washington rich, but a wealthy widow would.

Washington met Martha at the home of the Chamberlaynes, well-to-do relatives of her late husband. He wasted no time riding out to her plantation, called White House.

Martha was in a unique position for a young woman in the New World. At twenty-seven, the five-foot-tall widow was attractive in appearance, disposition, status, and family. She was petite, buxom, and had already given birth to two children—Jack, age four, and Patsy, age two—which signaled she was capable of bearing more for her future husband. Her father-in-law, half-brother-in-law, and late husband had died, the last without a will, leaving her one of the wealthiest women in Virginia—and free of meddling trustees. Martha was recognized as a so-called feme sole under English common law and had the right to legally conduct business as any man would. There were plenty of suitors milling about, eager to control her estate, which included around 290 enslaved people and almost eighteen thousand acres of land.

Among them was Charles Carter, a widower almost twice Washington's age. As a wealthy tobacco planter in her social circle, he was a relatively safe choice. In his letters, he seemed genuinely infatuated with her and eager to share his bed with another wife. But he came with his own children—twelve of them, to be exact. Martha declined his advances. If she chose to remarry, she would do so for love, and Washington, whose military renown she had most certainly heard of, was just the man to tempt her. At 6'2", he towered half a foot over any rival.

By all accounts, her marriage to Daniel Parke Custis, her first husband, had been happy. Yet Custis had been twenty years her senior, whereas Washington was seven months her junior. She seemingly took no issue with Washington's inferior birth and standing, perhaps because, years earlier, Custis's father had objected to her on the very same grounds. Maybe it wasn't a bad thing that Washington's father had died and his mother was a decent horse ride away. Martha may also have enjoyed the idea of being the wealthier spouse.

At twenty-seven, Washington was ready to marry. He had *been* ready for it, as his financial ledgers show. He was expanding his farmhouse at Mount Vernon, ordering hundreds of windowpanes, a marble mantelpiece for the fireplace, a mahogany dining room table and china to lay upon it—just the sort of spread a genteel wife would expect. And not just any genteel wife; before he met Martha, Washington may have fantasized about another woman.

"HEAVING THROBBING ALLURING"

Washington wrote when he was fifty-four that "there is moral certainty of my dying without issue."[1] He left nothing behind to indicate anything to the contrary (possibly because he was sterile), and if he had had premarital (or, later, extramarital) sex, there's almost nothing in the archives to imply it. A letter from George Mercer, a surveyor and an officer in the Virginia militia, suggests that sex wasn't something young Washington deigned to discuss. In 1757, Mercer reported that the women in South Carolina had a "bad Shape," and that "many of Them are crooked & have a very bad Air & not those enticing heaving throbbing alluring Letch exciting plump Breasts common with our Northern Belles." Yet he acknowledged that this sort of coarse talk was sure to have "tired your Patience." It seems he was right; Washington did not respond. [2] Another letter, from officer William La Péronie, provides some evidence that Washington did have premarital sex. Four years before he and Martha wed, La Péronie imagined him "plung'd in the midst of dellight heaven can aford & enchanted By Charms even stranger to the Ciprian Dame (+ M's Nel)."[3] "Ciprian Dame" was eighteenth-century-speak for a sex worker, but she may have been a barmaid or a mistress or a slave. It is therefore possible that Washington had a sexual relationship with a woman other than Martha, and that possibility includes nonconsensual sex with an enslaved woman.[4]

Sally Fairfax, a belle of Virginia society, had married into the same family as Lawrence Washington. Unlike him, however, she came from one of the state's oldest and wealthiest clans. Her marriage to George William Fairfax was typical of the time, designed to unite families and estates but not necessarily hearts. The union had yet to produce children, and in the end never would. Something, perhaps just a flirtatious friendship, quickly blossomed between Washington and Sally. She taught him to dance the minuet, coached him on conversations with influential men, and trained him to charm their wives and daughters.

But whatever he felt for Sally seemed to have faded when Washington began calling on Martha. It is clear the pair felt an instant connection, one that delayed his return to Williamsburg after a stroll around her estate; perhaps he saw how she doted on her children, something his own mother had never done, and made easy play with Jacky and Patsy. Martha must have liked what she saw, because she extended a dinner invitation, with her visiting sister and brother-in-law as chaperones. His notes from the trip show that he tipped her household staff well, perhaps for a full night's service. Whether he left White House late that night or the next day is less important than the date he came back, which is widely believed to be March 25—less than a week later.

Eighteenth-century courtship moved quickly. Martha and Washington would have spoken frankly about their estates during that visit, right before he was due to head back into the Ohios, where the French and Indian War was still being fought. He would have told her that he had inherited Ferry Farm, but his mother still lived there with his youngest brother, and they used the 260-acre farm to support themselves. He was renting Mount Vernon from Lawrence's widow; she had remarried and her daughter had died, but according to Lawrence's will, the property still belonged to her.

Washington, between his military career and the profit he made from Mount Vernon, primarily through its tobacco crop, was better off than many; but he could be doing much better if he quit the military and became a full-time planter, a transition Martha could make possible.

To the great disappointment of their biographers, we don't know

"A SENSIBLE WOMAN CAN NEVER BE HAPPY WITH A FOOL"

"In my estimation more permanent & genuine happiness is to be found in the sequestered walks of connubial life," Washington wrote, "than in the giddy rounds of promiscuous pleasure, or the more tumultuous and imposing scenes of successful ambition."[5] Later in life, for his beloved step-granddaughters Eliza, Martha, and Nelly Custis, Washington wished "a good husband when you want, and deserve one," and offered them plenty of advice.[6]

Don't be a reckless flirt	"It would be no great departure from truth to say that it rarely happens otherwise, than that a thorough coquette dies in celibacy, as a punishment for her attempts to mislead others, by encouraging looks, words, or actions, given for no other purpose than to draw men on to make overtures that may be rejected."[7]
Make sure he's really into you	"Have I sufficient ground to conclude that his affections are enjoyed by me?"
Let him come to you	"[T]he declaration without the most indirect invitation *on yours*, must proceed from the *man*, to render it permanent & valuable. And nothing short of good sense, and an easy unaffected conduct can draw the line between prudery & coquetry."
Get to know your prospective spouse*	"Retain the resolution to love with moderation . . . at least until you have secured your game."
Love blinds—and fades	"Love is a mighty pretty thing; but like all other delicious things, it is cloying; and when the first transports of the passion begins to subside, which it assuredly will do, and yield—oftentimes too late—to more sober reflections, it serves to evince, that love is too dainty a food to live upon *alone*."

*A real "Do as I say, not as I did" moment

Do a background check	"Is he a man of good character? A man of sense? . . . What has been his walk in life? Is he a gambler? a spendthrift [(wasteful)], a drunkard?"[8]
It's easier to love a rich man than a poor man	"Is his fortune sufficient to maintain me in the manner I have been accustomed to live?"[9]
Get advice from your loved ones	"[I]s he one to whom my friends can have no reasonable objections?"[10]
Be realistic	"Do not, then, in your contemplation of the marriage state, look for perfect felicity before you consent to wed. Nor conceive, from the fine tales the poets and lovers of old have told us, of the transports of mutual love, that heaven has taken its abode on earth; nor do not deceive yourself in supposing, that the only means by which these are to be obtained; is to drink deep of the cup, and revel in an ocean of love."
Life is long, and people change	". . . there is no truth more certain, than that all our enjoyments fall short of our expectations; and to none does it apply with more force, than to the gratification of the passions."

what passed between Martha and Washington when he left that spring, or over the next few months. The couple destroyed all their correspondence, with the exception of a few forgotten letters posthumously discovered in the backs of desk drawers and other lucky places. But their next moves tell us their discussions were serious.

Before returning to his troops, Washington asked George Fairfax, Sally's husband, to oversee the addition of a second floor at Mount Vernon, along with a grand staircase, and new chimneys. The additions doubled the number of rooms and made for a far more imposing outward appearance. He must have told Fairfax that he was expecting Martha and her children to join him, and Sally, perhaps sad to lose a virtuous admirer, or the drama of an illicit temptation, not only stopped writing to him but apparently forbade him to write to her.

And then, on May 4, 1758, Washington ordered a ring from Philadelphia.[11] He may have proposed with it when military business conveniently called him to Williamsburg in June. That was, perhaps, their third meeting. Martha's first husband had been dead a year. She was ready to move on.

She wrote to her London purveyor, Robert Cary & Company, to send her new gloves, a bit of fine lace, a silver chain, perfumed powder, shoes in a deep purple hue with a tiny heel, and new clothes that could be considered "grave but not Extravagent nor to be mourning."[12] She hired a mason, who erected a monument when Custis's tombstone arrived from England. Then she waited for Washington to return from war.

CHAPTER 6

"I Cannot Speak Plainer"

[A]LL IS LOST!–ALL IS LOST BY HEAVENS! OUR ENTERPRIZE Ruind," Washington wrote on August 2, 1758.[1] He was in command of the 1st Virginia Regiment, once again reporting to a British man with whom he was at odds.

Like Braddock, General John Forbes wanted to construct an entirely new road, which Washington found wasteful and unnecessary. So did the Cherokee and Catawba tribes supporting them. Rumor had it that the Indians would abandon the British if construction went ahead. But when Washington voiced his concerns, Forbes punished him for it. Washington's regiment was tasked with working on the road in bad weather as food supplies dwindled and disease spread.

It was Washington's third expedition against the French around what is now Pittsburgh, Pennsylvania. His first two—the Battle of Fort Necessity in 1754, and the Battle of Monongahela in 1755—had been disasters, and the stakes were high enough that the British Army had doubled its troops. But nothing about this experience, it was clear from Forbes's behavior, would be that different on the ground.

Back home in Virginia, everything about Washington's life was changing—even when he was off fighting in the French and Indian War. His first attempt to claim a seat in the House of Burgesses had failed, but this time George Fairfax and friends campaigned on his behalf, which in the eighteenth century meant plying voters with beer and spirits. And it worked. Washington would represent Frederick County during the 1758–1761 legislative session. No doubt rumors about his impending marriage helped his image as a well-to-do planter.

Now that Washington was officially engaged, Sally Fairfax broke her own no-contact rule and sent him what must have seemed a curious letter. It has been lost—perhaps he didn't think it was the kind of thing he should have hanging around—but his bold response on September 12, 1758, survives.

Yes, Washington admitted, he was eager to return to Virginia, and to the "annimating prospect of possessing Mrs Custis." But neither that nor the disaster he was facing under General Forbes was the source of "my anxiety."

> Tis true, I profess myself a Votary to Love—I acknowledge that a Lady is in the Case—and further I confess, that this Lady is known to you. . . . I feel the force of her amiable beauties in the recollection of a thousand tender passages that I coud wish to obliterate, till I am bid to revive them.—but experience alas! sadly reminds me how Impossible this is . . . the World has no business to know the object of my Love, declard in this manner to—you when I want to conceal it.[2]

Perhaps Sally wasn't ready to let go. She sent him another letter, which was again lost. His reply is somewhat terse.

> Do we still misunderstand the true meaning of each others Letters? I think it must appear so, tho I woud feign hope the contrary as I cannot speak plainer without—but I'll say no more, and leave you to guess the rest.[3]

With that, Washington, consumed by a busy, happy life with his new family, left the youthful crush behind him.

Sally would not be as fortunate. After the Revolution, the Fairfaxes moved to London, where her husband's noble relatives snubbed her; the state claimed their property back home as a penalty for remaining loyal to the crown, and her brother lost the family fortune. She later wrote to her sister-in-law, "I now know that the worthy man is to be preferred to the high-born."[4]

☆ ☆ ☆

On November 12, 1758, a French and Indian party approached British troops guarding cattle and horses. General Forbes ordered Washington to block the attack. He'd managed to take a few prisoners when, in the failing light, a second contingent materialized out of nowhere. His troops panicked. Virginians were suddenly firing on Virginians, mistaking their fellow colonists for the enemy. Fourteen of Washington's own men were dead before he managed to stop the bloodshed. And by the time he finally reached Fort Duquesne, the French had burned it to the ground and moved on.

Washington may have found some pleasure in the French departure, but it was an anticlimactic resolution. Although the war continued, the campaign was over, and so was his military career.

On January 6, 1759, Martha and Washington were married. She wore a yellow brocade dress over a white silk petticoat, he a civilian suit. They would not stay in the area long. Washington, now a man of great wealth and stepfather to two young children, would make a proper home of Mount Vernon.

A month earlier, he had ridden to Williamsburg and resigned his commission. He'd given up on the British military and, though he did not yet realize it, the British Empire. The French and Indian War set colonists, who had undergone their own cultural and social development in the New World, on the path to independence. They were learning that their goals and values differed from those of the crown, and that their concerns, even when voiced by the most ambitious, gifted, and loyal among them, fell on deaf ears.

"My inclinations are strongly bent to arms," Washington had written in 1754, when he was twenty-two, but he just couldn't satisfy that desire in His Majesty's forces. The next time he would join them on the battlefield, it would be to destroy them.[5]

CHAPTER 7

"What Manner of Man I Am"

IN 1772, THIRTEEN YEARS AFTER WASHINGTON HUNG UP THE UNI-
form of a colonel in the Virginia militia, he squeezed himself back
into it. Martha had chosen the artist Charles Willson Peale to paint his
portrait, but it was Washington who had decided to pose as a military
man. It was a curious choice, considering that he'd spent the intervening years as a gentleman farmer, and had the fine imported clothes to
prove it. Those clothes would surely have fit him much better; in the
portrait, the uniform appears slightly snug around his midsection,
which had grown paunchier with lifestyle and age. His hair, though, was
still reddish-brown, unpowdered beneath his campaign hat.

It was Peale's job, Washington wrote, to describe "to the World
what manner of man I am," but the sword slung around his waist and the
musket poking out behind him sent a clear message: George Washington was still very much "bent to arms."[1]

His transition from rising military star to gentleman farmer, husband, and father had been smooth; his youthful renown, wealthy wife,
considerable land holdings, and large plantation and home hit all the

right notes in Virginia society. The House of Burgesses sessions had become, among other things, a good excuse for the relatively private Washingtons to party with the Williamsburg gentry—which George and Martha did, dancing the nights away, playing cards, and going on fox hunts. And he had established deep ties with the community, serving as churchwarden, town trustee, and justice of the court.

Washington spared no expense when it came to Jacky and Patsy in part because those expenses were deducted from the Custis estate. His stepchildren were tutored at Mount Vernon until Jacky, at thirteen, was sent around six miles away to school. Patsy stayed at home, where her parents showered her with adoration. Perhaps, as Washington's ledgers indicate, she persuaded him to stop ordering books on Latin grammar in favor of those on music composition and song. He indulged her with regular dance lessons, too.

The ledgers also pinpoint the beginning of Patsy's decline. In 1768, the doctor's bills began to accumulate, as did the prescriptions. Patsy took powders, pills, and herbs, but was still "sezied with fits." Washington began tracking their frequency, length, and severity in his diary. During the summer of 1770, she had them on twenty-six different days, one "very bad."[2] The seizures, which we would now call epilepsy, must have been terrifying. Patsy most certainly lost consciousness and control of her limbs. She may have bitten her tongue or injured herself when, inevitably, they struck her when she was standing, causing her to fall down. Washington hired a live-in housekeeper, who was probably a nurse, to look after her at all times. He took her to Warm Springs, and to specialists. He wrote to experts for advice and new concoctions. Some seemed to work at first, giving the Washingtons hope, but then another fit would strike and send Patsy to bed.

When Patsy was well, she lived a full life. Washington ordered her finery from London, including a firestone necklace and satin dancing slippers. He took her riding and to church. She read *Lady's Magazine* with her mother, called on friends, and went to a ball in Alexandria. But in a miniature portrait painted in 1772, Patsy, aged sixteen, looks pale and tired. A year later, she was dead.

The next day, Washington managed to write a heartbreaking letter to Burwell Bassett, who was married to one of Martha's younger sisters, Anna Marie.

> It is an easier matter to conceive, than to describe, the distress of this Family; especially that of the unhappy Parent of our Dear Patcy Custis, when I inform you that yesterday removd the Sweet Innocent Girl into a more happy, & peaceful abode than any she has met with, in the afflicted Path she hitherto has trod.
>
> She rose from Dinner about four Oclock, in better health and spirits than she appeard to have been in for some time; soon after which she was siezd with one of her usual Fits, & expird in it, in less than two Minutes without uttering a Word, a groan, or scarce a Sigh.—this Sudden, and unexpected blow, I scarce need add has almost reduced my poor Wife to the lowest ebb of Misery. . . . [3]

From then on, Martha wore Patsy's miniature, set in a gold locket bracelet, on her wrist, and worried endlessly about the health of her remaining child.

From the very beginning, Washington had been excited to watch Jacky, heir to his late father's sizable fortune, benefit from all the advantages his own father's death had denied him. He provided Jacky with the best tutors, clothes, and introductions, but he could never give his stepson what he needed most: adversity.

Much to Washington's dismay, his sweet, precocious boy grew into a pampered, rowdy, undisciplined teenager with an affinity for "Dogs, Horses and Guns."[4] He could have sent the boy abroad, either to school or, like Abigail and John Adams did with John Quincy, to be a teenage diplomat-in-training, but Martha preferred that he stay close to home. So Washington sent Jacky to a boys' school in nearby Caroline County, Virginia, and spent the next few years receiving frustrating updates from the Reverend Jonathan Boucher. He had tutored a generation of wealthy ne'er-do-wells, but Jacky may have surpassed them all. "I must confess to You I never did in my Life know a Youth so exceedingly indolent, or so surprizingly voluptuous," Boucher wrote on December 18, 1770. "One wd suppose Nature had intended Him for some Asiatic Prince."[5] In letters, Washington coached, pleaded, lectured, and encouraged Jacky through the Boucher years, with some success; he managed to complete his early schooling, and agreed to continue his education. When Patsy died, Washington had just returned from dropping off Jacky at the College of New York—though he wouldn't last there long.

Jacky's squandered opportunities were hardly Washington's sole frustration. Civilian life offered him far more opportunities to acquire wealth and prestige, yet he kept butting up against the same obstacle that had driven him to quit the army in the first place: unequal treatment of colonists. As a member of the Burgesses' Committee on Propositions and Grievances, he was overwhelmed by petitions from soldiers and businesses to whom the crown owed money and land. And he had some personal grievances, too.

At Mount Vernon, Washington felt victimized by predatory merchants in London. His letters to Robert Cary & Company—a supplier that would not have dignified him with a response, let alone an account, before he took over Martha's fortune—had become increasingly hostile over the years. He regularly accused them of attempting to "palm some-times old, and sometimes very slight and indifferent goods upon us, tak-ing care at the same time to advance the price."[6] There was no return policy on the second-rate goods they sent colonists, and no alternative option. Americans were dependent on London purveyors for every-thing from clothing to plows, the latter of which Washington com-plained bitterly "coud only have been us[e]d by our Forefathers in the days of yore."[7]

Washington also blamed Cary & Co. for endangering his liveli-hood. The law required that colonists sell any tobacco they grew through England, but his crops fetched prices far lower than he deemed fair—not that Mount Vernon's soil, regularly tested by drought and heavy rain, grew especially good tobacco. Like many land-rich, cash-poor Vir-ginia planters, including Thomas Jefferson, Washington got behind on his payments to London purveyors, and was soon in debt.

He spent the 1760s and early 1770s attempting to break the cycle, which was only possible because his marriage to Martha had brought with it hundreds of enslaved people. Washington purchased additional slaves and indentured servants, and leased others from nearby planta-tions. While they worked, the man they called "Master" holed up in the mansion house, inhaling books and pamphlets on agriculture and man-ufacturing. He hoped to diversify his crops and maybe produce some artisanal goods.

Mount Vernon's large enslaved community, of whom more than half originally belonged to the Custis estate, labored from sunup to sun-down, six days a week, under the careful watch of overseers. Although estates like Mount Vernon are called "plantations," it's a word inflected with genteel romanticism. If we look at what actually occurred there, we see them for what they were: forced-labor camps.[9]

"Keep everyone in their places, and to their duty," Washington instructed an overseer in 1789. To do so, these white men (and, on occasion, enslaved black men) carried whips, and when they deemed it necessary, used them. "I am determined to lower [Charlotte's] Spirit or skin her Back," Anthony Whitting wrote in 1793 to Washington, who found the farm manager's use of a hickory stick "very proper."[10]

Washington did not just give others permission to physically abuse people he held in bondage; he sometimes assaulted them himself. Decades after his death, his nephew Lawrence Lewis recounted a story that had been told to him by an enslaved carpenter named Isaac. Washington had ordered Isaac to roll over a large log in order to cut it; he was strong, but not strong enough to lift it himself, so the cut was imperfect. When Washington saw, he "gave me such a slap on the side of my head that I Whirled round like a top & before I knew where I was Master was gone." It was not an isolated incident.[11]

Washington urged his overseers to use physical punishment sparingly—not for the enslaved person's well-being, but because an injured slave was less productive. He expected a lot from people who were motivated by nothing but the will to survive. They planted fields of barley, corn, and wheat; they pruned the orchards and vineyards; they bred horses; they operated a textile factory, a cider press, a flour mill, a sawmill, and a distillery. To supplement their lean diets, they were allowed to fish from the Potomac on Sundays, their only day off. When Washington learned of their impressive yield, he added that commodity to Mount Vernon's portfolio, too. He shipped goods to England, the West Indies, and Portugal, though whenever possible he attempted to sell and trade within the colonies.[12]

But the British Parliament was constantly frustrating Washington. A month after he joined the Mississippi Land Company, hoping to expand the colonies west from Ohio to Tennessee, the crown banned colonists from the area, citing the importance of fur trading with the

SLAVE QUARTERS

By Washington's death in 1799, there were 317 slaves and about 25 hired or indentured white servants living at Mount Vernon. They were housed in "small villages," as his presidential home calls them today, across Washington's five farms. In 1797, a visitor "entered one of the huts of the Blacks" and described what he saw: "the husband and wife sleep on a mean pallet, the children on the ground; a very bad fireplace, some utensils for cooking, but in the middle of this poverty some cups and a teapot."[8]

LOCATION	SIZE (ACRES)	ESTIMATED POPULATION	HOUSING TYPE
Mansion House Farm	500	90	The slave quarters closest to Washington's mansion were reserved for house servants and skilled workers. The two-story building had a chimney on each end and glazed windows. It was torn down in the 1790s, and most of the slaves were relocated into four 600-square-foot rooms in the Greenhouse's brick wings. The housing was better here than on the outlying farms, but the privacy was far worse; slaves lived alongside many other families, whereas in the farther-flung cabins no more than two shared a dwelling.
Dogue Run Farm	650	45	The standard slave cabins, on this farm and the four below, were made of wood daubed with mud. Each had a chimney, and consisted of one room or two. They were leaky and poorly constructed.
Muddy Hole Farm	476	41	Same as above.
River Farm	1,207	57	Same as above.
Union Farm	928	76	Same as above.

Indians. In 1765, Parliament passed the Stamp Act, which placed a tax on paper and printed material; practically everything Washington touched, from newspapers to playing cards, had a brand-new premium.

The colonists were livid. They complained to the royal governor and sent letters to Parliament; on the ground, the situation turned violent. In Williamsburg, the townspeople burned their tax collector in effigy. Washington would never act out in such a manner, but he began to rebel in his own ways. He became convinced that a meaningful effort to curtail the colonists' addiction to European luxury goods would stimulate local industry—including, conveniently, Mount Vernon. But before he could realize any meaningful profit, Parliament abandoned the wildly unpopular Stamp Act.

The colonists, an ocean away from the seat of power, blamed greedy nobles and lords in Parliament and thanked good and fair King George III for intervening. It would take years for them to realize their mistake.

☆ ☆ ☆

The Virginia elite returned to their old spendthrift ways, amassing even more debt and crippling interest. Advertisements for insolvent estates in the New World filled the gazettes. Then, just two years later, Parliament came back for more with the Townshend Acts, which taxed not just paper but also paint, glass, and tea.

This time, all of the Burgesses demanded a full repeal, and they weren't alone; New Yorkers and Philadelphians were just as outraged. Bloodshed "should be the last resource," Washington wrote, but if it came to that, no colonist should "hesitate a moment."[13] Thoroughly committed to the belief that King George was being misled by his advisers and Parliament, the Burgesses attempted to cut out the middlemen and wrote to him directly, "praying the royal interposition in favor of the violated rights of America."[14]

Lord Dunmore, the royal governor of Virginia, was infuriated; in order to remind them of his power, he dissolved the House of Burgesses. But he couldn't stop them from meeting elsewhere. They decamped to nearby Raleigh Tavern and agreed, with surprising enthusiasm, to boycott British goods. Although Washington wished the proposal were "ten times as strict," he was happy they were moving forward with a punitive plan of their own.[15]

The boycott didn't last long. Even Washington had trouble curtailing his spending, or perhaps getting Martha to. But as always, when the goods they ordered arrived from England, he was disappointed, and there was nothing he could do about it. He was beginning to realize that the only way to rid himself of the rigged system was to drive it out entirely.

Events in Boston in 1773 accelerated his thinking. Massachusetts colonists dressed as Indians boarded three ships moored in Boston Harbor and cast hundreds of crates of tea into the water. (Although the Townshend Acts had by then been repealed, a tax remained on tea.) Washington was uneasy with the Boston Tea Party's destructive methods, but smiled on their rejection of the tea tax.

It was Parliament's response—the Intolerable Acts (also known as the Coercive Acts)—to the protests that he found unforgivable. They shut down the port of Boston, followed by the democratic town meetings, where desperate colonists gathered to address the onslaught of starvation. British officials were exempted from criminal prosecution. Colonists were told they must house troops in their homes. London policymakers expected them to shrink back in terror, but the blatant misrule had the opposite effect. It mobilized them, and it radicalized Washington.

"I think the Parliament of Great Britain hath no more Right to put their hands into my Pocket, without my consent, than I have to put my hands into your's, for money," he lectured a friend. "And this being already urged to them in a firm, but decent manner by all the Colonies, what reason is there to expect any thing from their justice?"[16]

CHAPTER 8

"The Shackles of Slavery"

I N SEPTEMBER 1775, WASHINGTON ONCE AGAIN PUT ON HIS OLD MIL-
itary uniform. He was done posing. He was done writing "humble
and dutiful" letters to London, as he had done for years in the House of
Burgesses; it hadn't made a difference then, and it made no difference in
1774, after the First Continental Congress in Philadelphia.[1] He was
done watching and waiting. It was time to make a move.

Washington rode to Philadelphia, along with Peyton Randolph and
Patrick Henry, to represent Virginia at the Second Continental Congress.
When he arrived, after four days of travel, he seemed to be everywhere.
He visited with like-minded colonists in their regal homes—thirty-one
regal homes, to be exact. He made an appearance in nearly every church,
from Anglican to Quaker. He drank in the local taverns. Wherever he
went, people took notice of his "soldier like air and gesture."[2] It was hard
to miss, in that uniform, but Dr. Benjamin Rush, who would later sign the
Declaration of Independence, wrote, "He has so much martial dignity in
his deportment that you would distinguish him to be a general and a soldier from among ten thousand people."

Washington was quietly campaigning before there was anything to officially campaign for, and it worked. His charisma—that rarest of gifts—charmed and fascinated everyone around him. Delegates found him to be "discreet and virtuous," and when he spoke they listened.

Parliament was using "despotism to fix the Shackles of Slavery upon us," Washington said. It was the American colonists' duty to resist such oppression on behalf of "mankind"—a category he understood to exclude mothers, sisters, wives, and daughters, along with millions of slaves.[3] It was an ironic choice of words considering *Somerset v Stewart*, a 1772 decision from the Court of the King's Bench in London, which held that chattel slavery was neither supported in common law nor authorized by statute in England and Wales—a clear victory for abolitionists, which terrified Southern colonists. If slavery was outlawed in America, their profits would plummet, as would the power they derived from bondage—including the luxury of rebellion.

In London, writer Samuel Johnson railed against the hypocrisy of "these demigods of independence" in a forty-page pamphlet asking, "How is it that we hear the loudest *yelps* for liberty among the drivers of negroes?"[4]

★ ★ ★

When hostilities broke out in the spring of 1775, only one side had an army—and a man to lead it. "Oh that I was a soldier!" bemoaned John Adams, a lawyer from Massachusetts, in a letter to Abigail Adams. "I will be. I am reading military books. Everyone must and will, and shall be a soldier."[5] But he wasn't, and he wouldn't be. Adams, like many of the intellectual and landed men who gathered in Philadelphia, had no experience in the field; the coming war would not change that.

Washington, on the other hand, knew how the Royal Army operated.

What's more, he had never served under any other flag. The same could not be said for Charles Lee, his main competitor for commander in chief; Lee had served in the British Army during the French and Indian War and, more recently, for the Polish in the Russo-Turkish War. He returned to America in 1773—minus two fingers he lost in a duel—and promptly took himself out of the running by demanding that he be compensated, in advance, for the property the British would confiscate should the revolution fail. (Lee's obsession with his Pomeranian, Mr. Spada, his foul language, and his sloppy presentation may not have helped matters.) Meanwhile, it was rumored, correctly, that Washington would serve without pay, as he had during the end of his service in the British military. "He is a complete gentleman," Massachusetts delegate Thomas Cushing wrote. "He is sensible, amiable, virtuous, modest, and brave."[6]

And rich. Washington was rich enough to pay his own way, and perhaps support others, too, but devoted enough to the cause to risk it all. That was the kind of man that colonists, no matter where they were from, wanted to lead them into a seemingly unwinnable war.

With the exception, that is, of John Hancock, a politician and mercantile heir from Boston. He thought himself so likely to be a contender for commander in chief, despite a bad case of gout and no military experience, that he sat expectantly during nominations. But the Continental Army could not be led by a New Englander; that region had already mobilized. The southerners, with their money and potential enlistments, would best respond to one of their own. Washington was a Virginian, the most famous among a long list of rising stars. (Future presidents Thomas Jefferson and James Madison had already earned reputations as great thinkers.) Divisions between the delegates over how aggressively the colonists should move toward independence had already sprung up and created tensions among the men, but Washington, as Connecticut delegate Silas Deane wrote, "remove[d] all jealousies, and that is the main point."[7]

In the aftermath of the battles at Lexington and Concord the previous spring—during which Massachusetts militias had defeated the British—there was an urgent need to move quickly. "[T]he once happy and peaceful plains of America are either to be drenched with Blood, or Inhabited by Slaves. Sad alternative! But can a virtuous Man hesitate in his choice?" Washington had written from Mount Vernon, and in London, the British were asking the same thing.[8]

Votes were taken. In Philadelphia, miraculously, the delegates reached a unanimous decision on June 15, 1775: They would raise an army, and George Washington would lead it.

Parliament took a vote, too, later that summer, but they were not united. Only 78 members voted for conciliation; 270 nobles and lords were eager to teach the rebellious colonists a brutal lesson.

Washington, forty-three years old, accepted the position but spoke as if he were signing his own death warrant. Few letters between Washington and Martha (whom he apparently called "Patcy" in private) survive, but one of the most dramatic speaks to his state of mind on June 18, 1775.

My Dearest,

I am now set down to write to you on a subject which fills me with inexpressable concern—and this concern is greatly aggravated and Increased when I reflect on the uneasiness I know it will give you—It has been determined in Congress, that the whole Army raised for the defence of the American Cause shall be put under my care, and that it is necessary for me to proceed immediately to Boston to take upon me the Command of it. You may beleive me my dear Patcy, when I assure you, in the most solemn manner, that, so far from seeking this appointment I have used every endeavour in my power to avoid it, not only from my unwillingness to part with you and the Family, but from a consciousness of its being a trust too great for my Capacity. . . . it was utterly out of my power to refuse this appointment without exposing my Character to such censures as would have reflected dishonour upon myself, and given pain to my friends—this I am sure could not, and ought not to be pleasing to you, & must have lessend me considerably in my own esteem. I shall rely therefore, confidently, on that Providence which has heretofore preservd, & been bountiful to me, not doubting but that I shall return safe to you in the fall.[9]

It would be, in reality, more than seven years before Washington would "return safe." And though he would repeat these humble sentiments for the rest of his life, the uniform he had at the ready for Philadelphia—and the busts of Julius Caesar, Alexander the Great, and other military heroes he had ordered after he retired over a decade earlier—suggested that he yearned for a military triumph. This time, there would be no Englishman above him.

For all Washington's talk of the "American Union and Patriotism," his arsenal of personal grievances cannot be underestimated. He had grown and changed over the previous sixteen years, but at his core, he was still a man eager to be recognized. As commander in chief of the Continental Army, he would be at the center of his country's story. It was the ultimate way to right past wrongs, to distinguish himself not by where he came from or whom he married but by what he had achieved. And there could not be a more auspicious start than a unanimous election.

Only Washington could deny himself the opportunity to drive the British out. Only the British could deny him victory. These were the odds he had always wanted, and he wasn't about to sit this one out.

✯ PART II ✯

*General George Washington's
American Revolution—
Off the Battlefield*

GENERALS *of the* AMERICAN REVOLUTION

"**A**n American planter was chosen by us to Command our Troops and continued during the whole War," Benjamin Franklin wrote, taunting an English friend. "This Man sent home to you, one after another, five of your best Generals, baffled, their heads bare of Laurels, disgraced even in the opinion of their employers."[1]

YEAR	AMERICAN GENERAL	BRITISH GENERAL
1775	George Washington	Thomas Gage
1776–1777	George Washington	Sir William Howe
1778–1781	George Washington	Sir Henry Clinton
1781	George Washington	Lord Charles Cornwallis
1782–1783	George Washington	Sir Guy Carleton

WASHINGTON'S
Revolutionary Battles
AT A GLANCE

First in war doesn't mean best in war. After Washington died, hundreds of eulogies praised his brilliance as a battleground tactician and strategist. But from the outset, Washington was well aware of his own limitations and anxious about those of his officers; even the Thigh Men acknowledge that Washington "lost more battles than any victorious general in modern history."[2] And yet, his performance as a military leader has been the subject of hundreds of biographies and thousands of books. This section will instead focus on his feats off the battlefield, with a brief review of his major battles in the table on the next page.

YEAR	BATTLE	OUTCOME	AMERICAN TROOPS & CASUALTIES	BRITISH TROOPS & CASUALTIES	SUMMARY
April 19, 1775– March 17, 1775	Siege of Boston	Won	Troops: 11,000 Killed or Wounded: 469 Captured: 30	Troops: 9,400 Killed or Wounded: 1,160 Captured: 35	"My God, these fellows have done more work in one night than I could make my army do in three months," British Commander General William Howe declared when daylight revealed that 49 patriot cannons were pointed at his men from Dorchester Heights. Howe, along with 11,000 redcoats and Loyalists, would leave on what would be known as "Evacuation Day."
August 27, 1776	Battle of Long Island	Lost	Troops: 10,000 Killed: 300 Wounded: 650 Captured: 1,100	Troops: 20,000 Killed: 63 Wounded: 314 Captured: 0	Despite Washington's attempt to fortify Brooklyn Heights and Lower Manhattan, Howe took advantage of the unguarded Jamaica Pass to the east and attacked Americans from the rear and sides. Washington, humiliated, was supposedly the last man evacuated from Brooklyn.
September 15, 1776	Battle of Kip's Bay	Lost	Troops: 450 Killed or Wounded: 60 Captured: 367	Troops: 4,000 Killed or Wounded: 12 Captured: 0	Burn or abandon New York? Washington's council of war urged him to evacuate, but as British-allied Hessians approached, he was seen hitting panicked militiamen with the flat of his sword to stop them from fleeing. When the enemy got too close, he finally listened to his aides and headed up to Harlem—with the British bugling "Gone Away," a fox-hunting tune celebrating an animal's imminent capture.

YEAR	BATTLE	OUTCOME	AMERICAN TROOPS & CASUALTIES	BRITISH TROOPS & CASUALTIES	SUMMARY
September 16, 1776	Battle of Harlem Heights	Won	Troops: 1,800 Killed: 30 Wounded: 100 Captured: 0	Troops: 5,000 Killed: 90 Wounded: 300 Captured: 0	During the first open battlefield victory for the Americans, Washington sent for reinforcements and successfully executed a flank attack.
October 28, 1776	Battle of White Plains	Lost	Troops: 13,000 Killed: 50 Wounded: 150 Captured: 17	Troops: 5,000 Killed: 47 Wounded: 182 Captured: 4	A flank attack by the British on Washington's encampment meant another withdrawal.
November 16, 1776	Battle of Fort Washington	Lost	Troops: 2,900 Killed or Wounded: 53 Captured: 2,818	Troops: 8,000 Killed or Wounded: 458 Captured: 0	Washington, stationed across the river, insisted on inspecting its defense, and left no more than thirty minutes before British and Hessian forces overwhelmed the fort's garrison.
November 20, 1776	Evacuation of Fort Lee	Lost	Troops: 2,000 Killed or Wounded: 0 Captured: 160	Troops: 4,000 Killed or Wounded: 0 Captured: 0	"Fort Lee was always considered as only necessary in connection with [Fort Washington]," the general wrote to John Hancock a day before ordering the fort's evacuation. That may have been true, but it also meant forfeiting dozens of cannons, hundreds of tents, and a thousand barrels of flour.

YEAR	BATTLE	OUTCOME	AMERICAN TROOPS & CASUALTIES	BRITISH TROOPS & CASUALTIES	SUMMARY
December 26, 1776	Battle of Trenton	Won	Troops: 2,400 Killed or Wounded: 0 Captured: 0	Troops: 1,500 Killed or Wounded: 22 Captured: 918	Following a series of defeats, Washington led a daring crossing of the Delaware River in the middle of the night—and a winter storm. His determined force attacked the Hessians at 8 a.m. The enemy, still recovering from Christmas celebrations, offered but a brief defense that left their commander mortally wounded.
January 2, 1777	Second Battle of Trenton	Won	Troops: 1,000 Killed or Wounded: 50 Captured: 5	Troops: 2,000 Killed or Wounded: 40 Captured: 5	The British returned to reclaim Trenton but, with only one bridge to attack from, were repelled three times. By the next morning, Washington had slipped away with the main body of his force for an attack on Princeton.
January 3, 1777	Battle of Princeton	Won	Troops: 4,500 Killed: 25 Wounded: 60 Captured: 0	Troops: 1,200 Killed: 20 Wounded: 60 Captured: 230	Washington's arrival reinvigorated fatigued patriot troops, who followed him into battle and successfully pushed the British back, threatening their supply lines and claiming much of New Jersey.
September 11, 1777	Battle of Brandywine	Lost	Troops: 14,600 Killed: 200 Wounded: 300–600 Captured: 400	Troops: 15,500 Killed: 583 Wounded: 93 Missing: 6	A devastating loss that allowed the British to conquer Philadelphia, then the capital of the United States.

YEAR	BATTLE	OUTCOME	AMERICAN TROOPS & CASUALTIES	BRITISH TROOPS & CASUALTIES	SUMMARY
September 16, 1777	Battle of the Clouds	Draw	Troops: 9,500 Killed or Wounded: 0 Captured: 0	Troops: 12,000 Killed or Wounded: 0 Captured: 0	Washington hoped to rebuff General Howe's advances, but was thwarted by a torrential downpour that dampened ammunition and washed out roads.
October 4, 1777	Battle of Germantown	Lost	Troops: 11,000 Killed: 152 Wounded: 521 Captured: 438	Troops: 9,000 Killed: 71 Wounded: 448 Missing: 14	When Howe divided his army and encamped outside of Philadelphia, Washington took a chance. The battle lasted five hours and shook the victors, but the Continental Army ultimately failed; their flanking columns were late to arrive and the British-occupied Cliveden mansion turned out to be as strong as a fortress.
December 6–8, 1777	Battle of White Marsh	Draw	Troops: 6,000 Killed or Wounded: 40 Captured: 0	Troops: 8,000 Killed or Wounded: 56 Captured: 0	Hoping for one decisive victory before winter, Howe marched his army sixteen miles from the capital to Washington's encampment. After skirmishes and failed flanking, Howe decided that his counterpart was stronger than he realized, and withdrew.

YEAR	BATTLE	OUTCOME	AMERICAN TROOPS & CASUALTIES	BRITISH TROOPS & CASUALTIES	SUMMARY
June 28, 1778	Battle of Monmouth	Draw	Troops: 12,000 Killed: 72 Wounded: 161 Missing: 130 Died of Heatstroke: 37	Troops: 10,000 Killed: 147 Wounded: 170 Died of Heatstroke: 60	When Sir Henry Clinton (who succeeded Howe) moved his troops from Philadelphia to New York, Washington instructed General Charles Lee (his principal subordinate) to harass them from the rear. But after just a few hours, Lee retreated. Washington, usually so self-controlled, loudly cursed him upon arrival. After night fell, the redcoats left for New York, but Washington was none the wiser, duped by burning fires masking their departure. Despite that, Washington claimed it was a victory.
September 15–October 19, 1781	Siege of Yorktown	Won	Troops: 20,000 Killed or Wounded: 400 Captured: 400	Troops: 9,725 Killed: 156 Wounded: 326 Captured: 7,980 Missing: 70	When the British withdrew a significant force from New York to reinforce troops in Yorktown, Virginia, Washington headed south. French allies helped Americans capture key points, and by sea, their ships, which controlled access to the Chesapeake Bay, prevented British naval assistance and reinforcements. Lord Cornwallis surrendered in less than thirty days.

CHAPTER 9

Hardball with the Howe Brothers

T HE BRITISH DIDN'T SEE THEMSELVES AS INVADERS IN 1776, BUT they showed up, just the same, with the largest invasion force they had ever mustered—400 ships carrying 32,000 troops, enough to block off America's key waterways and starve it of military supplies.

The flotilla was led by Admiral Richard Howe, who'd earned the nickname "Black Dick" because he was said to smile only when a lot of people were about to die. With help from Loyalists on the ground, Black Dick would teach a violent lesson to the "rascally banditti" and "fire-brands of sedition" who had taken up arms against the sovereign.[1] He announced his arrival on the Hudson with a two-hour cannonade.

George Washington, meanwhile, had little artillery, no cavalry, and no naval support; a total of perhaps 19,000 troops served under his command.

King George III had told his ministers that "blows must decide" whether the Americans "submit or triumph," but Parliament decided to make one last attempt at diplomacy—or the appearance of it, anyway.[2] It instructed William Howe, general of the Royal Army and brother to

Black Dick, to offer the commander in chief of the Continental Army (which one imagines he said while miming scare quotes) a final chance to avoid leading the thirteen colonies into certain death, destruction, and degradation. He entrusted a letter to Lieutenant Philip Brown, who set out to deliver it on a small boat bearing a white flag.[3]

The British were eager to reach a resolution. War was always expensive, but in this case there was a small chance it could be ruinous; the enemy's power was unknowable. What if the patriots had made soldiers of the two million male colonists in America? Even if the Continental Army had managed to enlist just 5 percent of the population, those 100,000 men would outnumber the Royal Army by a factor of four to one. And although the patriots' lack of a navy put them at a distinct disadvantage, their great advantage was supplying locally, whereas those of

IDEALISM DOESN'T PAY THE BILLS

Massachusetts firebrand Samuel Adams argued the cause of liberty would sustain an army, but Washington worried that volunteer soldiers would lead to frequent turnover. Unlike Adams, whose politically active father prospered in real estate and the brewery business, Washington knew that idealism couldn't feed a soldier's family or pay his debts. "After the first emotions are over," he warned John Hancock, untrained civilian recruits could not be expected to forfeit "private interest to the common good." (After all, that's how the British Army had lost him.) "To expect then the same Service from Raw, and undisciplined Recruits as from Veteran Soldiers is to expect what never did, and perhaps never will happen."[4] And he was right; by mid-1776, half of the Continental Army had deserted. It would take years before Congress—wary of the cash and land grants it would take to secure a trained, professional army—gave Washington what he wanted.

the British were 3,000 miles away.[5] There would be travel delays, to be sure, exacerbated by however long it took Parliament to approve every replenishment. The conflict would drag on, and the longer it did, the weaker Britain would become, perhaps tempting the French or Spanish to get involved. And if that happened, the British would be fighting a war against both their own colonies and their old enemies.

Washington was expecting Howe's overture. He dispatched Colonels Henry Knox, Joseph Reed, and Samuel Webb, who approached to rendezvous with Brown's boat between Staten Island and Governors Island. Brown, the British lieutenant, said that he had a letter for "Mr. Washington," to which Reed replied, "Sir, we have no person in our army with that address." Brown asked him to look at the letter, addressed to "George Washington, Esqr.," and again Reed rejected it. "You are sensible, sir, of the rank of General Washington in our army?" he asked. "Yes, sir, we are," Brown admitted.

Acknowledging Washington's rank would mean recognizing America as a sovereign nation, and that was a nonstarter. The Howe brothers, for all their guns and ships, and ships with guns, didn't have much bargaining power. The Royal Army was open to reconciliation or battle, and nothing else. They could offer Washington pardon, but only in exchange for a total and complete "dissolution of all rebel political and military bodies, surrender of all the forts and posts, and restoration of the King's officials."[6] It was a bad offer for Washington as an individual and for America as a country. He refused.

"So high is the vanity and the insolence of these men!" Ambrose Serle, General Howe's personal secretary, declared. But Howe didn't share Serle's disdain.[7] If anything, he was curious about this previously loyal colonist, who was already proving fearless in the face of a global superpower. He sent another letter, this time generously adding two "etceteras" to the address. "George Washington, Esq, etc., etc." was

WASHINGTON'S LIFEGUARDS: "CONQUER OR DIE"

On March 11, 1776, during the siege of Boston, Washington issued a "General Order to Colonels or Commanding Officers," in which he asked them to select four men. Washington had a very specific vision for his personal guards, down to their height:

> His Excellency depends upon the Colonels for good Men, such as they can recommend for their sobriety, honesty, and good behavior; he wishes them to be from five feet, eight Inches high, to five feet, ten Inches; handsomely and well made, and as there is nothing in his eyes more desirable, than Cleanliness in a Soldier, he desires that particular attention may be made, in the choice of such men, as are neat, and spruce.[8]

Washington put Caleb Gibbs, of the 14th Massachusetts Continental Regiment, in charge of the new unit, which he called "My Guards." Soldiers called them "His Excellency's Guard" and "Washington's Body Guard," but most of his men called them "the Life Guards." They dressed in blue and buff uniforms with leather helmets bearing a white plume. Gibbs had the buttons on his uniform engraved with "USA"—the first known record of the abbreviation.

Under the motto "Conquer or Die," Gibbs trained his men to protect Washington, as well as the army's cash and official papers. They foiled at least one assassination attempt, fought in battles, and performed military demonstrations. They were mostly furloughed after Yorktown, but their last mission was one of the most important—ensuring that the six wagons filled with Washington's belongings and official war records reached Mount Vernon.[9]

promptly declined again, but this time Washington agreed to meet British Colonel James Paterson. Colonel Paterson was blindfolded and taken to Knox's temporary home in New York, at No. 1 Broadway. Washington insisted that his Life Guards, a sort of proto–Secret Service, stand watch.

Paterson likely knew that nothing would come from the meeting, but he seemed happy to take it. In a letter to his wife, Lucy, Knox reported that Paterson stood before Washington "as if he was before something supernatural." He described a reverent scene in which "Every other word was 'May it please your Excellency,' 'If your Excellency so please' . . . " But Paterson had nothing new to offer except flattery. "Etc.," he argued unconvincingly, meant "everything," a sign of Howe's esteem for his American colleague. Washington could not abide this contention. What's more, he told Paterson, "the Americans had not offended, and therefore they needed no pardon."[10] If peace between two coequal nations wasn't on the table, there was nothing more to discuss.

Still, Paterson lingered, hoping for a message he could take back to the Howe brothers. Washington replied, smolderingly, "My particular compliments to both."[11] That swagger, from the leader of a far inferior, ill-trained army facing the greatest military power in the world, was all Washington. He'd lacked a cool head when he'd fought for the British, but in the seventeen years since he'd grown into a statesman.

Washington then sent a letter to John Hancock, explaining why he'd dug in his heels. "I deemed It a duty to my Country and my appointment," he wrote, "to insist upon that respect."[12] This wasn't about superficial decorum. It was about what the United States of America was willing to put up for negotiation, and that emphatically did not include its independence—or the laws of war.

If America was not a sovereign nation, its soldiers were "rebels,"

SIDESTEPPING THE RULES OF WAR

Captive soldiers, according to the rules of war, were meant to be treated like one's own—fed, housed, and cared for, at the expense of the army to whom they belonged—and violations of these rules made for good propaganda. When Washington heard Lieutenant William Martin and six of his men had been brutally hacked to death after they injured a couple of Hessian mercenaries, he ordered Martin's mutilated body be cleaned and exhibited for all to see. John Robert Shaw, a seventeen-year-old British soldier who rode to the Hessians' rescue and witnessed the subsequent killing of Martin's men, wrote that "the shrieks and screams of the helpless victims whom our saved fellow soldiers were butchering, were sufficient to have melted into compassion the heart of a Turk or a Tartar." He saw some "having their arms cut off, and others with their bowels hanging out crying for mercy." One patriot escaped, with the redcoats on his heels and a bayonet sticking out of his arm. He made it to a Continental Army camp in Paramus, New Jersey. "It is evident," Alexander Hamilton, Washington's aide at the time, wrote to New York Congressman John Jay, "that the most wanton and unnecessary cruelty must have been given him when utterly out of a condition to resist." That story ended up in the patriot newspapers, with harrowing details about how Martin had asked for quarter (clemency or mercy) and instead received "a most barbarous butchery."[13] And if Washington had not already made his point clear—to the Americans as much as the British—he had Martin's corpse placed in a cloth-covered casket and delivered to enemy headquarters. He included a note condemning the killers' "spirit of wanton cruelty."[14]

which meant the British didn't have to follow established rules on the treatment of prisoners. They'd answer to no one but themselves.[15]

Washington's insistence on being addressed by his title reminds us that he could be a brilliant tactician, but his strategic and intellectual victories *off* the battlefield have been totally overshadowed by his military triumphs during the Revolution. He won the war, but he didn't do it with sheer force alone.[16] He couldn't have.

If Washington had tried to match the Howe brothers in experience or armed forces, the war would not have been the second longest in American history.[17] There likely wouldn't *be* an American history. To pigeonhole him as a military leader is to underestimate how much the fledgling government needed Washington as a diplomat and political strategist. His ability to manage large-scale combat while also running spy rings and shadow and propaganda campaigns in enemy-occupied areas is a significant—and often overlooked—part of the Revolutionary War.

CHAPTER 10

The Court of Public Opinion

IN 1777, A "GREAT NUMBER OF SOLDIERS BELONGING TO THE BRITISH Army" went to Edmund Palmer's Pennsylvania farm and demanded to "speak to" his thirteen-year-old granddaughter, Abigail Palmer. There was no reason to allow it. Aside from her unfortunate proximity to a British encampment, Abigail played no role in the hostilities. Edmund refused.

A soldier "dragged her in the back room and she screamed." Abigail kept screaming, though they threatened to "knock her eyes out if she did not hold her tongue." More soldiers came and went. Her grandfather pleaded that they not "use a girl of that age after that manner," but they did, for three days.

Mary Phillips, Abigail's pregnant aunt, was also raped by the redcoats. So were the Cain sisters, who were visiting the Palmer farm. When fifteen-year-old Elizabeth and seventeen-year-old Sarah resisted, the soldiers threatened to run bayonets through their hearts, or poison them, or "kill the family & fire the house & barn." They took the youngest girls, Abigail and Elizabeth, "into the same room where they ravished them both," then brought them back to camp.[1] There, they were repeatedly raped by more soldiers until their pleas fell on a sympathetic ear, and they were returned to Palmer's farm.[2]

REPORTING SEXUAL ASSAULT

In early America—as, indeed, in later America—victims rarely reported a sexual assault. During peacetime, the public humiliation and blame that such an accusation was guaranteed to bring the woman and her family was a strong deterrent. War introduced further obstacles. The aggressor might be an enemy soldier traveling through town, a stranger the victim could not identify. Even if she could, would it matter to the man's commanding officer?

While few letters on the subject of sexual violence have survived, those that can be found in the archives are disturbingly consistent. In one example, Francis Rawdon-Hastings, an aide-de-camp to British general Sir Henry Clinton, wrote to his uncle:

> A girl of this island made a complaint the other day to Lord Percy of her being deflowered, as she said, by some grenadiers. Lord Percy asked her how she knew them to be grenadiers, as it happened in the dark. "Oh, good God," cried she, "they could be nothing else, and if your Lordship will examine I am sure you will find it so."

Throughout the letter, he marvels at the virile redcoats, whose American victims "are so little accustomed to these vigorous methods that they don't bear them with the proper resignation."[3]

Washington let it be known that he wanted horrific stories "on the subject of the Enemy's brutality" collected and sent to him. "[I]t is expected that humanity and tenderness to women and children will distinguish brave Americans, contending for liberty, from infamous mercenary ravagers, whether British or Hessians," Washington wrote in

1777 to William Livingston, the governor of New Jersey.[4] Accounts about the "infamous mercenary ravagers" were then pieced together and printed in congressional reports, placed with no less care or intention than troops on the battlefield.[5] And at a time when there were no real war correspondents, those dispatches from the front—or, as in the Palmer farm case, from men like Jared Saxton, a justice of the peace in western New Jersey—were of great interest to newspapers throughout the country.

Their circulation numbers were small, and they rarely contained more than four pages, but their reach was enormous—and the propaganda they disseminated was integral to the success of the Revolution. They were read aloud in meeting houses, coffee shops, and taverns. Washington got his hands on as many editions as he could—requesting they be sent from other cities and that visitors bring them to him—and studied them carefully. He even talked Congress into funding the *New Jersey Journal*, over which he could exert total editorial control, spreading stories about American good deeds and British evil. Benjamin Rush, a prominent physician who served briefly as surgeon general, described these newspapers as "equal to at least two regiments."[6]

In lieu of putting one man on trial, accounts like Abigail Palmer's managed to put the enemy on trial, for the world to judge. While the British Army did occasionally court-martial and even execute rapists, they did so inconsistently enough that American propagandists could easily portray the morality of the British Empire as deficient all around; they could no more be trusted to keep American wives and daughters safe than they could anything else.

☆ ☆ ☆

White Americans' enthusiasm for liberty and "humanity and tenderness" was mostly reserved for people who shared their skin color. They had no plans to abolish slavery. That left them vulnerable to the British, who'd promised freedom for slaves who fought for the crown. Washington, who owned several hundred people himself, recognized the power of the pledge—not only in the reality it promised but also in what it signified to the rest of the world. A weapon he needed to ward off criticism arrived just in time, in 1776, right after he had been appointed commander in chief. That was when Phillis Wheatley, an enslaved poet who'd been named after the boat that brought her from West Africa to Boston, wrote an affecting ode in praise of the Revolution. The final stanza was dedicated "To His Excellency George Washington."

Proceed, great chief, with virtue on thy side,
Thy ev'ry action let the goddess guide.
A crown, a mansion, and a throne that shine,
With gold unfading, WASHINGTON! Be thine.

Washington wasted no time exploiting the poem for political purposes. He included it in a letter to Colonel Joseph Reed on February 10, 1776, writing that he had considered publishing Wheatley's poem "With a view of doing justice to her great poetical Genius," but feared it would look vain. Reed took the not-so-subtle hint and promptly sent her ode out to editors, who published it widely.[7]

Just as Wheatley's support reassured colonists, news of Indian oppression was essential to Washington's hearts-and-minds campaign throughout the colonies. At times, the crown had made peace treaties with the Indians that curtailed westward expansion, and the colonists saw themselves as the victims. In an attempt to reassure them, and with the full support of Congress, Washington undertook a campaign of genocide against the Six Nations, the northeast Iroquois confederacy. On May 31, 1779, he allocated a third of his army to General John Sullivan, writing:

> The immediate objects are the total destruction and devastation of their settlements and the capture of as many prisoners of every age and sex as possible. It will be essential to ruin their crops now in the ground and prevent their planting more.[8]

When the press reported the attacks, they did so with high praise for Washington. The news was so well received, Benjamin Franklin and Marquis de Lafayette set about developing a series of prints to teach children about the kind of Indian-British-Loyalist inhumanity that necessitated such a response.

The most powerful and enduring story from the Revolution, however, was Washington's crossing the Delaware River on Christmas night, 1776. Rain, hail, and snow fell on Washington and his men, and ice floes blocked their path, but they landed safely and marched straight to Trenton, New Jersey, successfully assaulting the Hessian encampment there and securing victory. None of Washington's struggles "fixed itself on my mind so indelibly as the crossing of the Delaware," wrote Abraham Lincoln, the man who saved the union Washington won, four score and a few years later. Lincoln added, "I am exceedingly anxious that the object they fought for—liberty, and the Union and Constitution they formed—shall be perpetual."

And so was the image of that Christmas night, recorded seventy-five years later in Emanuel Gottlieb Leutze's painting *Washington Crossing the Delaware.* The painting's inaccuracies abound—the flag Monroe carries has yet to be introduced, the ice is much too thick—but it hardly matters.[9] Leutze managed to capture a certain against-all-odds spirit, which seemed to persuade the world that America was born righteous, so Washington along with it.

CHAPTER 11

George Washington, Agent 711

W E SHALL REMAIN ABSOLUTELY SILENT ON THE SUBJECT," JOHN
Jay, incoming president of the Second Continental Congress,
wrote to Washington in 1778.[1] Jay couldn't get him what he was looking
for—"a liquid which nothing but a counter liquor (rubbed over the
paper afterwards) can make legible"—but his brother could.[2] Sir James
Jay, a physician in New York, had developed a "sympathetic stain" for
secret correspondence.

Washington called the invisible ink "medicine" and advised those
he supplied with it to write "on the blank leaves of a pamphlet . . . a common pocket book, or on the blank leaves at each end of registers, alma-
nacs, or any publication or book of small value." Scraps of paper were
easier to come by than the ink: Sir James refused to disclose his recipe
to anyone, including his brother.[3]

"Much will depend on early Intelligence, and meeting the Enemy
before they can Intrench," Washington had written to William Heath, a
general in the Continental Army, on September 5, 1776.[4] When it came
to spying, the Americans lagged too far behind their enemy. The crown

had centuries of experience in espionage, as it did in warfare, but Washington had the means to play catch-up in only one realm.

Good spies are hard to come by. The job attracts risk-takers, fabulists, escapists, idealists, adventurers, and worse. Early American history is littered with the names of men who swiftly learned they lacked the instinct or constitution for espionage. Perhaps the best known is Nathan Hale, who ventured into British-occupied Long Island in September 1776 with no training, no handler, no safe house, and no extraction plan. He was promptly caught.[5]

Washington needed better operatives in the field, and that wouldn't come cheap. There were plenty of Continental soldiers contemplating rebellion over missing back pay and want of provisions, but that didn't stop him from requesting funds for spies. On December 30, 1776, Washington wrote to Robert Morris, the financier of the war, "We have the greatest Occasion at present for hard Money, to pay a certain set of People who are of particular use to us."[6] But he wasn't after the kind of cash the Continental Congress printed. American currency would incriminate the spies if they were caught with it, and that was assuming they even wanted it; the new money was unstable, in large part because the British printed millions of counterfeit bills during the war. Ultimately Morris sent Washington forty-one Spanish dollars, two English crowns, ten shillings, and two sixpence.[7]

Washington had learned a lesson from Hale. Sending spies behind enemy lines was short-sighted and risky. Recruitment and case work should come from a trusted officer who had longstanding relationships with people in occupied territory—like Major Benjamin Tallmadge, who would go by the code name "John Bolton." The Yale graduate was intelligent, loyal, and dependable, and though he had no experience in

JAMES ARMISTEAD LAFAYETTE

Not all operatives worked for money alone. James Armistead Lafayette, a double agent, moved among the British with relative ease—as did the tens of thousands of other slaves who became Loyalists in hopes of freedom. Lafayette was so successful, he managed to get close to Benedict Arnold after his defection.

Benjamin Quarles, a scholar of African American history, estimates that the British evacuated four thousand slaves from Savannah, six thousand from Charleston, and four thousand from New York after the war, but cautions "these figures are a bit low." The British likely "carried away" another five thousand people before the surrender at Yorktown, and an unknown number left with the French.[8] Lafayette was not among them. He remained in America, still enslaved and considered three-fifths of a person. In 1782, Virginia, where Lafayette was from, passed a manumission act allowing any slave to be emancipated by his owner. When the man who enslaved Lafayette made no move to free him, he made it himself. With the following testimonial from Marquis de Lafayette, he submitted a Manumission Petition to the Virginia General Assembly on November 30, 1786.[9]

> This is to certify that the bearer by the name of James has done essential services to me while I had the honor to command in this state. His intelligences from the enemy's camp were industriously collected and faithfully delivered. He perfectly acquitted himself with some important commissions I gave him and appears to me entitled to every reward his situation can admit of.
>
> Done under my hand, Richmond,
> November 21st, 1784.
> Lafayette

While most slaves would have to wait until the end of the Civil War in 1865 and the ratification of the Thirteenth Amendment to be out of bondage, Lafayette was granted freedom. He also received a pension for his service during the war.

espionage, he had grown up in Setauket, one of the many towns the Continental Army had been forced out of after the Battle of Long Island. His family and friends still lived there and could provide a way in.[10]

Setauket was not known for patriot sympathy, but the British soon changed that. They took over everything—pubs, restaurants, boarding houses, and churches—and became an overwhelming, frightening burden. For some residents, the American cause was a fight for a quiet way of life. Their help became essential to the untrained intelligence operatives' success.

Tallmadge knew exactly whom to tap. He began with Abraham Woodhull, a young man he'd known for his entire life, who reported under the name "Samuel Culper," or "Samuel Culper, Sr." Woodhull would make dead drops of vital intelligence on his farm, and his neighbor, Anna Strong, the wife of a patriot judge, would arrange the laundry on her clothesline when it was ready for pickup. Patriots on the Connecticut shore would interpret the handkerchiefs and petticoats through a spyglass, then send someone to pass on the message.

That person was often Caleb Brewster, a rough-mannered whaleboat captain. Spies were required to be brave, but Brewster was exceedingly bold. He was known to sign his real name on intelligence reports, and once captured two British vessels before he was struck on the head with an iron cannon rammer and shot by a musket.[11]

The Culper ring had a far-flung member they called "Samuel Culper, Jr." who lived even deeper undercover in British-occupied New York. The operative, Robert Townsend, was a practicing Quaker who wrote passionate essays in the *New York Royal Gazette,* a Tory newspaper, and operated a coffee shop favored by British soldiers.[12] It was the perfect cover, allowing Townsend to eavesdrop on customers, who often discussed military business. A courier shuttled intelligence sixty miles east to Setauket, where it made its way to Tallmadge and, not infrequently, to the commander in chief.

Washington went by the name of Agent 711 and exchanged enough letters with Woodhull to grow tired of his lengthy asides about how brightly the American cause for liberty and freedom burned. Time was of the essence, and Washington was after crucial information about British troop deployments, supplies, and strategy. The intel would be best delivered through a code, one complicated enough to deceive the average reader but not too arduous for Washington and his aides-de-camp to decipher. Tallmadge devised a solution, mapping nearly a thousand different numbers onto various words. To reveal the numbers, Washington would apply a reagent to a piece of white paper, exposing invisible ink.

On October 17, 1780, Tallmadge wrote to inform Washington that English regiments had left New York and "intended to make a diversion in Virginia or Cape Fear in No. Carolina, to favour Lord Cornwallis." Three days later, Washington responded with follow-up questions, eager to learn more about the enemy's movements.

SAMPLE OF THE CULPER RING'S CODE

0. 8th	114. Contradict	339. Jealous	499. Pervert	701. Woman
10. Absent	125. Damage	335. Indians	487. Pleasure	711. Washington
14. Adore	130. Dispatch	397. Misery	618. September	727. New York
38. Attack	192. Fort	403. Mercenary	619. Surrender	729. Setauket
55. Boat	194. Famine	415. Night	647. Vain	744. England
58. Baker	245. Haste	459. Overthrow	670. Unarm.	763. Headquarters [13]

Of what number of Men and of what Corps the late embarkation consisted? Whether Sir Henry Clinton went with them? Whether a reinforcement arrived lately from Europe—the number, and whether of whole Corps or Recruits? In what manner the British army is at present disposed—designating as nearly as possible the Corps which lay at the different places? I am anxious to receive intelligence of the foregoing particulars, and you will oblige me by obtaining it speedily.[14]

"Cu. Shall be immediately notified of the Questions which Your Excellency wishes to have resolved," Tallmadge responded on October 23. Woodhull, the senior Culper, soon sent word that the British forces had split up, with one continuing into Virginia and another moving farther south. Townsend, the junior Culper, also had news. A British fleet was headed straight for Lafayette and the Comte de Rochambeau, who were attempting to land some six thousand desperately needed troops in Newport, Rhode Island. Washington acted immediately, sending a double agent to New York with letters supposedly detailing the Continental Army's next move.[15] The agent was intercepted and the letters mined for information; as a result, British ships were rerouted, clearing the way for the French (who were by now aiding the Americans) to land.

On December 22, 1776, Continental soldiers captured John Honeyman, a former British soldier. Washington had told him exactly where to be found, should he need an immediate audience. They both played along when the soldiers delivered Honeyman to camp in Bucks County, Pennsylvania, where Washington declared him a "notorious" turncoat and insisted on interrogating the prisoner himself. Thirty minutes later, he ordered that Honeyman be thrown in the guardhouse. In the morning, he would hang.

But the next day, Honeyman was nowhere to be found. The watchmen swore they had no idea how he had slipped out, but Washington did: He'd handed Honeyman a key to the door during their "interrogation" and told him the fastest route out. The escape had to look real, just like the capture and interrogation, lest there be informants among them. And even if there weren't, Honeyman needed a plausible story to report back to Johann Rall, the colonel in charge of about twelve hundred Hessians in Trenton, New Jersey.

Washington's camp was in a sorry state, Honeyman told Rall. The Continental soldiers were hungry, shirtless, and shoeless. There were deficits of every kind, of weapons and of ammunition. Rall was overjoyed at the news, which meant he and his men might be returning home soon. In the immediate future, they could at least celebrate Christmas, and celebrate it hard, with all the drink and women they could round up.

Honeyman had been working Rall for weeks. By the time he was "captured," he knew the garrison's schedule and the location of stationed guards, all of which he reported back to Washington, who now had the intelligence he needed for a successful attack. By December 26, Rall was dead, his troops were captured, and New Jersey had been loosened from the crown's grip.

Although Washington was often a successful spymaster, he suffered bitter intelligence failures, too, and numerous close calls—many of which involved Major John André, who ran British intelligence operations out of Philadelphia, where he occupied Benjamin Franklin's house. Washington failed to ferret out André's finest agent, Ann Bates, the wife of a British soldier who passed as a peddler in his own camp.[16] But she wasn't the one who caused Washington the greatest misery. That honor went, of course, to Benedict Arnold.

History has reduced Washington and Arnold to two-dimensional characters—God above, Lucifer below—but in the beginning, when they shared a place in the nation's first class of American heroes, they didn't look all that dissimilar.[17] Both men were obsessed with honor and thus extremely sensitive to slights; neither was much of an orator, lacking the education afforded to so many of the founders; and both found success on the battlefield.

As time went on, though, their differences began to show. All successful American military men were micromanaged, painstakingly audited, and occasionally court-martialed by the distrustful Continental Congress. The politicians feared that a celebrity general would emulate Oliver Cromwell and seize power. Washington, who'd learned to hold his tongue as an adult, bore these bureaucratic impositions well; Arnold never did.[18] In a May 1779 letter to Washington, just days before he began corresponding with André, Arnold wrote:

> If Your Excellency thinks me Criminal For Heavens sake let me be immediately Tried and If found guilty Executed, I want no favor I ask only for justice. . . . I little expected to meet the ungrateful Returns I have received from my Countrymen, but as Congress has Stamp'd ingratitude as a Current Coin I must take it.

Washington sympathized with his complaints but not with his too-public recitation of them. He called Arnold's conduct "Impudent and Improper." Earlier a military tribunal had called them "illegal, illiberal and ungentlemanlike"—and that was one of Arnold's better hearings.[19]

Insult, alienation, and want of money made him easy prey for

André, who passed messages between Arnold and British general Sir Henry Clinton. For what would now be around half a million dollars, Arnold agreed to hand over West Point—the patriots' strategically key fortress on the Hudson River—to the British, along with Washington himself.[20] Had Washington been captured, he would likely have been taken to London, tried, and hanged. Coupled with the loss of West Point, which Washington called "the most important Post in America," Arnold's betrayal might have ended the Revolution.[21]

André came exceptionally close to claiming that victory. In 1780, he was sneaking away from West Point with Arnold's treasonous instructions hidden in his boots when three patriot militiamen stopped him. Their supervising officer, following protocol, was about to turn him over to the commanding district officer—Benedict Arnold—when the transfer was halted by none other than Major Tallmadge of the Culper ring. He knew how to spot one of his own kind. André was ultimately court-martialed and sentenced to death. Yet because he was widely admired, Washington's inner circle suggested that André be exchanged for Arnold. The British refused the deal, and André was hanged.

It took Washington a year to give up on catching Arnold, who was now serving as a brigadier general in the British Army. At one point, he ordered Sergeant Major John Champe to cross enemy lines, posing as a deserter. Champe managed to land a job in Arnold's house; he planned to knock him unconscious one night while he was relieving himself in the garden, spirit him away to a boat, and deliver him to Washington. When the perfect moonless night arrived and Arnold indeed went to pee, Champe came close—but in a dramatic turn of events, just before the perfect moonless night arrived, Arnold's American legion was suddenly called to raid Richmond, Virginia.

Arnold escaped punishment for his treason. He'd inconvenienced the patriots and damaged their morale, but he accomplished very little for the British. He knew, for instance, that there were spies in New York, but Washington had never told him their names.[22]

"Washington did not really outfight the British," the British spymaster Major George Beckwith said. "He simply outspied us."[23]

CHAPTER 12

Eight Years Away

ICAN HARDLY THINK THAT LORD DUNMORE CAN ACT SO LOW, & unmanly a part, as to think of siezing Mrs Washington by way of revenge upon me," Washington wrote to Lund Washington, his third cousin, in 1775. Lund, who was five years his junior, served as Mount Vernon's estate manager throughout the war, although Washington often micromanaged from afar.[1] The general was in Cambridge, his headquarters during the Siege of Boston, when he felt, for the first time, how vulnerable the war made him and everything he cared about. He was still years away from fully realizing the price he would pay in family, estate, and fortune, but rumors that Lord Dunmore, the last royal governor of Virginia, had plans to sail up the Potomac and kidnap Martha reached him immediately. It seemed everyone was concerned for Martha's safety at home—except for Martha herself.

"'Tis true many people have made a Stir about Mrs Washingtons Continuing at Mt Vernon," Lund responded, but "she does not believe herself in danger."[2] Martha, then forty-four, wasn't even at home when they corresponded. She had taken a carriage to Mount Airy, her daughter-in-law's family plantation in Maryland, to attend to the birth of her first grandchild.

In the end, Martha remained safe, but the British did come to Mount Vernon during the war. The HMS *Savage* had been burning great homes along the Potomac when their patriotic owners refused to supply it with provisions—with offers of sheep, hogs, and poultry, the British warship left with more than just the livestock Lund gave them. In 1781, seventeen people enslaved by Washington—fourteen men and three women—bolted for the ship when it docked, and there was nothing Lund could do about it. At the beginning of the war, Dunmore issued a proclamation that many Virginians had tried and failed to keep quiet, declaring "all indented Servants, Negroes, or others (appertaining to Rebels) free, That are able and willing to bear Arms, they joining his Majesty's Troops."[3] If they fought against American liberty, they were fighting for their own freedom.

It didn't take long for the news to reach Washington. "When the Ennemy Came to your House Many Negroes deserted to them," wrote Marquis de Lafayette, who would later urge Washington to free or allow the people he enslaved to work as free tenants. "This piece of News did not affect me much as I little Value property. But You Cannot Conceive How Unhappy I Have Been to Hear that Mr. Lund Washington Went on Board the Ennemy's vessels and Consented to give them provisions." In peacetime, Washington would have pursued the escaped slaves, but now he targeted Lund. Echoing Lafayette, Washington wrote him a dramatic letter of censure: "It would have been a less painful circumstance to me, to have heard, that in consequence of your non-compliance with their request, they had burnt my House, and laid the Plantation in ruins."[4]

The letter stands as an exception to their otherwise warm and conspiratorial correspondence. While Lund's widow burned much of their

MOUNT VERNON SLAVES WHO ESCAPED
ONTO THE *SAVAGE*[5]

In 1781, there were nearly seventy enslaved men, fifty enslaved women, and fifteen hired and indentured men at Mount Vernon. (Nonworking enslaved adults and children weren't counted.) Washington estimated that there were between two hundred and three hundred enslaved workers at the plantation over the course of the war, and records show there were at least fifty births during that time.[6]

NAME	AGE	JOB/ DESCRIPTIONS	FORCIBLY RETURNED TO MOUNT VERNON AFTER THE REVOLUTION
Peter	"old"		
Lewis	"old		
Frank	"old"		x
Frederick	"about 45"	"overseer and valuable"	x
Gunner	mid-40s	brick maker	x
Harry	around 40	stableman	
James	"about 25"		
Tom	"about 20"	"stout and Healthy"	
Sambo	"about 20"		x
Stephen	"about 20"	cooper	
Lucy	"about 20"		x
Watty (or Wally)	"about 20"	weaver	
Daniel	"about 19"		
Esther	"about 18"		x
Thomas	"about 17"	house servant	x
Deborah	"about 16"		
Peter	"about 15"		

correspondence in 1796, we know that Washington's cousin sent him weekly dispatches about Mount Vernon, which seemed to serve as the general's wartime escape. As busy as he was, he always found time to think about his plantation. He drew up architectural plans to extend both ends of the house, ordered the replacement of "existing outbuildings with larger structures, creation of service lanes, development of the bowling green, and enlargement of the formal gardens."[7] But the execution was left to Lund, whom he trusted with all his affairs. (When Lund asked for a raise in 1778, Washington replied, "[I]t is my first wish that you should be satisfied."[8]) Washington wouldn't see it with his own eyes until 1781, when he was on the way to Yorktown, the last decisive battle of the war.

Eight years away from Mount Vernon was a price Washington was willing to pay, but as many away from Martha was not. He wanted his wife by his side, which meant she would have to face one of her greatest fears: medical intervention. "Mrs Washington is still here, and talks of taking the Small Pox, but I doubt her resolution," Washington wrote to his brother John Augustine, from New York, in 1776.[9]

There were plenty of rumors and anecdotal evidence to bolster Martha's fears. Her sister-in-law Anne Steptoe Allerton, Samuel Washington's fourth wife, died after receiving the inoculation. When Jacky received the treatment in 1771 (ahead of a European tour that never happened), Martha, according to Washington, was far too anxious to hear the details. She wished her son would just do it "without her knowing of it," her husband wrote, so that "she might escape those Tortures which Suspense wd throw her into, little as the cause might be for it."[10]

"THIS MOST DANGEROUS ENEMY"

The British and the Hessians brought smallpox with them when they arrived to quell the Revolution, and though Washington had been immune since contracting the disease in Barbados in 1751, he quickly learned that almost everyone around him was vulnerable. "I am very much afraid that all the Troops on their march from the Southward will be infected with the small pox, and that instead of having an Army here, we shall have an Hospital," he wrote to General Horatio Gates in early 1777.[11] The Virginia legislature, worried that inoculation would spread rather than contain the disease, made inoculation illegal. But the epidemic, which Washington called "this most dangerous enemy," threatened to defeat the patriots; by 1776, 20 percent of his army had suffered or died from smallpox.[12] Variolation, a new technique, was risky; at best, it put soldiers out of commission for weeks at a time. Still, Washington decided to move ahead with compulsory mass inoculations. Smallpox-related fatalities of soldiers and recruits dropped by 17 percent as soon as inoculation was introduced; by the end of the war, it had reached 1 percent.

In the end, Martha's desire to be with her husband outweighed her fears. When she finally assented to the inoculation, though, she passed up the military doctors in favor of civilian specialists in Philadelphia. There, John Hancock vied with other signers of the Declaration of Independence to see her through her recovery. Benjamin Randolph, who often rented out his lodgings to high-profile delegates and their wives—and who, coincidentally, had built the lap desk on which Thomas Jefferson drafted the Declaration—"has not any Lady about his House to take the necessary Care of Mrs. Washington," Hancock informed

Washington.[13] But Martha never left Mount Vernon without her favored enslaved servants, and always traveled with at least one member of Washington's military staff. She chose to convalesce at Randolph's over Hancock's, which seemed to be relatively brief and easy. Thirteen days after Martha was inoculated, Washington happily reported to Burwell Bassett, her brother-in-law, that she had made it through her "Fever and [had] not more than about a dozen Postules appearing."[14] Martha was soon reunited with Washington in New York, and would ultimately remain by his side for half of the war.

Yet Washington's most constant companion when he was away from home wasn't Martha. It was William Lee, his enslaved manservant. Washington bought Billy Lee in 1768 for 61 pounds, 15 shillings; he paid an additional 50 pounds for his younger brother, Frank. They were described as "mulatto" in his ledgers, which suggests their father was a white man, possibly Colonel John Lee, whose widow, Mary, sold the brothers upon her husband's death.[15] Even before the war began, Billy Lee's days were long and demanding. He would get up before Washington, who was an early riser himself, and prepare and lay out the general's clothes. When Washington woke, Lee shaved his face and powdered and curled his hair. Lee, who was known as an accomplished horseman, rode alongside Washington on many of his outings, from surveying to foxhunting. During the war, he was as responsible for everything Washington needed, from his spyglass to his papers.

Billy Lee is often noted and praised by contemporaries and historians for his constant presence during the war, without any reflection on or seeming awareness of the irony: Lee had no choice in the matter. The figurehead of American liberty was never far from a representation of its (and his own) deep-seated hypocrisy. And of course there wasn't any question of Lee enjoying the same battlefield perks as his master. He received only one update about his family during the war: "If it will give

Will any pleasure he may be told his wife and child are both well," Lund wrote to Washington in late 1775.[16] After that, there are no more references to Lee's family.

☆ ☆ ☆

"I am at a loss how to account for your long silence," Betty, Washington's sister, wrote to him. Their mother seemed so unsure of her own survival, she turned to Lund in desperation.[17] "I shall be ruined," Mary Washington wrote in 1778. "I never lived soe poor in my life butt if I can gitt Corn I am contended."[18] For eight years, Mary and Betty rarely heard from Washington and never saw him. They seemed to feel his absence and silence as much as the relentless wartime deprivations and instability they faced in Fredericksburg, Virginia.

Mary, who would be seventy-five by the time the Revolution ended, had no shortage of fears and concerns to fuel her already anxious disposition. She watched Betty and Fielding Lewis, her daughter and son-in-law, stake their fortune on the war, and then she watched it ruin them. When she struggled to pay taxes and make ends meet, she could not ask them for help any more than she could her other sons; Charles, John Augustine, and Samuel were in similar straits—or far worse. ("In Gods name how did my Brothr. Saml. contrive to get himself so enormously in debt?" Washington wrote in 1783, when confronted by his younger brother's burden. "Was it by purchases? By misfortunes? or shear indolence and inattention to business?"[19]) Mary tried to make do with what she had, selling her livestock and tools, but the profits weren't enough.

And her family kept dying on her. In 1775, at the age of fifteen, her grandson Charles Lewis succumbed to disease; he was one of five Lewis children who died before adulthood. Six years later, his father, Betty's husband, died of tuberculosis. Within weeks, Samuel was gone, too, another victim of tuberculosis. Mary, like her son George, was strong and athletic, but there were dangers other than disease to worry about. Lord Dunmore often ordered or threatened military attacks on the populace; Mary also feared that her slaves would listen to his entreaties to rise up.

In 1781, life in Virginia got much scarier. Benedict Arnold, fighting for the British, took control of Governor Thomas Jefferson's Richmond, then the capital of Virginia. Jefferson moved his operations to Monticello, while other Virginians fled the colony; everyone who remained was vulnerable—especially Washington's family. Lafayette was concerned enough about a British attack on Fredericksburg that he made plans to evacuate them. Ultimately, though, the redcoats never came close to paying Mary a visit.

But Washington did, unexpectedly, the one time Mary left town to accompany Betty, whose health deteriorated during the war, to the country for recovery. She was devastated. In a letter, Mary thanked him for the effort, although her tone was catastrophic: "I am afraid I Never Shall have that pleasure again," she wrote, before signing, with unusual emotion, "Loveing & affectinat Mother."[20]

The war deprived Mary of security and family, and intensified her natural thriftiness and well-earned paranoia—which she talked about openly and often. Word of the widow Washington's hardships and delinquent taxes reached Benjamin Harrison, who succeeded Jefferson as governor. The Virginia Assembly, hoping to ease the dire effect of currency inflation on the older population, had been supplementing their living with pensions. In 1781, Harrison wrote to Washington that officials discussed offering Mary one as well.[21]

He was mortified. Admitting he was "but little acquainted with her *present* situation," Washington responded with a lengthy, defensive letter. He had, "at her request but my own expence, purchased a commodious house, Garden & Lotts (of her own choosing) in Fredericksburg, that she might be near my Sister Lewis, her only daughter." He also passed the buck to Lund, the "Steward" he had tasked with caring for her while he was at war. And then he blamed taxes, "being the most unequal (I am told) in the world." Mary was fine, Washington assured Harrison, and even if she wasn't, he and his siblings "had the means of supporting her." Any talk of a pension, he wrote, "may be done away, & repealed by my request."[22] And with a closing reference to "that arch traitor, Arnold," the matter was closed.

In the spring of 1783, he realized—far too late—that the overseer at Mary's farm had, in Washington's own words, "provided the most wretched management[,] equally burhensome to me, and teazing to her."[23] Whether he admitted as much to his mother, we'll never know, but he did give her one thing she desperately wanted: a visit.

Washington and Mary were finally reunited in 1784, when he came to Fredericksburg to be honored by the mayor. He arrived at the celebration with his mother on his arm, but she had to excuse herself early. Her son, perhaps finally understanding she was indeed struggling in her old age, was seen escorting her home.[24]

☆ ☆ ☆

Jack Custis, Washington's stepson, spent the war years as he had those before—being the playboy heir to the Custis fortune. Jack was "making a ruinous hand of his Estate," Washington complained, as he continued to hear about his stepson's thoughtless behavior. "[I]t is in your power to be punctual in your attendance," Washington lectured him in 1781, after Jack showed up late for a meeting of the Virginia House of Burgesses.[25] Jack never finished college, traveled to Europe, or made careful, studied decisions, but against all odds, he succeeded in an unlikely realm.

When Washington went to war, the person closest to being his son became a father, and a decent one at that. Jack seemed to take father-hood seriously—although his eldest daughter would later recall that he taught her some "very improper" songs and made her perform them for his dinner guests.[26] Jack and Nelly's first child, a daughter, was born in 1775 but died before they named her. Twin girls, born in 1780, would not make it three weeks. But four of their children lived until old age: Eliza (1776–1832), Patsy (1777–1854), Nelly (1779–1852), and George Washington Parke Custis (1781–1857). Throughout it all, Jack appeared to be by Nelly's side.

Perhaps it was the birth of a son that prompted Jack to suddenly decide, after spending the entire Revolution as a civilian, to join Washington in Yorktown. If he died, at least he had a male heir to take over the estate. Jack never officially enlisted, but he was readily accepted by Washington's inner circle. "His patriotism led him to camp to partici-pate in some degree of the dangers of his amiable and illustrious father," explained Henry Knox.[27] Or it was an attempt to finally please the man who had raised him since the age of four. In 1776, following the birth of his first surviving daughter, Jack had written a touching letter to Washington.

I am extremely desireous (but I am at Loss for Words suffi-ciently expressive) to return you Thanks for your parental Care which on all Occasions you have shewn for Me. It pleased the Almighty to deprive me at a very early Period of Life of my Father, but I can not sufficiently adore His Goodness in send-ing Me so good a Guardian as you Sir; Few have experience'd such Care and Attention from real Parents as I have done. He best deserves the Name of Father who acts the Part of one. I first was taught to call you by that Name, my tender years unsusceptible of the Loss I had sustaind knew not the contrary;

your Goodness (if others had not told Me) would always have prevented Me from knowing, I had lost a Parent—I shall always look upon you in this Light, and must intreat you to continue your wholesome Advice and reprimands whenever you see Occasion. I promise you they shall not be thrown away upon Me, but on the contrary be thankfully receiv'd and strictly attended to; I often wish'd to thank you personally, but my resolution fail'd Me; I thought I cou'd more strongly express my Gratitude in this Manner, but my slender Capacity cannot afford Words expressive enough to convey the high Idea I entertain of the many Obligations I have receiv'd from you. This you may depend on; I shall with the greatest Eagerness seize every Opportunity of testifying that sincere regard & Love I bear you; in which Nelly begs Leave to join Me.[28]

We don't know whether Washington's response was loving and generous, or scolding and demanding; that letter has never been found.

During the monthlong Battle of Yorktown, Jack's role could generously be described as "civilian aide." He spent much of the time updating his mother on Washington's health ("tho in constant Fatigue, looks very well") and trying to spot runaway slaves fighting for the other side.[29]

When the British surrendered on October 19, 1781, the battlefield was littered with the rotting corpses of soldiers and their horses, which polluted the water and the air, spreading "camp fever," or typhus. Jack quickly fell ill, but Washington wouldn't have him treated in an overcrowded, malaria-infested makeshift hospital; he ordered Jack be spirited by carriage to his aunt's home in Eltham, Virginia, thirty miles away, and sent word for Nelly and Martha, who were headed to camp to dance at the victory ball, to meet him there. And then, in an illuminating demonstration of priorities, Washington abruptly left Yorktown, where negotiations over the British surrender were underway, to be with his family. He went silent. His aides waited nervously, unsure of what to do until, at long last, a letter that Washington wrote to Jonathan Trumbull Jr. arrived.

> I came here in time to see Mr. Custis breathe his last. [A]bout Eight o'clock yesterday Evening he expired. The deep and solemn distress of the Mother, and affliction of the Wife of this amiable young Man, requires every comfort in my power to afford them—the last rights of the deceased I must also see performed—these will take me three or four days; when I shall proceed with Mrs Washington and Mrs. Custis to Mount Vernon.[30]

The heartbreak didn't end after Yorktown. Washington had grown fond of the men who served under him, and he spent the next year saying goodbye, in one way or another, to many of them. "I often asked myself, as our Carriages distended, whether that was the last sight, I ever should have of you? And tho' I wished to say no—my fears answered yes," he wrote to Lafayette, who, having secured independence and nationhood for the United States, returned to his native France, eyes firmly fixed on the monarchy. Alexander Hamilton went to Congress in New York. Others died in the waning skirmishes of the war. "Poor Laurens is no more," Washington wrote to Lafayette in 1782, upon learning John Laurens, who had served as his aide-de-camp, was killed by redcoats while foraging (or plundering, as the British argued in their defense) in South Carolina.[31]

When Washington finally returned home to Mount Vernon two years after Yorktown, the mansion house was bigger, fuller, and poorer than ever. At first, the recently widowed Nelly lived there with her four children. When she remarried two years later, she left the two youngest, Nelly and Washy, to be raised by their grandparents. Washington also took on three of Samuel Washington's children, for a total of five children to clothe, educate, and feed—and he was solely responsible for paying off his late brother's debts.[32] Worse, Lund had incurred large debts keeping Mount Vernon up and running during the Revolution, but had failed to collect "many years arrears of rent" from the estate's tenants.[33] And worst of all, Lund had not paid himself a wage since Valley Forge, hoping the estate would recover from crop failure and inflation by the time the war ended; it had not. Washington owed his cousin five years' back pay. It was a shocking turn of events for a man who had been so financially comfortable at the beginning of the war that he refused to take a salary.

CHAPTER 13

"From Whence No Traveller Returns"

THE LONG WAR AGED WASHINGTON. WHEN IT BEGAN, HE WAS forty-four years old, spent most nights at Mount Vernon, and his hair, auburn in his youth, was a deep shade of brown, powdered white by Billy Lee. By the time it ended, Washington was fifty-two. He had slept in nearly 280 different beds, never for very long. His hair had grayed and his face was deeply creased; he suffered from rheumatism and poor eyesight; his stomach had given in to gravity, and his teeth were worse than ever. Martha, seven months his senior, was feeling it, too. "Billous Fevers & Cholic's attack her very often, & reduce her low," Washington wrote to George William Fairfax.[1]

And yet, Washington managed to use diminished health to his advantage, succeeding where failure—and even mutiny—seemed all but guaranteed. There was unrest among the ranks over inaction and late pay. Congress was too distracted by peace negotiations, brokered by the French in Versailles, to take Washington's countless letters about wages seriously. But to him, on the ground, it was obvious that "[t]he temper of the Army is much soured."[2] When he discovered that field officers were circulating a paper that urged mass desertion if the fighting continued—or, worse, a refusal to lay down arms when peace was achieved—he gathered them in Newburgh, New York, and read a lengthy letter about the various reasons their pay was delayed. They were justifiably unmoved until Washington, having stammered through line after line, took out his glasses.

"Gentleman, you must pardon me," he said, putting on his new spectacles. "I have grown gray in your service and now find myself growing blind."[3] Softened by his sincerity, the soldiers accepted their fate. Some would wait for years after the war to be paid, but others would sign away their future earnings to parasitic lenders, settling wherever they could.

The British were resigned to a similar fate. As the redcoats departed the colonies for London and European theaters of war, they staged fire sales, some of which the Washingtons partook in, picking up French wine, beer, olives, nuts, water glasses, and china as they moved between Philadelphia, New York City, and West Point. They would save them for, at long last, private life—which they planned on starting as soon as the treaties were ratified. It was the only thing standing between Washington and the permanent retirement he craved, "from whence no Traveller returns."[4]

★ ★ ★

When the time came, would Washington actually transfer power from the military to the civil government, or did he secretly aspire to be Caesar? The world had only known kings, despots, and dictators, and Washington held unprecedented authority in a new republic. Although he always spoke the language of democracy, his letters to Hamilton and other members of Congress made it hard to tell how ready he was to step down. These letters sometimes numbered five pages or more, touching on governmental concerns far outside a general's purview. He didn't like the Articles of Confederation, which had guided the United States through the latter years of the war. He worried about financial solvency, economic vitality, and the constant bickering and squabbling among state representatives. All of it signaled division and weakness rather than unity and strength.

But after the peace treaty—negotiated by John Adams, Benjamin Franklin, Henry Laurens, and John Jay—was finally signed in Paris on September 3, 1783, Washington moved quickly. Whatever concerns he had were outweighed by his desire to return to Mount Vernon in time for Christmas. Within days of hearing about the treaty, he issued a farewell address to his army. When the last redcoat evacuated New York in November, he formally turned the city over to George Clinton, the new American governor. And when Congress was finally ready to accept his resignation, he left the means up to them. On December 20, 1783, he wrote to its president, Thomas Mifflin, asking for guidance: "[I]t is essential for me to know [Congress's] pleasure, and in what manner it will be most proper to offer my resignation, whether in writing, or at an Audience; I shall therefore request to be honored with the necessary information, that being apprized of the sentiments of Congress I may regulate my Conduct accordingly."[5]

He also provided them with his intended address, which inspired delegates Thomas Jefferson, James McHenry, and Elbridge Gerry to plan a public event at the State House in Annapolis, Maryland. It was an opportunity to demonstrate to skeptics worldwide that the new republic would remain as mannered, honorable, and righteous as any European power.

Washington made the journey to Maryland with a small entourage of fewer than a dozen men, including Billy Lee, a handful of his most trusted officers, and their slaves. It was an eye-opening ride.

Washington had grown accustomed to the reverence he felt as he moved among his troops, but that paled in comparison to being America's first real celebrity.

Everywhere he went, crowds celebrated the man who had united the colonies and made a nation out of them; they cheered at word of his approach, and when he arrived, they thrust letters and accolades and toasts at him. Washington received it all with just enough grace for onlookers to note, but if one reads between the lines of their hagiographic descriptions, it's easy to see a man who is deeply uncomfortable with attention. "[Y]ou must permit me to say, that the genuine approbation of my fellow-Citizens is far more satisfactory, than the most lavish encomiums could be."[6] By the time Washington was welcomed to Annapolis by thirteen blasts of cannon fire followed by thirteen dinner toasts, he had likely reached his limits. In his own speech, he got right to the point: "Competent powers to Congress for general purposes," he said.

The next stop, a ball, was far more tolerable. "The general danced every set, that all the ladies might have the pleasure of dancing with him, or, as it has since been handsomely expressed, *get a touch of him*," Dr. James Tilton wrote on Christmas Day. First up was Martha Rolle Maccubin, a twenty-two-year-old belle who wore her hair in thirteen carefully crafted curls. No one noted the time he left, but he was up early enough the next morning to write Baron von Steuben, who had served him as inspector general and chief of staff, "the last Letter I shall ever write while I continue in the service of my Country." It was dated December 23, and "the hour of my resignation is fixed at twelve this day; after which I shall become a private Citizen on the Banks of the Potomack."[7]

First, though, there was the small matter of his farewell address, which a congressional committee had been choreographing. There was no precedent, and no protocol. It was the first time in Western history that a general would be addressing his civilian superiors as he left military service.

Washington arrived in military dress shortly before his call time, and was seated on the dais. In the audience, twenty representatives watched from their seats, careful not to rise, hats securely on their heads; the British would have considered them commoners, and demanded they pay their respects by standing, heads bare, genuflecting in the direction of royal and noble birth. After that, the freemen and women of Maryland crowded into the hall, with ladies seated in the gallery and men gathered wherever they could, to watch the performance.

REPORT OF A COMMITTEE ON ARRANGEMENTS FOR THE PUBLIC AUDIENCE

[22 December 1783]

Order for a publick Audience of General Washington.

1st. The president and Members are to be seated and covered, and the Secretary to be standing by the Side of the president.

2dly. The Arrival of the General is to be announced by the Messenger to the Secretary, who is thereupon to introduce the General attended by his Aids to the Hall of Congress.

3dly. The General being conducted to the Chair by the Secretary, is to be seated with an Aid on each side, standing, and the Secretary is to resume his place.

4thly. After a proper Time for the Arrangement of Spectators, Silence is to be ordered by the Secretary if necessary, and the president is to address the General in the following Words *"Congress sir are prepared to receive your Communications"* Whereupon the General is to rise and address Congress, after which he is to deliver his commission and a Copy of his Address to the president.

5thly. The General having resumed his place, the president is to deliver the Answer of Congress, which the General is to receive standing.

6thly. The president having finished, the Secretary is to deliver the General a Copy of the Answer from the president, and the General is then to take his Leave.

N. B. When the General rises to make his Address, and also when he retires, he is to bow to Congress, which they are to return by uncovering without bowing.[8]

Following the stage directions, Washington rose to deliver his speech. His voice was surprisingly ragged and his hands were shaking, but the words he spoke were consistent with everything he'd said before: He was unworthy of the role of general, but aspired to the cause, and succeeded because of Divine Providence and the men who served under him.

"I consider it an indispensable duty to close this last solemn act of my Official life, by commending the Interests of our dearest Country to the protection of Almighty God, and those who have the superintendence of them, to his holy keeping," he said. "Having now finished the work assigned me, I retire from the great theatre of Action." He concluded, "[A]nd bidding an Affectionate farewell to this August body under whose orders I have so long acted, I here offer my Commission, and take my leave of all the employments of public life."[9]

"Many tears were shed" in the audience as Washington reached into his blue uniform coat, shoulders laden with gold tassels. He took out his original commission papers and handed them, along with his speech, to Mifflin. (Later, he asked for the papers back, hoping to give them to his "Grand Children some fifty or a hundd. years hence for a theme to ruminate upon.") Then, turning to Congress, he bowed and ceded the stage.[10]

Mifflin read a response "without any shew of feelings, tho' with much dignity."[11]

> The U.S. in congress assembled receive with emotions too affecting for utterance this solemn deposit of the authorities under which you have led us with safety and triumph through a long, a perilous, and a doubtful war.[12]

With that, Washington bowed again and, with each handshake he exchanged with delegates, moved closer to the door. He didn't linger, and made it back home just in time for Christmas. Nothing is known about his first dinner home, but he probably enjoyed a festive meal and the squealing joy of his young wards far more than his wartime Christmases, which he spent eating drab camp fare.

The country celebrated his voluntary resignation, and in London, subjects of the British crown marveled over "a Conduct so novel, so inconceivable to People, who, far from giving up powers they possess, are willing to convulse to the Empire to acquire more." King George himself allegedly said, upon hearing of the plan, "If [Washington] does that, he will be the greatest man in the world." America would spark an age of revolutions. When France experienced its own, led by Napoleon Bonaparte, he did not step down from power, but rather declared himself emperor. Years later, he would say, "They wanted me to be another Washington."[13] But he couldn't be. No one could.

✦ PART III ✦

Mr. President

FRENEMIES

When Washington assumed the presidency, his reputation was beyond reproach. Everywhere he went, the public celebrated him, and everyone he met respected him, wanted to be his friend, and seemed eager to serve him in any capacity. But by the end of two terms in office, Washington was estranged from three of his four original cabinet members, as well as three out of four future presidents. Half the country considered itself politically opposed to him.

	BEFORE WASHINGTON BECAME PRESIDENT	AFTER WASHINGTON BECAME PRESIDENT	FINAL RELATIONSHIP STATUS
John Adams	"I glory in the character of Washington because I know him to be an exemplification of the American character."[1]	"Too illiterate, unlearned, unread for his station and reputation."[2]	Friends
Thomas Jefferson	"In War we have produced a Washington, whose memory will be adored while liberty shall have votaries, whose name will triumph over time, and will in future ages assume its station among the most celebrated worthies of the world."[3]	"His colloquial talents were not above mediocrity, possessing neither copiousness of ideas, nor fluency of words. in public when called on for a sudden opinion, he was unready, short, and embarrassed."[4]	Estranged
Thomas Paine	"I shall never suffer a hint of dishonor or even a deficiency of respect to you to pass unnoticed."[5]	"And as to you, Sir, treacherous in private friendship (for so you have been to me, and that in the day of danger) and a hypocrite in public life, the world will be puzzled to decide whether you are an apostate or an impostor; whether you have abandoned good principles, or whether you ever had any."[6]	Estranged
James Madison	"The conduct of Washington does equal honor to his prudence and to his virtue."[7]	"[Washington's conduct is] improper & indelicate."[8]	Estranged
James Monroe	"I have a boundless confidence in him, nor have I any reason to believe he will ever furnish occasion for withdrawing it."[9]	"[T]he labours of y[ou]r more early life contributed to promote the liberties of y[ou]r country; but those of y[ou]r latter days to enthral[l] & enslave it."[10]	Estranged

CHAPTER 14

Unretirement

B Y LATE 1785, WASHINGTON HAD HAPPILY RETREATED INTO PRI-vate life, and all the small dramas that went with it. That October, he and Martha had thrown George Augustine, Washington's favorite nephew, and Fanny Bassett, Martha's favorite niece, a champagne-soaked wedding. The young couple had each lost a parent, and so they lived at Mount Vernon, where the Washingtons watched them grow closer over the years. George Augustine stayed on as Washington's plantation manager, and Martha's attachment to Fanny deepened. "She is a child to me," Martha wrote to Elizabeth Powel, a friend in Philadelphia, "and I am very lonesome when she is absent."[1]

Then, in December, after a couple of failed attempts, Washington finally got the jackass he'd always wanted. He believed that mules—a cross between a male donkey and a female horse—were the future of American farming, because they could do an equivalent amount of work to horses with less food and water. The best donkeys in the world came from Spain, but it was illegal to export them. Fortunately, Thomas Jefferson, then U.S. minister to France, had informed the Spanish king about Washington's mule mania. Charles II ordered "two of the very best to be procured & sent you as a mark of his respect."[2] Only one donkey survived the voyage; Washington named him Royal Gift, and ran ads in the local papers offering the stud's services. There were plenty of takers who were, at first, disappointed by the animal's lukewarm libido. America's mares just didn't seem to do it for him. As Washington remarked to his nephew Bushrod, "at present he seems too full of royalty, to have anything to do with a plebeian race."[3] Eventually, though, Washington had a breakthrough: Royal Gift was a big fan of females of his own species, so if a couple of American jennies were in view "by way of stimulus, when he is in those slothful humours," he would successfully perform with horses.[4] For a small price, of course; Washington charged five guineas a season.

Washington wanted nothing more than to make some of those recently issued United States dollars. "Having closed all my transactions with the public, it now behooves me to look into my own private business, no part of which seems to call louder for attention, than my concerns with you," he wrote to Gilbert Simpson in 1784. Together, he and Simpson owned a hundred and fifty acres of Pennsylvania meadow, which included an apple orchard and a gristmill; the property should have been a moneymaker but had not brought in a dime. Washington blamed Simpson for being "much more attentive to your own interest than to mine" and ultimately put the land up for auction.[5] He then headed out west of the Appalachians, where he collected overdue rent and forced squatters off his forty thousand acres there. And on and on it went. Since returning home, he'd had to address one frustrating discovery after another.

There was never enough time. Being a living legend and international sensation was a constant distraction. "Many, mistakingly, think that I am retired to ease, & that kind of tranquillity which would grow tiresome, for want of employment, but at no period of my life—not in the eight years I served the public, have I been obliged to write so much *myself* as I have done since retirement," he complained to Richard Henry Lee, who had called for the colonies' independence from the British Empire in 1776.[6] Congress had waived postage fees on any letters addressed to Washington, which meant he was inundated with mail, but was, for the first time, without a secretary. He eventually hired Tobias Lear, a twenty-three-year-old Harvard graduate with good handwriting, to handle his correspondence and tutor his grandchildren.

"The general has adopted them and loves them deeply," Marquis de Lafayette wrote of Eleanor "Nelly" Parke Custis and George Washington "Wash" Parke Custis. The two youngest children of the late Jacky Custis remained with their grandparents after their mother remarried and moved to Alexandria with her two older children. "It is quite funny when i arrived to see the curious looks on those two small faces who had heard nothing but talk of me the entire day and wanted to see if I looked like my portrait," Lafayette reported back to his wife, Adrienne, during a trip to Mount Vernon in 1784. "[T]he general loved reading your letter and that of Anastasie," he added. (Anastasie, their seven-year-old daughter, had sent a sweet letter from France: "I hope that papa whill com back Son here. . . . i am very sorry for the loss of him, but I am very glade for you self."[7]) The Washington that Lafayette described to Adrienne indulged in the silly, tender cares of young children and was thoroughly content in his retirement. And the Washington he described to Philippe de Noailles, a French aristocrat (and soon-to-be victim of the guillotine), knew how to have a good time: "[T]he general and I got a little tipsy."[8] That may have made their predawn rides around his five farms challenging, though Lafayette must have found the sight sobering; he hoped that Washington would emancipate his slaves and, in so doing, set an example for the country. By 7 a.m. each day, they were back at the mansion house eating breakfast, and then out again. Washington probably showed him the greenhouse he had constructed to house all the rare plants and flowers sent to him.

But Washington himself was Mount Vernon's most popular specimen. There was a steady stream of fans and opportunists who walked right up to the mansion house, hoping for a glimpse of or a word from the living legend. On occasion, Washington indulged "the doorkeepers of the temple of fame," and even found some of the attention enjoyable. Martha was apparently unaware of artist Joseph Wright's process: "Whilst in this ludicrous attitude, Mrs. Washington entered the room, and seeing my face thus overspread with the plaster, involuntarily exclaimed. Her cry so excited in me a disposition to smile, which gave my mouth a slight twist or compression of the lips, that is not observable in the busts Wright afterwards made."[9]

For the most part, though, Washington tried to avoid his celebrity. He had a back stairway built inside the house, which allowed him to slip away unnoticed. When his mother was in need of money in 1787, he claimed he wasn't in a position to help her financially, but invited her to live with him and collect rent on her home—though she should be warned that life at Mount Vernon "may be compared to a well resorted tavern." She should be prepared to "always be dressing to appear in company" or "be as it were a prisoner of your own chamber."[10] Mary wouldn't like it, and he didn't either. But much as he did truly wish to focus on happenings at home and around the Potomac, he could not help but look beyond.

"From the high ground on which we stood—from the plain path which invited our footsteps, to be so fallen!—so lost! is really mortifying," Washington had written John Jay in May 1786. He blamed the country's many woes on the Articles of Confederation, which allowed the states to "laugh" at congressional requisitions. "Retired as I am from the world, I frankly acknowledge I cannot feel myself an unconcerned spectator. . . . having happily assisted in bringing the ship into port & having been fairly discharged." Still, Washington added, "it is not my business to embark again on a sea of troubles."[11]

Jay nonetheless sent him copies of the "Injunctions of Secrecy" in June, which was a list of ways the individual states were failing to uphold the treaty of peace with Great Britain. "[W]e are going and doing wrong," Jay wrote, "and therefore I look forward to Evils and Calamities."[12] America had failed to pay back British debts and to treat remaining Loyalists well, all of which the British foreign secretary noted in a steady stream of embarrassing and very public correspondence. And that wasn't all: The British were threatening American interests by occupying forts in New York and the Northwest Territory, the area bordering the Great Lakes that would eventually become the states of Ohio and Michigan.

Until the North and the South could agree on real powers for a central government, it would be impossible to collect taxes to pay the debts, or to function at all for much longer. And if the United States looked unstable to the rest of the world, foreign countries would exclude it from international affairs, including trade—but that was as much Washington's concern as his neighbor's. He was trying his best, for the sake of the country, to participate in national politics as a private citizen.

"We are either a United people, or we are not," Washington had written James Madison in November 1785.[13] America had always intended to succeed without a king, a dominant church, or a military leader, let alone an arthritic retiree with blurry vision, fogged hearing, a couple of teeth, and limited cash flow. Washington was no longer an ambitious youth with something to prove but a fifty-four-year-old man with everything to lose.

But his contemporaries didn't let up; they kept writing, asking for him to get involved with increasing urgency. "It is the general wish that you should attend," Henry Knox wrote of the upcoming Constitutional Convention in Philadelphia.[14] If he could help the delegates address the deeply flawed Articles of Confederation and strengthen the central government, they might avoid an impending crisis.

Martha, however, wouldn't even entertain the idea of attending. "Mrs. Washington is become too Domestick, and too attentive to two little Grand Children to leave home," he had written earlier in early May 1787.[15] She was also comforting Fanny, who had buried her first child only two weeks after his birth. Experience had taught her this: Family was fleeting, and when Washington went to big meetings in Philadelphia, whatever tranquility they had come to know was about to be completely disrupted.

In May 1787, Washington headed to Philadelphia with Billy Lee, where he was quickly disabused of any notion that he was just another attendee: The delegates unanimously elected him to be the convention's president.

Washington sat in a tall wooden chair on an elevated platform, once again in an old military uniform. He tried to observe in silence, except when debates became too heated or it was time to vote on an article. He kept a diary during this time, but his entries offer no clear insights into his thinking. We know from the letters and notes of others, however, that slavery loomed as a major obstacle for the founders. At this point in his life, Washington no longer bought slaves, but he was nowhere near favoring manumission. Like pretty much all the delegates, he wanted to defer difficult decisions; he probably was in favor of allowing the slave trade to continue for another twenty years and counting slaves as three-fifths of a person for the allotment of representatives.

But outside of the sessions, during dinners with trusted delegates, he spoke freely and often to a rapt audience, most often at Mayor Samuel Powel's home. Powel's lively wife, Elizabeth, ran a sort of salon, and Washington had long been fond of her, always taking the time to visit whenever he came to town. He found an unlikely ally in Gouverneur Morris, a war veteran who also believed in a strong central government. (Morris was perhaps better known for his scandalous affairs. He lost a limb in a carriage accident in 1780, but people gossiped that his peg leg was the result of an injury sustained when he leaped from a lover's balcony to avoid her husband, who had unexpectedly returned home.) In the mornings, Washington took a constitutional with the enslaved people he traveled with before the crowds formed; one excursion included a stop by "the old Cantonment" of the Continental Army at Valley Forge, which he found to be "in Ruins."[16]

All in all, it was a pleasant trip that concluded with consensus around the Constitution of the United States, with a preamble written by Morris.[17] When the time came to sign it, Washington was the first; he was likely the first to depart Philadelphia, too. He did so satisfied that, with minimal interference, and at the expense of just a few weeks of neglecting private affairs, the country had been set on the right path. Now he could return to Mount Vernon for good.

Unfortunately for Washington, he was the only one left with that impression. Alexander Hamilton, who had served as his aide-de-camp until 1781, argued that, by attending, Washington had "*pledged* to take a part in the execution of the government." The majority of delegates voted for a single executive, versus three, based on the assumption that Washington was going to be the first president. They figured that he'd define the role through precedents. They could see no other way of establishing the office. If he refused, there was no backup choice.

"It cannot be considered as a compliment to say that on your acceptance of the office of President the success of the new government in its commencement may materially depend," Hamilton wrote, keeping the pressure on.[18] "You *must* be the President," echoed Morris.[19]

James Madison took a more personal approach. He visited Mount Vernon in the summer of 1788—the same summer, in fact, that Washington saw his mother for the last time.[20] When one visit didn't do the trick, Madison returned in December for Christmas. Time was of the essence: The electoral college was going to pick a president soon. Whatever Madison said worked. Martha complained to Fanny that "we have not a single article of news but pollitick which I do not concern myself" while Washington, fifty-six, began quietly getting his affairs in order.[21]

As one of his favorite writers, Joseph Addison, wrote in a play called *Cato*, "Thy life is not thy own, when Rome demands it."

CHAPTER 15

The Presidency; or,
"The Place of His Execution"

THE FIRST PRESIDENTIAL ELECTION IN THE UNITED STATES WAS its least dramatic. There were no debates and no campaigns; when the Senate and the House of Representatives met for the first time on April 6, 1789, in New York to tally the votes, there were no surprises. George Washington appeared on every ballot and received sixty-nine electoral votes to secure the presidency. He easily beat John Adams, who garnered thirty-four votes, the top total among ten other also-rans. Second place gave the vice presidency to Adams. (By 1804, the Twelfth Amendment required that electors name both a president and a vice president on their ballots.)

The Virginian and the New Englander made for an odd couple. Washington was tall and athletic, whereas the much shorter Adams had already earned the nickname "His Rotundity." People either loved or grudgingly respected Washington, whereas Adams was a more divisive figure. One had mastered the art of self-control, offering his opinions only when he judged it wise, whereas the other could not restrain himself. And when it came to the daunting roles they were about to assume, Washington was focused on big issues, like establishing enduring norms for his office and addressing foreign debt, whereas Adams was obsessed with essentially meaningless formalities, like the president's title.

Adams argued that Washington be called "His Highness, the President of the United States of America, and Protector of the Rights of the Same." When Jefferson got word in Paris, where he was serving as U.S. minister to France, of the spectacle, he wrote in code that it was *"the most superlatively ridiculous thing I ever heard of."* Ben Franklin had described Adams, Jefferson added, as *"Always an honest man, often a great one, but sometimes absolutely mad."*[1] And Jefferson was a *friend* of Adams.

Adams, and practically every vice president who followed, suffered the consequences of his faux pas. Washington did not easily trust or forgive, and this inauspicious beginning ensured Adams wouldn't become a confidant. "My Country has in its Wisdom contrived for me, the most insignificant Office that ever the Invention of Man contrived or his Imagination conceived," Adams later wrote to his wife, Abigail. "I can do neither good nor Evil, I must be born away by Others and meet the common Fate."[2]

☆ ☆ ☆

Eight days after Washington's unanimous election as president, Charles Thomson's carriage passed through the whitewashed gates of Mount Vernon. They were expecting him.

Henry Knox had sent word that the outgoing secretary of the Continental Congress was on his way with news of the election, to which Washington sent a dramatic, even fatalistic reply on April 1, 1789: "My movements to the chair of Government will be accompanied with feelings not unlike those of a culprit who is going to the place of his execution." He worried that he lacked "that competency of political skill—abilities & inclination which is necessary to manage the helm."[3] In the name of service to his country, he agreed to trade "a peaceful abode for an Ocean of difficulties."[4]

The family gathered outside, watching Thomson's carriage approach the mansion house. Martha and Jacky had seen Washington become the commander in chief of America's first army, and now Martha and Jacky's children, Nelly and Wash, would see him become the first president.

After they greeted Thomson, they led him inside, to the New Room, the finest in the house, where he read a speech written by Congress, much of which must have made the flattery-averse Washington squirm:

> I have now Sir to inform you that the proofs you have given of your patriotism and of your readiness to sacrifice domestic ease and private enjoyments to preserve the liberty & promote the happiness of your Country, did not permit the two houses to harbour a doubt of your undertaking this great, this important Office to which you are called not only by the unanimous votes of the Electors but by the voice of America, I have it therefore in command to accompany you to New York where the Senate & the house of Representatives of the United States are convened for the dispatch of public business.
>
> In executing this part of my commission where personal gratification coincides with duty I shall wait your time & be wholly governed by your convenience.[5]

Washington had prepared a comparatively grave statement of his own, sticking to logistical matters:

Upon considering how long time some of the gentlemen of both Houses of Congress have been at New York, how anxiously desirous they must be to proceed to business, and how deeply the public mind appears to be impressed with the necessity of doing it immediately, I cannot find myself at liberty to delay my journey. I shall therefore be in readiness to set out the day after to-morrow, and shall be happy in the pleasure of your company.[6]

Washington and Thomson left two days later. "When, or wheather he will ever come home again god only knows," Martha wrote to her nephew John Dandridge. "I think it was much too late for him to go in to publick life again, but it was not to be avoided. . . . I must soon follow him."[7] A month later, she set out for New York with Nelly, Wash, and six of their slaves: Molly and Oney Judge, Martha's maids; Austin (Oney's half brother) and Christopher Sheels, their waiters; and Giles and Paris, Washington's coachmen.

Robert Lewis, the twenty-year-old son of Washington's sister Betty, escorted the group on the roughly eight-day journey. He was to remain in New York, to serve as his uncle's junior secretary. Mary had lent her grandson her carriage for the trip, but made him promise that he would eventually return it to Betty, to whom she had willed it. Mary had often declared herself near death, but this time she was right. It must have been obvious to Lewis, too, who "experienced the most disagreeable sensations imaginable with the reflections of parting with an Aged Mother and Grandmother."[8] Mary had breast cancer, and had been living on borrowed time since 1787, when a letter arrived at Mount Vernon

BILLY LEE'S FORCED RETIREMENT

Billy Lee, the slave who was Washington's manservant for the entirety of the war, was left behind when he could no longer keep up. After he was crippled due to injuries sustained in service to Washington, Lee was demoted to shoemaker.

The year before his first accident, he'd convinced Washington to bring Margaret "Peggy" Lee to Mount Vernon. They had met during the war, and while Washington clearly didn't care for her, he nonetheless wrote to Clement Biddle in an attempt to bring her to Virginia.[9]

Mount Vernon July 28th 1784
Dear Sir,

The Mulatto fellow William who has been with me all the War is attached (married he says) to one of his own colour a free woman, who, during the War was also of my family—She has been in an infirm state of health for sometime, and I had conceived that the connection between them had ceased—but I am mistaken—they are both applying to me to get her here, and tho' I never wished to see her more, yet I cannot refuse his request (if it can be complied with on reasonable terms) as he has lived with me so long & followed my fortunes through the War with fidelity.

After promising thus much, I have to beg the favor of you to procure her a passage to Alexandria either by Sea, by the passage Boats (if any there be) from the head of Elk, or in the Stage as you shall think cheapest & best, and circumstances may require—She is called Margaret Thomas als Lee (the name which he has assumed) and lives at Isaac & Hannah Sills, black people who frequently employ themselves in Cooking for families in the City of Phila. I am—Dr Sir Yr Most Obedt Hble Servt
    Go: Washington

For whatever reason, Peggy never arrived. It seems that Lee never did remarry.

urging Washington to get to Fredericksburg as soon as possible. She survived that scare, but there was little doctors could do for her. Perhaps she dulled the pain with opium or wine, but most often she sought solace in her Bible.

☆ ☆ ☆

If Washington had been a king, Americans waiting to celebrate him on the road to New York would have bowed, but since the country had evicted the monarchy, it was Washington who bowed to them. And they loved him for it. Hundreds of people walked alongside his small caravan to Baltimore, where he stayed the night. Well-wishers took him all the way to Wilmington, Delaware, the next day, and the day after that a military escort accompanied him to the Pennsylvania border. There the state president, Thomas Mifflin, escorted him, along with two cavalry units and a company of around a hundred men, into Philadelphia.

Once in town, Washington ditched the carriage for a white horse. The crowds went wild. They cheered him on as he boarded a commercial ferry, crossing into New Jersey along the same passage he had on that Christmas night in 1776, when a much-needed victory at Trenton restored belief that the war could be won; this time, the ride and weather were much more accommodating. He rode under a bridge with a sign that read "The Defenders of the Mothers will also Defend the Daughters"; it was covered in flowers, more of which were thrown at his feet. He was so moved by the gesture that he immediately had a thank-you letter sent "To The Ladies of Trenton."

> General Washington cannot leave this place without expressing his acknowledgments, to the Matrons and Young Ladies who received him in so novel & grateful a manner at the Triumphal Arch in Trenton, for the exquisite sensation he experienced in

that affecting moment. The astonishing contrast between his former and actual situation at the same spot—The elegant taste with which it was adorned for the present occasion—and the innocent appearance of the *white-robed Choir* who met him with the gratulatory song, have made such impressions on his remembrance, as, he assures them, will never be effaced.[10]

When Washington arrived in New York, he found it hadn't changed much since he left in 1783. It was still more of a haphazard village than an orderly city, crowded with thirty thousand residents. At night, two thousand slaves emptied "night soil," as waste disposal was called, onto the streets, some of which were paved, some of which were still dirt. There were patches of farmland all over the noisy, sometimes riotous city; you were as likely to find hogs in someone's house as European royalty. It was all quite different from life in Virginia, where Washington obsessed over the perfectly manicured gardens and farms bordered by wilderness.

After dinner at the governor's mansion and a fireworks display, Washington, surely exhausted, settled into his new home at 3 Cherry Street, hoping to take advantage of the days before the inauguration. He was immediately thwarted. Everyone in New York seemed to know where he lived, and many showed up unannounced, looking for favors. Washington doled them out carefully, especially when it came to family members; he could abide entry-level nepotism for his nephew Robert Lewis, but he declined to offer a legal job to another nephew, Bushrod, because his "standing at the bar would not justify my nomination," and "the eyes of Argus are upon me, and no slip will pass unnoticed that can be improved into a supposed partiality for friends or relations."[11] During his first week, Washington was so overwhelmed by office-seekers that he could barely achieve his actual agenda, which was simply to pay respects to members of Congress. Long visits were out, but he did the best he could with almost comic brevity: Washington rode up to each house, quickly got off his horse, bowed, and got right back on to ride off to the next residence.

That wasn't the only problem with 3 Cherry Street, which his secretary Tobias Lear had secured. It was supposed to function as his home and office, but it wasn't even big enough to house his family and their slaves and servants. Samuel Fraunces, the former owner of Fraunces Tavern, where Washington had said farewell to his officers at the end of the war, was hired to help Martha run the president's social life—which required an additional two dozen servants. She, too, was forced to play constant hostess. But unlike her husband, she found a friend in the Adams family; Abigail was a frequent visitor, and described Martha in the most glowing terms to her sister, Mary Smith Cranch.[12]

> Mrs Washington is one of those unassuming Characters which Creat Love & Esteem, a most becomeing plasentness sits upon her countanance, & an unaffected deportment which renders her the object of veneration and Respect, with all these feelings and Sensations I found myself much more deeply impressd than I ever did before their Majesties of Britain.

The best thing about the house was that Congress paid the yearly rent of $845. Washington argued, as he had during the war, that he should cover his own living expenses, which was great for optics but terrible for his pocketbook. Fortunately for him, the Constitution required compensation and Congress allotted him a twenty-five-thousand-dollar annual salary plus the cost of living. But the new government didn't pay in advance, and like most Virginians, Washington was land rich and cash poor. In order to make it to New York, he had to secure a loan from

Alexandria merchant Richard Conway.[13] Plenty of stately homes and gratis accommodations were available to him, had he wanted to be someone's guest, but he was determined to pay his own way. Washington was defining the role of president as he occupied it, and from the very beginning, it seems, he was sure about one thing: He wasn't going to owe anyone any favors.

Inauguration Day, April 30, couldn't have come soon enough. Washington was growing impatient; it was time to put ceremony behind him and get to work.

He awoke to church bells and cannons on a day that promised to be both plain and extravagant, and he took care to match his outfit to the day. Washington's tailored suit, made of brown Connecticut broadcloth he had special-ordered for the occasion, was embellished only with buttons bearing the American eagle; it was an aberration from his usual dress, which was usually made from the finest materials he could order from European vendors. He wore a dress sword at his waist, and from the knees down, he was all flash—white knee-high silk stockings, shoes adorned with a silver buckle and diamonds. His hair was powdered white and curled under his hat. For once, he was in civilian dress in a sea of soldiers. Five hundred of them accompanied him through the throngs of onlookers to Federal Hall, which held the House of Representatives on the ground floor and the Senate on the second floor.

After an awkward hour during which senators tried to figure out whether to sit or stand, Adams, who hesitated and balked inelegantly, finally escorted Washington out to the balcony, which was crammed with sixteen other men. He bowed to the thousands of people gathered below, a crowd-pleaser that was quickly becoming his signature move. Samuel Otis, secretary of the Senate, awkwardly balanced a Bible that had been, as an afterthought, borrowed from St. John's Masonic Lodge, which teetered atop a red pillow. Washington, who had been a Mason since 1752, placed his hand on it and, at Chancellor of New York Robert R. Livingston's prompting, recited the oath of office.[14] When he finished, Otis lifted the pillow up to Washington, who had no idea what he meant by the gesture. After an uncomfortable moment, he motioned for Otis to lower it, and bent down to kiss it.

"Long live George Washington, President of the United States!" Livingston shouted, prompting the crowds to erupt in cheers. A flag signaled an artillery salute, and Washington delivered his inaugural address. David Humphreys, a former aide-de-camp and an enthusiastic poet who inclined toward lengthy odes, had written a seventy-page draft back at Mount Vernon; Washington had opted to go with James Madison's far shorter version, which clocked in at five hundred words. He spoke in general terms, promising to follow the Constitution and lead on behalf of the people.

No one thought Washington looked very happy to be there. He would have preferred the modest sort of celebration that greeted "Lady Washington" (the title "First Lady" had yet to be introduced) when she arrived weeks later, but instead, he got a daylong affair.

From Federal Hall, Washington went to St. Paul's Chapel. He was private about his religious views; he often spoke of "Providence," rarely "God" and "Jesus" or "Christ." He was most likely a deist, which meant he believed that God was responsible for the creation of the world, but does not intervene in it. Above all, he firmly believed in religious freedom; during his presidency, he would write as much to the Hebrew Congregation of Newport, Rhode Island.

The festivities finally came to a close that evening with a fireworks display. Eighteenth-century pyrotechnics were reportedly advanced enough to represent his face, along with images of America's glorious beginnings, in the sky. With Washington leading them forward, the people expected nothing short of a spectacular show, with no end date to his term on paper or in sight.

As an adult, Washington had often proved to be a negligent son, and the busy spring and summer of 1789 were no exception. By the time Betty wrote to say that their mother wanted to know how he was doing, he had long reached New York. Mary could have read about it in the papers, but according to Betty, "she will not believe you are well until she has it from under your hand."

Betty wasn't just after a letter. "The doctors think if they could get some hemlock, it would be of service to her breast," she explained.[15] They hoped he could find some in New York, but Washington was too preoccupied with his own illness for several weeks to pay attention to his mother's.

"I Am not afraid to die, and therefore I can hear the worst," Washington reportedly told his doctor, Samuel Bard, some seven weeks after his inauguration.[16] According to Bard, he suffered from the cutaneous form of anthrax, which caused a carbuncle (an infection of the soft tissue) in his upper thigh. Washington did his best to avoid eighteenth-century medicine, which often left patients worse off than they began, but was in too much pain to object to Dr. Bard's insistence: He must drain pus out of the infected tissue. Washington was bedridden for six weeks, during which time he wrote no letters and received few guests. A slow recovery followed, allowing him just an hour a day to ride with Martha in the carriage, after it had been modified to allow him to lie down.

He eventually recovered, only to be taken ill again and again during his presidency; there was a repeat abscess in his thigh, and later, his cheek; he experienced regular fevers, inflammation of the eye, and back strains; he fell off a horse and had to use a crutch to move around. In the spring of 1790, during a flu outbreak in New York, he became infected. Although he experienced a high fever, delirium, and bloody sputum, Martha wrote that he "seemed less concerned himself as to the event than perhaps almost any other person in the United States."[17]

Washington was pragmatic through it all; he had already outlived most of the men in his family, and he'd lived some of those years hard, which apparently showed. "Time has made havoc upon his face," observed Fisher Ames, a congressman from Massachusetts, during the inauguration.[18] It may have been a pained reaction to all the attention, but such comments would only become more frequent—and be made about every president who followed.

Even if Washington had managed to procure hemlock for his mother when she first asked for it, it would have made no difference. Betty's letter arrived in July, and by August 10, 1789, Mary had stopped speaking. She died fifteen days later. The town crier rang the bell at St. George's Episcopal Church eighty-one times: twice because she was a woman, and seventy-nine for every year she lived. Washington, by then busy with the presidency, replied to Betty with a quick note of comfort and advice on estate proceedings; he did not share his feelings past remarking the obvious.

"Awful, and affecting as the death of a Parent is, there is consolation in knowing that Heaven has spared ours to an age, beyond which few attain, and favored her with the full enjoyment of her mental faculties, and as much bodily strength as usually falls to the lot of four score," Washington wrote. "Under these considerations and a hope that she is translated to a happier place, it is the duty of her relatives to yield due submission to the decrees of the Creator—When I was last at Fredericksburg, I took a final leave of my Mother, never expecting to see her more." True to form, he rarely spoke in Christian terms; there was no mention of judgment, redemption, and while he mentions heaven, he leaves out a key Christian idea: a future reunion there.

Mary spoke with ease when it came to her faith, but not her feelings; her will, however, showed whom she cared for most. Her eldest son received the best of everything: Mary gave Washington the property her father had left her, just as she'd given him her late husband's surveyor tools. She also left him what appears to be her marriage bed, the very one she shared with his father, along with a quilt and other prized household goods.[19] Her slaves received a most cruel goodbye, no doubt a reflection of their life with her: She separated families, sending couples and parents and children in different directions.

Washington ordered black cockades and ribbons for his household staff. Out of respect, women wore black ribbons and necklaces, and government officials wore black capes. New York City mourned for his loss, and formal functions were cancelled for three weeks. Washington wore black for months.

CHAPTER 16

Infant Nation

"THIS DEFEATS EVERY PURPOSE OF MY COMING HERE!" WASHING-
ton yelled "in a Violent fret," according to Senator William Maclay
of Pennsylvania.

On Saturday, August 22, 1789, Washington arrived at the Senate
chambers in Federal Hall. Article II of the Constitution said that the
president should make treaties "with the advice and consent of the Senate," and that's exactly what he was trying to do—consult with them
ahead of upcoming negotiations with the Creeks, the Cherokees, and
the Carolinas about ongoing violence between tribes and white settlers.
The Continental Congress was wholly responsible for the conflict; it
had effectively stolen large swaths of indigenous land, claiming that the
Indians had forfeited their right to it by supporting the British during
the Revolution. (In reality, only a handful of tribes had actually done so.)

Washington handed an address to Vice President John Adams, a
summary of the treaties and current issues Washington had sent them
ahead of the session. Adams, acting in his constitutional capacity as
president of the Senate, tried to read it, but was completely drowned

out. The windows were open, a relief on the hot summer day, but one that made it impossible to hear over the pounding of hooves and the creaking of carriages along Wall Street. The doorkeeper shut the windows, then Adams tried again.

> [I]t would be highly embarrassing to Georgia to relinquish that part of the Lands, stated to have been ceded by the Creeks . . . its Citizens who settled and planted thereon untill dispossessed by the Indians.[1]

The Creeks, who had made significant land cessations in 1783, 1785, and 1786, were no longer honoring the treaties they'd signed. "It is however painful to consider that all the Indian tribes once existing in those States . . . have become extinct," Henry Knox, secretary of war, had written to Washington. "In a short period the Idea of an Indian on this side the Mississippi will only be found in the page of the historian." Washington sided with the settlers, of course, but believed the solution was to send missionaries to teach Indians, who believed in using land in ways that left little lasting impact, to farm and raise animals. "It has been conceived to be impracticable to civilize the Indians of North America," Knox acknowledged. "This opinion is probably more convenient than Just."[2]

When Adams finished, Washington turned expectantly to the senators. Nothing the vice president said should have been new to them. He'd expected to move on quickly to a variety of questions he had for them, and had brought Knox along to answer any they might have.

"There was a dead pause," observed Maclay. The senators shifted awkwardly. They moved papers around and cleared their throats, but they asked no questions and answered none of Washington's. Finally, Maclay spoke up and asked that *all* the items Washington had sent ahead be read aloud. He was trying to buy his colleagues time; Washington was a powerful presence, and Maclay worried that he would "over awe the timid and neutral part of the Senate," leaving "no chance of a fair investigation of subjects." His fear proved well founded: When Maclay "cast an Eye at the President of the United States, I saw he wore an aspect of Stern displeasure."

Maclay eventually proposed that the Senate convene a special committee to discuss the issue at a later date. "We waited for him to withdraw, he did so with a discontented Air. Had it been any other, than the Man who I wish to regard as the first Character in the World, I would have said with sullen dignity," Maclay generously concluded.[3]

On the way out, Washington supposedly vowed to never return—and he didn't. But the summit was mere weeks away, and needed advice now. He wanted to represent everyone's interests (all the land-owning white men, that is) and to govern by consensus (of the same land-owning white men). The Constitution offered two ways forward for the president. The first—seeking counsel from the Senate—clearly hadn't worked.

Washington had better luck with the second: The president "may require the Opinion, in writing, of the principal Officer in each of the executive Departments, upon any subject relating to the Duties of their respective Offices." The framers were wary of formal councils that met in person; it sounded too close to the King's ministers, whom they blamed for Parliament's unfair policies. The paper trail would provide transparency if future developments required investigation. But so much of Washington's presidency was trial and error, with twists and turns that nobody foresaw; theory rarely survives experience unscathed, and his practical needs would often alter or overcome abstract desires.

By the second year of his presidency, Washington had assembled an executive dream team with "Mr Jefferson at the Head of the Department of State, Mr Jay of the Judiciary, Hamilton of the Treasury and Knox of that of War, I feel myself supported by able Co-adjutors, who harmonise extremely well together," Washington wrote to Marquis de Lafayette.[4] But that wasn't yet the case in 1789; going in to the negotiations, he had to rely solely on information from Knox, whose jurisdiction included Indian affairs. (The peace treaty eventually drawn up with the southern Indians marked the official beginning of the tortured—if not outright genocidal—relations between tribal nations and the federal government.)

After the first session of Congress ended, Washington marked up his personal copy of the Constitution, writing "President" next to the sections that applied to him. He was extremely careful to satisfy every requirement of the office; a false move might kill the infant nation in its crib.[5] What's more, his decisions would shape how future presidents wielded power; he was determined that "precedents may be fixed on true principles."[6] The Constitution had been written by men he knew well, and could now call on to consult with, but it was ultimately up to interpretation. The first year of government was like the fourth trimester of a pregnancy; Washington had carried the baby to term, but now he had to figure out how to keep it happy, healthy, and growing.

America was born with enough wartime debt to crush it to death. The government owed forty million dollars to its own citizens, who had loaned it money, and twenty-five million to individuals around the world. France, now in the throes of its own revolution, was the United States' main overseas creditor, and a sensitive one at that. It was already feeling unappreciated by the United States, and delayed repayment would only aggravate that feeling. But in general, all foreign nations had to be kept happy; they were key to trade and diplomatic recognition.

Alexander Hamilton, secretary of the treasury, was in charge of solving the debt problem. Emulating the British system, he proposed setting up a central bank. It would issue currency, oversee the national banking system, and assume the interest payments on states' debts—but the principal loan would never be paid back. And while the federal government would run the Bank of the United States, it wouldn't own it. A small group of investors would, making relief of the national debt integral to their own prosperity.

The plan inflamed regional tensions. Southerners had paid off nearly all their wartime debts already, thanks in large part to slave labor. They disliked ceding a measure of their financial autonomy to the federal government, and they were smarting about the debate over a permanent location for the capital; the majority of the sixteen proposed sites were in the north. Southerners were looking at a situation in which they'd be saddled with others' debts (thanks to Hamilton, a New Yorker) *and* stripped of political influence (because of the likely northern capital location).

James Madison, representing Virginia in the House, led the fight against Hamilton's plan. His fellow representatives balked at a system inspired by Great Britain, their old oppressors. Because of the way the bank was structured, any time citizens needed help from the government, they would have to appeal to unelected power brokers. This all but guaranteed corruption. They had *just* broken the cycle, and now Hamilton was trying to trap them back in it.

There had been a time when Hamilton and Madison had worked together with great success, publishing, along with John Jay, eighty-five essays that would collectively be known as the Federalist Papers (and that, ironically, had Madison advocating for a stronger federal government). In June 1790, Jefferson invited them to dinner, and while little is known about what transpired, by the end of the night, they'd made a deal. Madison and Jefferson agreed to Hamilton's financial plan. In exchange, the northerner agreed to a southern location for the permanent seat of government.

Washington was pleased by the Compromise of 1790—in no small part because it moved the capital fifteen miles north of Mount Vernon. He signed the Residence Act in July (and the Funding Act a month later), creating a federal district around Georgetown in Maryland and Alexandria in Virginia, on his beloved Potomac. He loved renovations and was excited to oversee the construction of Federal City. In the meantime, the seat of government would move to Philadelphia, a city that he—and, perhaps more importantly, Martha—much preferred.

"I sometimes think the arrangement is not quite as it ought to have been," Martha wrote to Mercy Otis Warren, a friend and political writer. Washington traveled often, and she seemed to resent him for leaving her alone in New York, where she had friends but few intimates; she missed Fanny, who remained at Mount Vernon. At times, she sounded not just burdened, but depressed and out of place, unhappily "occupy[ing] a place with which a great many younger and gayer women would be prodigiously pleased."[7]

Martha had never taken to the city, but her young grandchildren Nelly and Wash had; they loved the lively streets and cosmopolitan schools, and they enjoyed whatever amusements came through town, including a certain Dr. King's "exhibition of animals," which featured sloths and porcupines. The Washingtons went to the theater on occasion, and attended Trinity Church on Broadway, but when they did, Martha felt as closely watched as the person delivering the sermon. "I think I am more like a state prisoner than anything else, there is certain bounds set for me which I must not depart from—and as I can not doe as I like I am obstinate and stay at home a great deal."[8]

Even at home, Martha had to play the part of Lady Washington, which required a fashionable wardrobe, full of kid gloves and fur cloaks, and the frequent attentions of a hairdresser. On Thursdays, she hosted a dinner party attended mostly by men, and although Tobias Lear and others helped, she would be judged for the quality of the soup, fish, meats, puddings, pies, iced creams, and jellies. On Fridays, she held a reception that largely consisted of people curtsying to her or Washington bowing to them. Philadelphia would offer her little relief from her role, but the city itself—so she thought—would bring her far more joy.

In Philadelphia, the Washingtons settled into a three-and-a-half-story brick mansion on Market Street. It had once served as British general Sir William Howe's headquarters, and then as Benedict Arnold's, just as he was being tempted toward treason; a financier named Robert Morris purchased it at the end of the war. Washington had been a guest there during the Constitutional Convention in 1787, and now he made it his own. The bathing room became the president's office. Martha installed a new bed in their room and expanded others.

Many of the men and women who had worked for them in New York were left behind. ("The dirty figures of Mrs Lewis and her daughter will not be a pleasant sight in view," Washington decided, ordering the dismissal of his kitchen maid and cook.⁹) Instead, the Washingtons would use people they enslaved—even though Philadelphia had recently passed the Gradual Abolition Act, which freed any slave who reached the age of twenty-eight or lived in the city for six months.

In the spring of 1791, while Washington was promoting national unity on a southern tour from Maryland to Georgia, Attorney General Edmund Randolph came to Martha with a warning. While it was well known that the slaves of congressmen, foreign ministers, and consuls were exempt from the Gradual Abolition Act—those officials could keep their slaves as property as long as they stayed in town—it seems Randolph's slaves were the first to figure out that the executive branch's slaves were *not* exempt. When they discovered the truth, they informed the attorney general they intended to claim their freedom. Randolph suggested that Martha send her slaves away to avoid the same fate; even a short trip would buy the Washingtons another six months.

"[T]he idea of freedom might be too great a temptation for them to resist," Washington wrote to Lear; it certainly was at Mount Vernon, where slaves attempted to flee with some regularity. "I do not think they would be benefitted by the change," he added. Their owner certainly wouldn't. "As all except Hercules and Paris are dower negroes"— meaning six of eight slaves in the Philadelphia house belonged to Martha—"it behoves me to prevent the emancipation of them, otherwise I *shall* not only loose the use of them, but may have them to pay for."[10] He was still cash poor and had not purchased a slave since 1775; if dower slaves escaped, he would have to reimburse Martha's estate.

Lear's response was full of magical thinking. He seemed to believe that Washington, or the country, would outlaw slavery within his lifetime, but he displayed a similarly paternalistic outlook—that Washington knew what was best for them, and they were better off owned by him than free to make their own decisions.

> You will permit me now, Sir, (and I am sure you will pardon me for doing it) to declare, that no consideration should induce me to take these steps to prolong the slavery of a human being, had I not the fullest confidence that they will at some future period be liberated, and the strongest conviction that their situation with you is far preferable to what they would probably obtain in a state of freedom.[11]

And so Lear talked himself into prolonging the bondage of Washington's slaves, starting with the one who seemed to concern them the most: Hercules, his chef, had become relatively well known for his outgoing personality and natty dress. At night, when he was done with his work, he would, according to Wash's recollection, take an "evening promenade" in his finery, purchased with money he earned selling kitchen leftovers.[12] "If Hercules should decline the offer which will be made him of going home [to Mount Vernon]," Lear wrote to Washington, "it will be a pretty strong proof of his intention to take the advantage of the law at the expiration of six months."[13]

Hercules, who had been with Washington since 1767, since he was just a teenager, "was mortified to the last degree to think that a suspicion could be entertained of his fidelity or attachment to you," Lear wrote to the president in June 1791. He had acknowledged "the motive for sending him home," had "made not the least objection to going," and, in Lear's assessment, "left no doubt of his sincerity."[14] Hercules took great offense at the idea that he would escape from the President's House in Philadelphia, where Washington had at the chef's own request brought his son, Richmond. (As Washington noted, he did so not because of Richmond's "appearance or merits I fear, but because he was the Son of Hercules & his desire to have him as an assistant."[15]) And his enslaved daughters Eve and Delia still lived at Mount Vernon; if Hercules ran away, he would probably never see his children again.

In the letter, Lear explained that he'd set up an arrangement by which Hercules would go back and forth between Mount Vernon and Philadelphia every six months with as much ease as he did anything else; his role of secretary extended to the entire household, including the desserts Martha had recently served to the Adams and Morris families. He described, in detail, the pastries a "Confectioner in town" had delivered for a recent soirée. The desserts were "very genteel & tastey," Lear wrote, and best of all, the baker would buy back the uneaten portions to minimize trouble and expense.[16] It seemed to be a good deal for the president, though Lear was anxious to see the bill.

Lear also updated Washington on the children's lessons. Nelly was educated in French, geography, music, dance, and art at home, sometimes with friends by her side—Abigail Adams's granddaughter, Caroline; Robert Morris's daughter, Maria; and Attorney General Edmund Randolph's daughter, Susan. Wash, it seemed, liked his new school in Philadelphia because he was learning very little. "Boys of his age are better pleased with relaxed discipline—and the inattention of their tutors, than with the conduct that brings them forward," Washington wrote to Lear. He remembered this from Jacky, Wash's father, and thought a different school might be better. "[B]efore you finally decide on this matter, it is my wish as Colo. Hamilton, Genl. Knox and the Attorney-General have sons in the same predicament (if they are not removed) that you would consult and act in Concert with them; & I shall be satisfied in whatever is done in consequence of it," he instructed Lear.[17]

Washington had spent the previous few years relying on these men's opinions for everything. Usually they wrote letters, but occasionally he would summon them to his office for individual meetings. He had instructed them, along with Vice President Adams, to meet should an emergency arise while he was away on the southern tour. Perhaps it occurred to him only then how much preferable it would be to gather together at the same time. A couple of months after he returned to Philadelphia, Washington sent out invitations for a group meeting, and the cabinet was born.

On November 26, 1791, Washington invited Hamilton, Jefferson, Knox, and Randolph to meet in person.[18] He had come to believe that the two

Virginians, one New Yorker, and one New Englander would give him the best range of viewpoints he could get. (Notably absent was Adams, who had never shaken his early reputation for loving all things monarchical; the latest gossip was that he rode with no fewer than six horses, as if he were a member of a royal court.)

WASHINGTON'S CABINET

	POSITION IN THE ADMINIS-TRATION	EDUCATION	OCCUPATION BEFORE THE REVOLUTION	POSITION DURING THE REVOLUTION	REGION
Thomas Jefferson	Secretary of State	College of William & Mary	Plantation owner	Virginia governor and delegate to Congress	Virginia
Henry Knox	Secretary of War	Self-educated	Bookseller	Artillery commander and general	Boston and Maine
Alexander Hamilton	Secretary of the Treasury	King's College (now Columbia University)	Bookkeeper	Artillery officer and Washington's aide-de-camp	New York City by way of the Caribbean
Edmund Randolph	Attorney General	William & Mary	Lawyer	Virginia attorney general, Williamsburg mayor, and delegate to Congress	Virginia

Washington would hold eight more meetings of the cabinet—a term coined by Madison—in 1791.[19] "[I]n these discussions, Hamilton & myself were daily pitted in the cabinet like two cocks," Jefferson later wrote.[20] His description turns meetings into a blood sport, with Washington as the referee and Jefferson and Hamilton the razor-beaked competitors.

By 1792, their fights spilled out of the cockpit. Jefferson and Madison, who were ideological allies, quietly funded Philip Freneau's *National Gazette,* which criticized all of Washington's policies and attacked Federalist supporters; he was, at least in the first term, far too popular with the people to assault directly. Just as they had blamed Parliament for misleading the king, they now blamed Washington's seemingly favorite adviser, Hamilton, for misleading the president. Hamilton was already promoting—and perhaps backing—John Fenno's *Gazette of the United States,* a pro-administration paper; he sometimes wrote for it under the name "An American."[21]

Neither publication bothered with the pretense of objectivity or balance. Most articles were written anonymously or pseudonymously, as was commonplace in early America; none were fact-checked, and everything, including personal lives, was fair game. Washington, who wished nothing more than to be a symbol of unity, was horrified. But the public couldn't get enough of the infighting. Similar newspapers launched all over the country, inflaming partisanship in even the most remote regions.

While Washington suspected that Jefferson was behind the attacks on his policies, Hamilton was convinced of it. He believed "... Mr. Madison cooperating with Mr. Jefferson is at the head of a faction decidedly hostile to me and my administration, and actuated by views in my judgment subversive of the principles of good government and dangerous to the union, peace and happiness of the Country," Hamilton wrote in code; the situation was so bad, he feared that his correspondence might be intercepted and read by partisan opponents.[22] (Because Washington had led him to believe he was integral to the presidency, Hamilton often referred to it as "my administration.")

And yet Washington still believed that regional prejudices were at the heart of their differences; he had mostly rid himself of such attitudes during the war, when he worked with a great many northerners. He did,

POLITICAL PARTIES IN EARLY AMERICA

Though Washington was sympathetic to the Federalists, he remains the only president who never claimed a political affiliation while in office. At the time, this may have been the pragmatic approach: The Constitution doesn't mention parties, and until 1804 the runner-up in the presidential election was automatically made vice president. Parties were also at odds with Washington's goal of unity. Nevertheless, two disparate visions for the country quickly emerged.

PARTY	ORIGIN	PLATFORM	DEMOGRAPHIC BASE
Democratic-Republican	The exact date is disputed, but most historians agree that Madison and Jefferson founded the party around 1791 in response to Hamilton's financial policies. (Madison had been a Federalist, but the debt crisis made him switch.)	Limit federal power and strengthen state governments; interpret the Constitution literally; anti-British; pro–French Revolution.	Farmers and southerners who wanted stronger rights for states. They tended to be less religious and believed in the separation of church and state.
Federalist	Also founded around 1791 as supporters of a strong federal government rallied around Hamilton's financial policies.	Strong central government; interpret the Constitution expansively; pro-Britain; anti–French Revolution.	Conservatives, businessmen, New Englanders—and most of the founders, including Hamilton and John Adams. Tolerated a lower barrier in the separation of church and state.

however, realize the situation was untenable. In the late summer of 1792, Washington finally addressed the tensions directly in separate letters, written three days apart. In a missive to Jefferson, dated August 23, he devotes a few paragraphs to small talk about the Spanish, then tells Jefferson, in his own way, that his infighting with Hamilton is ruining everything:

> My earnest wish, and my fondest hope therefore is, that instead of wounding suspicions, & irritable charges, there may be

liberal allowances—mutual forbearances—and temporising yieldings on *all sides*. Under the exercise of these, matters will go on smoothly, and, if possible, more prosperously. Without them every thing must rub—the Wheels of Government will clog—our enemies will triumph—& by threwing their weight into the disaffected Scale, may accomplish the ruin of the goodly fabric we have been erecting.

I do not mean to apply these observations, or this advice to any particular person, or character—I have given them in the same general terms to other Officers of the Government— because the disagreements which have arisen from difference of opinions—and the Attacks wch have been made upon almost all the measures of government, & most of its Executive Officers, have, for a long time past, filled me with painful sensations; and cannot fail I think, of producing unhappy consequences at home & abroad.[23]

On the 26th, Washington wrote much the same to Hamilton, if in a softer tone:

How unfortunate would it be, if a fabric so goodly—erected under so many Providential circumstances—and in its first stages, having acquired such respectibility, should, from diversity of Sentiments . . . brought us to the verge of dissolution— Melancholy thought! But one, at the same time that it shows the consequences of diversified opinions, when pushed with too much tenacity; exhibits evidence also of the necessity of accomodation; and of the propriety of adopting such healing measures as will restore harmony to the discordant members of the Union, & the governing powers of it.[24]

The men responded quite differently. Hamilton promised that "if any prospect shall open of healing or terminating the differences which exist, I shall most chearfully embrace it; though I consider myself as the deeply injured party." He listed the many ways "I *know*" Jefferson had wronged him, but promised "not directly or indirectly [to] say or do a thing, that shall endanger a feud."[25]

Jefferson's letter was about three thousand words longer, and ended with his resignation. He reviewed the many ways Hamilton had manipulated and wronged him, starting with the Compromise of 1790: "I was duped into by the Secretary of the treasury and made a tool for forwarding his schemes." He strongly denied any involvement with partisan newspapers: "not a syllable of them has ever proceeded from me . . . no cabals or intrigues of mine have produced those in the legislature." And then Jefferson gave his notice. He would serve Washington until the end of his first term and then retire to his plantation, Monticello.[26]

When Washington had the same idea earlier that spring, Jefferson had talked him out of returning to Mount Vernon after four years in office. "North and South will hang together, if they have you to hang on."[27] On this point, Hamilton agreed, and so did everyone Washington came into contact with. He spoke at length about resigning with Elizabeth Powel, one of his closest friends in Philadelphia, who followed up with a dramatic letter; it would be the end of him, she said, and the end of the country.

> Your Resignation wou'd elate the Enemies of good Government and cause lasting Regret to the Friends of humanity. The mistaken and prejudiced Part of Mankind, that see thro' the Medium of bad Minds, would ascribe your Conduct to unworthy Motives. They would say that you were actuated by Principles of self-Love alone—that you saw the Post was not tenable

with any Prospect of adding to your Fame. The Antifederalist would use it as an Argument for dissolving the Union, and would urge that you, from Experience, had found the present System a bad one, and had, artfully, withdrawn from it that you might not be crushed under its Ruins—that, in this, you had acted a politic Part.

Near the end of the letter, Powel also pointed out that Washington was often wrong about where and when he would find peace. He'd spent his last retirement, for instance, fretting from afar about the state of the country.

Have you not often experienced that your Judgement was fallible with Respect to the Means of Happiness? Have you not, on some Occasions, found the Consummation of your Wishes the Source of the keenest of your Sufferings?[28]

Had Washington left after one term, it would undoubtedly have been on a high note. "We are in a wilderness without a single footstep to guide us," Madison had written to Jefferson in 1789, at the beginning of Washington's first term.[29] By 1792, the first president had set up a functioning executive branch and established conventions for future presidents to either follow or reform. He had overseen the passage of the Bill of Rights; appointed all ten Supreme Court justices, thirty-eight federal judges, and twenty-eight district judges; declared the first Thanksgiving; welcomed Rhode Island, Vermont, and Kentucky into the union; formed armies under federal regulation; and signed the Naturalization Act, which granted citizenship to any free white person who had been in the country for at least two years.[30] There were banks and an official currency, a Copyright Act and a capital city underway.

But he didn't leave. Washington, then sixty, was once again named on the ballot of every presidential elector.[31] He did not so much agree as capitulate to a second term, a decision Washington must have regretted on March 4, 1793, when he took his second oath of office against a backdrop of such immense international unrest, it threatened America's very ability to survive.

CHAPTER 17

"Political Suicide"

ON APRIL 11, 1793, WASHINGTON BURIED GEORGE AUGUSTINE, HIS favorite nephew and heir apparent, at Mount Vernon. The young man had died from tuberculosis, leaving Fanny a widow with three children to raise. She was so distraught that she asked the Washingtons to postpone filing her husband's will in court; she wasn't ready to face the realities of life after him. Washington had little time to comfort her.

His second inauguration had passed uneventfully only a little more than a month earlier, but as the spring air slowly warmed and flowers bloomed, a series of conflicts threatened to become crises. Two days after George Augustine's funeral, Washington received a letter from Hamilton: France had declared war on Great Britain. The president called an emergency meeting of the cabinet at his house in Philadelphia on April 19.[1] He sent thirteen questions in advance, but one was the most important: Had America's 1778 treaty with France been guillotined a few months earlier alongside King Louis XVI?

Washington was inclined to ignore the treaty and declare neutrality;

he felt that the country shouldn't be bound by an agreement that the Continental Congress, which no longer existed, had made with the French crown, which also no longer existed. America's land forces could offer nothing meaningful to the conflict, and there were almost no sea forces to speak of; he wouldn't even sign the Naval Act into law for another year, and those six frigates had yet to be built.

Even a declaration of public support was risky; it was likely to encourage American privateers to attack the ships of the opposing side, which would surely drag the government into the conflict. And the prospect of war was already causing divisions in the young and volatile country. As soon as news of it reached America, citizens declared their allegiances. To some people, the French motto "Liberty, equality, fraternity" sounded an awful lot like their own "life, liberty, and the pursuit of happiness"; they often gathered, wearing red, white, and blue ribbons, to celebrate news of French military victories. Great Britain's supporters, who wore golden eagles or black rose-shaped badges, were just as loyal, if not more orderly.

But Washington wasn't just being careful. He was being savvy. If America remained neutral, it could sell goods to *both* nations.

The issue split the cabinet down the middle. Hamilton was a known Anglophile, but he argued for neutrality. Although often alone in his own ideological corner, he won the support of Henry Knox, the secretary of war. According to Jefferson's notes, Knox sided with Hamilton even as he acknowledged, "like a fool as he is, that he knew nothing about it."[2]

Jefferson, whom Washington had persuaded to stay on as secretary of state for a few months into the president's second term, surprised everyone: After voicing his support for the French Revolution, even as thousands of people were being executed and imprisoned, he suggested that America play coy. France and Great Britain, he said, should come to them and make an offer; American loyalty would go to the highest bidder.

On April 22, Washington issued a Neutrality Proclamation that Attorney General Edmund Randolph put into final form. The document declared that the United States "should with sincerity and good faith adopt and pursue a conduct friendly and impartial toward the belligerent powers" and warned "the citizens of the United States carefully to avoid all acts and proceedings whatsoever, which may in any manner tend to contravene such disposition." At Washington's request, Jefferson distributed printed copies of the proclamation to state executives and diplomatic officials in European capitals.[3]

Washington had to follow the rules, too. He chose not to receive Marquis de Lafayette's brother-in-law, who arrived with other counter-revolutionary émigrés, and agonized over what to do when the marquis's son, Washington Lafayette, landed in 1795. He quietly arranged for him to enroll at Harvard—"The expence of which, as also of every other mean for his support, I will pay"—but young Lafayette instead chose to join Hamilton in New York, hoping the trip would be a quick stopover before an invitation to the President's House materialized.[4]

Washington, meanwhile, sought advice on the French visitor from those most likely to be critical of him: Madison and his Republican-dominated House of Representatives. They were surprisingly supportive; Lafayette was a reminder of the Revolution, something they could all still rally around, and his son was very welcome in America. "A few jokes passed between the President and young Lafayette, whom he treats more as his child than a guest," Benjamin Latrobe, one of the architects who designed the U.S. Capitol, recorded in his diary.[5] He ended up living quietly with Washington for two years.

☆ ☆ ☆

Jefferson did emerge with one diplomatic win: Washington agreed to receive Edmond-Charles Genêt, the first ambassador from the French Republic. But when Genêt arrived in the spring of 1793, he didn't go straight to Philadelphia, as he should have, to pay his respects to the president. Instead, the young redheaded ambassador began a month-long anti-neutrality tour from Charleston, South Carolina, to New York. He urged Americans to openly defy Washington—whom he described as "a man very different from the character emblazoned in history"—by pressuring Congress to declare support for France, sending privateers to seize British merchant ships, and wresting control of Florida and Louisiana from the Spanish, who were now also at war with France.[6]

Crowds gathered wherever he went; his words agitated citizens and critics alike. "The Spirit of 1776 is roused again," the editors of the *National Gazette* wrote in a taunting open letter to Washington, who had once been the embodiment of that spirit.[7] "You certainly never felt the Terrorism, excited by Genêt, in 1793," John Adams recalled in a letter to Jefferson in 1813, "when ten thousand People in the Streets of Philadelphia, day after day, threatened to drag Washington out of his House, and effect a Revolution in the Government, or compel it to declare War in favour of the French Revolution, and against England."[8]

Washington, slowed with illness, had plenty of time to stew about it. Jefferson described his situation to Madison in a letter on June 9.

Little lingering fevers have been hanging about him for a week or ten days, and have affected his looks most remarkably. He is also extremely affected by the attacks made and kept up on him in the public papers. I think he feels those things more than any person I ever yet met with. I am sincerely sorry to see them. I remember an observation of yours, made when I first went to New York, that the satellites and sycophants which surrounded him had wound up the ceremonials of the government to a pitch of stateliness which nothing but his personal character could have supported, and which no character after him could ever maintain.[9]

But after the French privateer *Embuscade,* hoping to tempt Americans into joining them, had the gall to send prizes it had captured into Philadelphia's port, even Jefferson agreed: Genêt had gone too far. It took Washington a full year to have him recalled.

Right after Washington refused to use military force against a foreign nation, he turned it on his own people in what would ultimately be the biggest overreaction of his life.

In 1794, the government was having trouble collecting an excise tax—a part of Hamilton's plan to pay back foreign debt—from distillers in the Kentucky and western Pennsylvania backcountry.[10] Whiskey was their main export and sole profitable activity past basic farming, they wrote in a petition to Congress. Higher prices would make their product less attractive to consumers, and the expectation that they, rural folk, should repay a disproportionate share of foreign debt was unfair and untenable.

When the petition didn't work, the peaceful gatherings began. The largest numbered around six thousand and took place on Braddock's Field in Pittsburgh, where, almost four decades before, a young

Washington had picked up the sash of his fallen commander and emerged a hero.

The distillers' complaints went unheard. Their frustrations mounted. The tax collectors closed in. Then, finally, violence erupted. Hamilton informed Washington that a crowd in Pennsylvania had seized an unlucky collector named Robert Johnson, "tarred and feathered him cut off his hair and deprived him of his horse, obliging him to travel on foot a considerable distance in that mortifying and painful situation." Another man, he said—no more than a messenger—was "seized whipped tarred & feathered, and after having his money & horse taken from him was blind folded and tied in the woods, in which condition he remained for five hours."[11] And around four hundred rebels set fire to the Pittsburgh home of John Neville, the collectors' supervisor.

Washington seems to have taken this personally. He was no king; he had not handed down the tax to fund his jewel habit or build a seventh castle. Rather, democratically elected officials had voted it into law. He saw these local attacks as a direct challenge to legitimate federal authority and was determined to quash the protest and have its participants tried for treason. But according to the Constitution, the commander in chief could send in troops only at the request of state officials, and Pennsylvania governor Thomas Mifflin wasn't ready to take that step.

Washington saw a rebellion, but Mifflin saw isolated (and largely whiskey-fueled) acts of desperation from a community that felt unheard. Only land-owning white men could vote, and land ownership in western Pennsylvania had fallen dramatically since the earliest period of white settlement. In some townships, none of the locals owned any land at all; their landlords—the ones who were allowed to vote—lived in the big cities. Much of the population covered rent and other necessities by bartering crops or whiskey. They rarely paid in cash, which was scarce in the region. For the majority of the population, then, even a low yearly tax would leave them with nothing.

Mifflin didn't make excuses for the rebels, but he believed the courts should decide how to resolve the impasse. Washington did not. In an extraordinary showing of executive overreach, he sidestepped both Mifflin and the Constitution, securing a judicial writ from Associate Justice James Wilson, called out state militia for federal service, and hired a tailor to make him a uniform modeled after the one he'd worn in the war.[12]

"Whenever the government appears in arms, it ought to appear like a *Hercules*," Hamilton would write in 1799, and the twelve thousand soldiers he led toward what is now Pittsburgh showed he meant it.[13]

Washington, sixty-two, was there, too. He became the first and only president to take up arms against his own citizens, and to come along for the ride—though he did so mostly from a carriage, dismounting only when it was time to review the troops. Knox, who had gone to Maine to see about a house he was building, was noticeably absent from the forces gathering in Pennsylvania. He had neglected, despite the situation, to communicate his personal plans in a timely fashion. When he finally offered to meet up with the president's party on the road, Washington was livid. It would have been nice to have Knox by his side, he wrote in a passive-aggressive letter on October 9, 1794, "if your return, in time, would have allowed it. It is now too late."[14] Excluding Adams from the business of the executive branch was one thing; telling the secretary of war he was unwelcome during a military campaign was quite another.

But in the end, the showdown with the insurrectionists of the Whiskey Rebellion never happened. When government troops arrived

A VIOLENT END TO INDIAN RESISTANCE

Knox was not completely missing in action. He had exchanged a handful of letters with Washington about another unfair fight.

In 1794, after diplomatic negotiations with the Indians in the Northwest Territory failed, Washington called General Anthony Wayne out of retirement and sent him to secure U.S. holdings. Wayne, popularly known as Mad Anthony, trained and led four thousand troops into the Ohio River Valley and overpowered the Ottawas, Shawnees, and other tribes that had been resisting white settlement. During the Battle of Fallen Timbers, the Americans destroyed their villages, burned their crops, and murdered an estimated forty Indians, including several war chiefs. Survivors—including a young Tecumseh—fled for nearby British forts. Fearing retribution, the British turned their old allies away. The following year, thirteen tribes ceded more than twenty-five thousand acres of land to the federal government, in exchange for $25,000 down and an annual payment of $9,500.

A year after that, Washington wrote a paternalistic letter to the "Beloved Cherokees" in which he suggested, at great length, that they be more like Virginia farmers:

"What I have recommended to you I am myself going to do. After a few moons are passed, I shall leave the great town, and retire to my farm. There I shall attend to the means of increasing my cattle, sheep, and other useful animals, to the growing of corn, wheat & other grain, and to the employing of women in spinning and weaving: all which I have recommended to you, that you may be as comfortable & happy as plenty of food, cloathing & other good things can make you."[15]

at Braddock's Field, there was no one to fight. (There was also no Washington; he'd thought better of his presence at the last minute and turned around.) "And what is equally astonishing," Jefferson later wrote to

James Monroe, "is that by the pomp of reports, proclamations, armies &c. the mind of the legislature itself was so fascinated as never to have asked where, when, and by whom has this insurrection been produced?"[16] The press was stunned by Washington's imprudence: The man famous for his self-control and judiciousness had neglected to consider whether military action was warranted. Couldn't he have simply threatened the poor civilians into submission—or, better yet, actually talked to them?

With some effort, the troops arrested one hundred and fifty whiskey rebels. But without much evidence, and with few people willing to testify, only two men, John Mitchell and Philip Wiegel, were found guilty of treason. Although Washington bragged about the peaceful resolution, he must have felt embarrassed about the situation, or at least the reception his overreaction had received; he used a presidential pardon for the first time in history, and let the men go.

But months later, Washington still had a point to make. During his sixth annual address to Congress, he blamed "Self created Societies" for inflaming dissent against the government and causing greater divisions across the country.[17] Federalist congressmen felt validated by the president's rare use of strong language, while Democratic-Republicans felt personally attacked; they had nothing to do with the rebellion, and furthermore, free speech and public debate were protected by the Constitution. In a letter to James Monroe, then US minister to France, Madison wrote that the "introduction of [Self created Societies] by the President was perhaps the greatest error of his political life."[18]

Jefferson, from retirement, continued to fuel the press attacks. From afar, it seems, he wore Hamilton down—as did life. In December, after his wife miscarried, Hamilton resigned. Knox followed twenty-seven days later, claiming he wanted to spend more time with his family.[19]

WASHINGTON'S SECOND–
AND ENTIRELY FEDERALIST–CABINET

NAME	POSITION IN THE ADMINIS-TRATION	EDUCATION	POSITION DURING THE REVOLUTION	OCCUPATION	REGION
William Bradford	Attorney General (January 1794–August 1795; died in office)	College of New Jersey (later Princeton)	Captain, then attorney general of Pennsylvania	Lawyer	Philadelphia
Charles Lee	Attorney General	College of New Jersey	Coastal trade official	Lawyer	Virginia
James McHenry	Secretary of War	Newark Academy (Del.)	Surgeon and then volunteer aide-de-camp	Physician	Pennsylvania and Maryland
Oliver Wolcott, Jr.	Secretary of the Treasury	Yale	Quartermas-ter's assistant	Comptroller of Connecticut, Auditor for the United States Treasury, and Comptroller for the Treasury	Connecticut and New York
Edmund Randolph	Secretary of State (January 1794–August 1795)	College of William & Mary	Virginia attorney general, Williamsburg mayor, and delegate to Congress	Lawyer	Virginia
Timothy Pickering	Secretary of State	Harvard	Adjutant general and quartermaster general	County judge	Massachusetts

✩ ✩ ✩

Neutrality was difficult to maintain. Congress, which had been quietly questioning whether the Constitution even allowed a president to declare neutrality on his own—after all, he could not unilaterally declare war—was on edge. In March 1794, after British ships in the West Indies seized hundreds of American merchant vessels carrying food, and forcibly conscripted the sailors into the Royal Navy, Congress placed an embargo on all British ships and vessels in U.S. ports for thirty days.

Hoping to avoid another war with the British, Washington sent John Jay, the chief justice of the Supreme Court, to London to negotiate a treaty. Given the slow pace of transatlantic mail, the administration would be unable to weigh in on negotiations in real time, so Jay traveled with a set of notes.

But they didn't come from his current cabinet. They came from Hamilton; he was now practicing law privately in New York, but that didn't stop Washington from constantly seeking his counsel. Jefferson had always failed to realize *why* Hamilton won almost all their battles; he typically attributed it to Hamilton's manipulation, or, as Washington aged, his inability to keep up, but in reality, it was a shared nationalistic worldview, and Hamilton's gift of clearly and forcefully articulating it. The way he did so, however, wasn't only loud and aggressive—compared to Jefferson's behind-the-scenes letter-writing campaigns and puppeteering—but sometimes reckless.

Hamilton couldn't just leave it to Jay, the actual negotiator, to handle discussions on his own. So he back-channeled with British leaders, assuring them America would not, as Denmark and Sweden had, defend its neutral stance with arms. The Brits' concern over direct engagement was the only card Jay had to play, and Hamilton showed them his hand.

A year later, the big concession Jay got out of the British was something they had failed to deliver the first time around in 1783—a total surrender of northwestern military installations. The promise to name the United States a "most favoured nation" in commercial trade applied only to ships under seventy tons; upon hearing the paltry weight limit, Madison supposedly joked that American merchants would have to trade from canoes.[20]

The terms got worse from there. Great Britain refused to recognize America's neutrality at sea; it would continue to seize any ship it suspected of carrying "contraband" for France. And it still expected to collect on debts incurred during the Revolution.

Jay knew the treaty wouldn't bring "universal satisfaction"; it squeaked by in the pro-administration, Federalist-controlled Senate by twenty votes to ten—without the weight limit. He was wrong, however, in thinking it wouldn't "administer occasion for calumny and detraction."[21] When anti-administration newspapers printed the treaty in full, people hurled stones at Hamilton on the street, burned effigies of Jay, and sent Washington an overwhelming amount of hate mail. "Tenor indecent—no answer returned," he wrote on one.[22]

"At present the cry against the treaty is like that against a mad dog and everyone, in a manner, seems engaged in running it down," Washington wrote to Hamilton, who was working behind the scenes publishing what would ultimately number twenty-eight pro–Jay Treaty essays under pseudonyms in various papers. "I have seen with pleasure," he continued, by way of thanks, "that a writer in one of the New York papers under the Signature of Camillus, has promised to answer—or rather to defend the treaty—which has been made with G. Britain."[23]

Washington called a cabinet meeting in the late summer of 1795, but Timothy Pickering, Knox's replacement as secretary of war, and

Oliver Wolcott, Jr., Hamilton's replacement as secretary of the treasury, had their own agenda. They presented him with a letter written by Jean Antoine Joseph Fauchet, the French ambassador to the United States, around the time of the Whiskey Rebellion. It was highly critical of Washington's foreign policy and, worse, contained a shocking—and frustratingly ambiguous—allegation: Edmund Randolph, Washington's only remaining original cabinet member, had apparently solicited a bribe from the French. Or maybe the French had made overtures to Randolph. Some kind of intelligence was provided . . . or could be provided. Fauchet's letter was confusing, likely because it was poorly translated. But Washington, too stressed from the treaty fiasco—which he had signed on August 15, 1795, despite the public outcry and his own reservations—was unable to tolerate even the suggestion of scandal.

A week after receiving the news, he called Randolph into his private study. The two men had known each other for decades; Randolph had served as Washington's aide-de-camp during the Revolution, then as his private lawyer, then as U.S. attorney general, and finally as secretary of state. Washington now accused him of treason. Randolph, outraged, quit on the spot. Perhaps he expected Washington to offer to launch an investigation or request that he stay on until a replacement was named. Instead, the president, whose main concern was to stop anti-administration newspapers from getting their hands on more embarrassing fodder, coldly demanded the resignation in writing. Randolph went back to his office, packed up his things, and sent a letter to Washington that same day.

> My sensations then cannot be concealed; when I find that confidence so immediately withdrawn, without a word or distant hint being previously dropped to me. This, sir, as I mentioned

in your room, is a situation, in which I cannot hold my present office; and therefore I hereby resign it.[24]

But it didn't end there. In December, Randolph published a pamphlet titled *Vindication*, the first tell-all from an American presidential administration. (Jefferson's copy, complete with his marginalia, resides at the Library of Congress.) He claimed innocence and included a retraction from none other than Fauchet.

Washington refused to comment on the story—he never responded to the press directly—but privately called Randolph's "long promised vindication" an "accusation." Yet Washington felt unsure enough to solicit the opinion of Hamilton, who dismissed Randolph and his supporters as "base" and reassured Washington that the spectacle would "do good, rather than harm to the public cause and to yourself."[25] Washington never spoke to Randolph again—though he was, in the end, mistaken. His old friend's outrage was genuine. Randolph had never sought to betray Washington to the French, or anyone else.

That scandal died after a few months, but the Republicans in the House, led by Madison, refused to let the Jay Treaty go, and a standoff ensued. In the spring of 1796, they demanded that the president share the diplomatic instructions Jay had received. Washington refused, asserting for the first time what would become known as executive privilege. The Republicans threatened to withhold the funds necessary to put the treaty into effect. Washington called that unconstitutional, arguing that the Senate and the president made treaties and the House could do nothing to veto them. He won on all fronts. Hamilton's notes stayed private, and the treaty was a success; trade expanded, and, once the British evacuated their northwest posts, so did settlements in Ohio.[26] As an added boon, Madison felt destabilized by the failed showdown, and contemplated retiring. "As a politician, he is no more," William

Cobbett—a British transplant who wrote political commentary under the pseudonym "Porcupine"—happily declared.[27]

And with that, Washington was no longer interested in inviting another Democratic-Republican into his cabinet, his confidence, or anywhere else. "I shall not, whilst I have the honor to administer the government, bring a man into any office of consequence knowingly, whose political tenets are adverse to the measures, which the *general* government are pursuing," he wrote to Timothy Pickering on September 27, 1795. "For this, in my opinion, would be a sort of political Suicide."[28]

The decision did not go unnoticed. In February of 1796, Washington's birthday—an event once celebrated in the streets—came and went without fanfare. Members of the House of Representatives voted against adjourning for thirty minutes to wish him well.[29]

CHAPTER 18

Farewell to "Cunning, Ambitious, and Unprincipled Men"

IN MAY OF 1796, WASHINGTON WAS GETTING READY TO ESCAPE Philadelphia for the summer. He had spent the previous few months, as his exhausting second term was winding down, checking in on the new window blinds and apple trees and structural repairs of the mansion house at Mount Vernon. Martha would be reunited with Fanny there, and Washington with Tobias Lear; the two had married the previous year and made a home nearby on the plantation.

The Washingtons were about to celebrate another marriage. Betsy, their eldest granddaughter, had "Suprize[d]" them with an engagement, as Washington wrote to her betrothed; he hoped that Thomas Law, a British citizen who had arrived from India with two of his three children, who were half-Indian, would be "fixed in America."[1] And to Betsy, he wrote to "bestow on you my choicest blessings," and the gift of a dower slave.[2]

Ona (Oney) Judge, a twenty-two-year-old "light mulatto girl, much freckled," was the daughter of Betty, an enslaved seamstress, and Andrew Judge, an indentured servant who became Washington's trusted tailor.

(We do not know whether the relationship was consensual or whether, at the end of his ten-year term of service, Judge tried to purchase Betty and their daughter from Washington; we only know that he left Mount Vernon without them.) Ona Judge had been Martha's personal maid since she was a girl of ten, and had been brought from Mount Vernon to Philadelphia to serve her. According to ledgers from the President's House, she led a relatively privileged existence when compared with the vast majority of the Washingtons' slaves. She dressed in fine gowns, shoes, stockings, and bonnets; in Philadelphia, she went to see a play and "the tumbling feats" at Ricketts' Circus, the first in America.[3]

And yet, as she moved through Philadelphia's free black community, she must have felt anything but lucky. On the way to the play or the circus, Judge might have seen things that would never be available to her as a slave. Free black couples strolling together. Black-owned businesses. The all-black congregation at the Mother Bethel African Methodist Episcopal Church. These people weren't going to be wedding gifts to anyone, let alone someone like Betsy, who had a notorious temper. "[I] was determined never to be her slave," Judge would later say.

Time was of the essence. The family would soon leave for Mount Vernon, and Judge feared that "if I went back to Virginia, I should never get my liberty." On May 20, as the Washingtons were eating dinner, Judge walked right out the door. "I had friends among the colored people of Philadelphia, had my things carried there beforehand," she said.[4]

Although Washington had once asked Lear to keep his slave-rotating scheme between the two of them, he did nothing to hide his pursuit of Judge. Two days after she "absconded" with "no provocation," Frederick Kitt, who served as Washington's household steward, placed an ad in the *Philadelphia Gazette and Universal Daily Advertiser* soliciting her capture. In it, Washington was named by title—"the President of the

United States"—as was the price he was willing to pay for her return: ten dollars.

☆ ☆ ☆

The Washingtons returned to Mount Vernon without Judge, but it was hardly the vacation they had hoped for. Every day, there was a new disaster. James Monroe, the American minister in France, had to be recalled; he had failed to defend the Jay Treaty, and was openly sympathetic to the French. Robert Morris, the financier, had fallen behind on payments for lots in the new Federal City, endangering the plan for the capital and Washington's own investments in the vital national venture. The *Aurora* and other Republican papers were relentless, and Washington now believed, despite Jefferson's denials, that the former secretary of state was behind the bad coverage.

"Your conduct has been represented as derogating," Washington wrote on July 6, 1796, his patience depleted. Jefferson, or at the very least his cohorts, had made him out to be Hamilton's puppet, "a person under a dangerous influence."[5] He sent his last letter to Jefferson the next month; it was an obligatory note, no more than five sentences long, appended to some papers he'd promised to forward.[6] They never spoke again.

Washington's list of estranged friends grew to include Thomas Paine. The English-born author had helped shape Washington's ideology, but he felt abandoned by the president, who had let him fester in a French prison during the revolution there, fearing every day was his last. On July 30, Paine penned an open letter bashing Washington on nearly every front.

> Monopolies of every kind marked your administration almost in the moment of its commencement. . . . Elevated to the chair

of the Presidency, you assumed the merit of everything to your-self, and the natural ingratitude of your constitution began to appear. You commenced your Presidential career by encourag-ing and swallowing the grossest adulation, and you traveled America from one end to the other to put yourself in the way of receiving it. You have as many addresses in your chest as James II. As to what were your views, for, if you are not great enough to have ambition, you are little enough to have vanity, they can-not be directly inferred from expressions of your own; but the partisans of your politics have divulged the secret . . . In what fraudulent light must Mr. Washington's character appear in the world, when his declarations and his conduct are compared together![7]

Just as Paine's *Common Sense* had won over the masses during the Revolution, his caustic letter was equally galvanizing—but not in the way he intended. Americans saw it as an attack on their living legend, and bristled at the disrespect. Federalists said it was proof that the French were trying to undermine the American government, a claim bolstered by additional evidence: Paine had written it at Monroe's resi-dence in Paris before the pro-French minister was recalled. (No matter that Monroe had actually tried to talk Paine out of sending the letter on Washington's birthday.)

To Washington, though, the damage was already done. At sixty-four, he wanted to retire, and this time, no one talked him out of it. The Constitution prescribed term limits of four years, but it did not restrict how many terms could be served; in choosing to stop at two, Washing-ton set a precedent that would endure into the twentieth century, when Franklin Delano Roosevelt went for a third. Once again, he would shock the world by giving up power, overseeing a peaceful transfer from one systematically elected official to another.

A few months before Washington publicly announced his decision, he sent Hamilton a copy of a valedictory address that Madison had written for him in 1792—the first time he had tried to retire from the presidency. It included his own edits and additions—many of which Hamilton, of all people, cut for sounding too bitter. But the drafts remain.

> As this Address, Fellow citizens, will be the last I shall ever make you, and as some of the Gazettes of the United States have teamed with all the Invective that disappointment, ignorance of facts, and malicious falsehoods could invent, to misrepresent my politics and affections; to wound my reputation and feelings; and to weaken, if not entirely destroy the confidence you had been pleased to repose in me; it might be expected at the parting scene of my public life that I should take some notice of such virulent abuse.[8]

Hamilton's version, which included only "reflections and sentiments as will wear well," was published in newspapers and distributed in pamphlet form in September 1796.[9]

It contained no surprises. Washington praised the infant country's rapid progress, which would continue if it focused on ambitions, not alliances; "the policy and the will of one country are subjected to the policy and will of another." Foreign influence was the enemy of American unity and prosperity, he wrote, because it whipped up "jealousy, ill-will, and a disposition to retaliate." He worried that "cunning, ambitious, and unprincipled men will be enabled to subvert the power of the people, and to usurp for themselves the reins of Government."[10] Political partisanship, Washington predicted, would reduce the government to a crowd of bickering representatives who were very good at thwarting each other but got very little accomplished for their constituents. And for all his talk of unity, he had come to see people as for or against his administration and had little patience for criticism. Unbridled partisanship was his greatest fear, and his greatest failure was that he became increasingly partisan.

Washington had two more seasons to go. In late fall, he observed the first contested, partisan election in silence. John Adams and Thomas Jefferson did not outwardly campaign for the presidency, but their respective corners did, with Washington's policies fueling the debate.

Federalists accused Democratic-Republicans of supporting the bloody French Revolution (the French ambassador's open support did not help matters) and Democratic-Republicans were just as quick to remind voters of the Jay Treaty, born from a monarchy-loving administration. Adams squeaked by with seventy-one electoral votes, mostly from the north, to Jefferson's sixty-eight; it would be the first and last time in which a president and vice president were elected from different parties.

The election did nothing to bridge the partisan divide during Washington's final winter in Philadelphia. After an innocuous final address to Congress on an icy day in December, a young Andrew Jackson, serving his first term in the House of Representatives from the newly inducted state of Tennessee, refused to salute or applaud Washington. Nothing was off base for the *Aurora*—they attacked his early career, reminding readers of de Jumonville's assassination back in the French and Indian War; his two terms in office; and the predicted aftermath of his policies.

"The President is fortunate to get off just as the bubble is bursting, leaving others to hold the bag," a resentful Jefferson complained to Madison. "He will have his usual good fortune of reaping credit from the good arts of others, and leaving to them that of his errors."[11]

His supporters remained loyal, and with the end of his presidency in sight, the Washingtons indulged them. They spent most of the winter going to social events thrown in his honor. Twelve hundred guests—including Elizabeth Powel, in black mourning dress for her husband—celebrated his sixty-fifth birthday in Philadelphia at Ricketts' Circus.

That same day, February 22, 1797, Hercules, originally considered the greatest flight risk among the president's slaves, ran away—but not from Philadelphia. He had been sent back to Mount Vernon after his son, Richmond (whom Washington begrudgingly brought to the city to make Hercules happy), had been accused of stealing from a guest the previous year.[12] Washington assumed the alleged robbery was a part of a plan to escape, and sent Hercules back to Mount Vernon—but not to the kitchen. Hercules spent the rest of 1796 and early 1797 crushing gravel, digging ditches, and doing whatever backbreaking work was assigned to him, under an overseer's watchful eye, and whip. This suggests he was telling the truth when he pledged fidelity to Lear six years earlier, and it was the punishment he received that prompted him to flee, leaving behind his three children.

It's unlikely Washington realized that; he only saw confirmation of his original suspicions. And when it came to Ona Judge, he was in complete denial. "[T]here is no doubt in this family," Washington wrote to Joseph Whipple, a customs collector in Portsmouth, New Hampshire, "of her having been seduced and enticed off by a Frenchman." He never considered that Judge was upset enough at her casual gifting to flee. (In her absence, her younger sister, Delphy, was given to Betsy.) "[T]he ingratitude of the girl, who was brought up & treated more like a child than a servant," complained Washington to Oliver Wolcott, Jr., his secretary of the treasury.[13]

Washington pursued both of his runaway slaves. "Continue your enquiries, I pray you, after Herculas," Washington wrote to Kitt, his household steward, "and if you should find it necessary, hire some one who is most likely to be acquainted with his haunts, to trace them out." He never got close to finding Hercules, but shortly after Adams was elected in November, Judge was spotted in New Hampshire, where slavery was abolished in 1783. Washington sent Whipple to compel her to return to Virginia.[14]

Judge actually agreed, but not without terms: She would remain with the Washingtons until they died; the end of their life would signal an end to her bondage. And she would not be gifted or sold to anyone. When Whipple wrote as much, Washington went apoplectic.

> To enter into such a compromise, as *she* has suggested to *you*, is totally inadmissible, for reasons that must strike at first view: for however well disposed I might be to a gradual abolition, or even to an entire emancipation of that description of People (if the latter was in itself practicable at this Moment) it would neither be politic or just, to reward unfaithfulness with a premature preference; and thereby discontent, beforehand, the minds of all her fellow Servants; who by their steady adherence, are far more deserving than herself, of favor.... If she will return to her former Service, without obliging me to resort to compulsory means to effect it, her late conduct will be forgiven by her Mistress; and she will meet with the same treatment from me, that all the rest of her family (which is a very numerous one) shall receive.[15]

"KEEP HIM HANDCUFFD"

Washington is often quoted as saying "I am principled [against] selling negros, as you would do cattle in the market," and that if he could find another way to part with them, he "would not, in twelve months from this date, be possessed of one, as a slave."[17] But he had sold his slaves on at least three occasions, and he did so knowing that the place he was sending them, the West Indies, would bring about a brutal change in their lives. They would likely work on sugar plantations under overseers who were quick to use their whips; their diets would be poor, their medical care worse. They were virtually guaranteed a premature death.

In 1766, Washington entrusted Joseph Thompson, captain of the *Swift*, with selling an enslaved man named Tom the Caribbean. Tom, it seems, was one of nearly fifty slaves who attempted to flee Washington during his lifetime as a slave owner.

> Sir,
>
> With this Letter comes a Negro (Tom) which I beg the favour of you to sell, in any of the Islands you may go to, for whatever he will fetch, & bring me in return for him
>
> One Hhd of best Molasses
> One Ditto of best Rum
> One Barrl of Lymes—if good & Cheap
> One Pot of Tamarinds—contg about 10 lbs.
> Two small Do of mixed Sweetmeats—abt 5 lb. each
> And the residue, much or little, in good old Spirits
>
> That this Fellow is both a Rogue & Runaway (tho. he was by no means remarkable for the former, and never practised the latter till of late) I shall not pretend to deny—But that he is exceeding healthy, strong, and good at the Hoe, the whole neighbourhood can testifie & particularly Mr Johnson and his Son, who have both

had him under them as foreman of the gang; which gives me reason to hope he may, with your good management, sell well, if kept clean & trim'd up a little when offerd to Sale.

I shall very chearfully allow you the customary Commissions on this affair, and must beg the favour of you (least he shoud attempt his escape) to keep him handcuffd till you get to Sea—or in the Bay—after which I doubt not but you may make him very useful to you.

I wish you a pleasant and prosperous Passage, and a safe & speedy return, being Sir, Yr Very Hble Servt

Go: Washington[18]

Washington could "resort to compulsory means to effect" Judge's return because he had signed the Fugitive Slave Act into law. Yet, since the Revolution, he had been saying that he wished "to see some plan adopted, by the legislature by which slavery in this Country may be abolished by slow, sure, & imperceptable degrees."[16] Washington always emphasized that emancipation be *gradual*; one could argue that this was to acclimate everyone to the notion, but it would, most importantly, lessen the financial blow to slave owners. Still, he did nothing to address the issue while he was in office.

In lieu of coercion from the federal and state governments, Washington could have freed his slaves as an individual, but always found a reason or excuse not to. The main issue was always money. According to a Virginia law passed in 1782, he could set any number of enslaved men, women, and children above forty-five years or under twenty-one (for men) and eighteen (for women) free *if* they could be "supported and maintained by the person so liberating them." If he failed to do so, the court would "sell so much of the person's estate as shall be sufficient for that purpose."[19]

Washington didn't have the cash. "My estate for the last 11 years have not been able to make both ends meet," he had written to Lund Washington in 1787, and little had changed since.[20] Crops regularly failed, meaning he not only couldn't sell his harvest but had to buy enough to feed his family, employees, and slaves. Those who owed him money were slow to pay him back, if they ever did at all. He struggled to pay taxes. And, of course, he and Martha had become accustomed to a certain standard of living.

It's hard to know how serious he had been over the years about liberating his slaves; when the topic came up in letters, he often said he would prefer to discuss it in person. Whether those discussions happened and how they went, we'll never know. What's clear is that, however Washington felt about owning human beings, he wasn't willing to part with everything he had to free them.

But in 1797, a sense of urgency was upon him. For one, as Judge had reminded him, death was inevitable, and, given his age, probably near. That led to concerns about legacy. Going into the presidency, Washington had feared that his reputation would take a hit, and that fear had been realized. He needed to take control, once and for all, of the story of his life.[21]

✭ PART IV ✭

"I Die Hard"

HOECAKES

Washington's Favorite Breakfast

"[Washington] ate three small mush cakes (Indian meal) swimming in butter and honey."

—NELLY PARKE CUSTIS,
WASHINGTON'S STEP-GRANDDAUGHTER

"The meal was without change to him whose habits were regular, even to matters which others are so apt to indulge themselves in endless variety. Indian cakes, honey, and tea, formed this temperate repast."

—GEORGE WASHINGTON PARKE CUSTIS,
WASHINGTON'S STEP-GRANDSON*

IN THE 1790s, WASHINGTON'S FAVORITE BREAKFAST WAS PREPARED by two enslaved house servants: Nathan, who slept in a bunk in the crowded greenhouse quarters, and Lucy, who lived in a nearby cabin with her husband, Frank Lee, a butler. Their days were long. They were expected to be in the plantation's mansion house kitchen by 4:30 a.m. to prepare Washington's breakfast. By 5 a.m., Lucy was stirring the hoecake batter she had prepared the night before, and by 6:30 a.m., she and

---

* Nelly Parke Custis and George Washington Custis quoted in Stephen A. McLeod ed., *Dining with the Washingtons: Historic Recipes, Entertaining, and Hospitality from Mount Vernon* (Chapel Hill, NC: UNC Press Books, 2011), 38. I adapted the recipe, with small changes, from the same book.

Frank were frying the hoecakes and preparing coffee, tea, and hot chocolate. They may have added cold cuts or leftovers from the night before to the breakfast spread. At 6:45 a.m., the plantation bell rung, alerting the Washingtons that their breakfast would soon be served, and by 7 a.m., Frank would bring the food to the table for it to be served by Marcus, another house slave. This, along with the sandwich Lucy prepared Washington for his daily eight- to fourteen-mile ride around Mount Vernon, would satisfy him until dinner.

Ingredients

½ teaspoon active dry yeast
2½ cups white cornmeal
3 to 4 cups water, room temperature
1 large egg, room temperature
Vegetable oil or lard
Salt

Directions

The night before: In a large bowl, mix the yeast with 1¼ cups of cornmeal. Stir in 1 cup of water for the consistency of pancake batter. If needed, add an additional cup of water. Cover the bowl and refrigerate overnight.

The next day: Preheat the oven to 200°F. Remove the batter from the refrigerator.

Lightly beat the egg in a small bowl. Add a pinch of salt. Stir it into the batter along with ½ cup of water.

Incrementally stir in the remaining cornmeal and water. Cover and let the batter rest for 20 minutes.

While the batter rests, heat a cast iron pan (or griddle) on medium heat for 5 minutes. When you're ready to start cooking, lightly grease the pan with oil or lard.

Ladle or pour ¼ cup of the batter onto the pan and cook until slightly brown (about 5 minutes) before flipping. If there's room, add additional hoecakes to the pan, and when each is completed, put them in the oven to keep warm. Makes about 15 hoecakes.

Serve with plenty of melted butter and honey. Washington washed them down with three cups of tea.

CHAPTER 19

Final Retirement

ABOUT FIVE MONTHS AFTER WASHINGTON RETIRED TO MOUNT Vernon for the third time, he and Martha received a wedding invitation from a nephew. Washington RSVP'd to Lawrence Augustine Washington with a bit of light fatalism: "Wedding assemblies are better calculated for those who are *coming in* to than to those who are *going out* of life, you must accept the good wishes of your Aunt and myself in place of personal attendance, for I think it not likely that either of us will ever be more than 25 miles from Mount Vernon again."[1]

Washington wanted to die there, and figured it would happen soon. He said so to practically everyone he corresponded with, including a gardener he aimed to tempt from Scotland: "I am once more seated under my own Vine and fig tree, and hope to spend the remainder of my days—which in the ordinary course of things (being in my Sixty sixth year) cannot be many—in peaceful retirement, making political pursuits yield to the more rational amusement of cultivating the Earth."[2] As he reminded his nephew Burgess Ball, "I was the *first,* and am now the *last,* of my fathers Children by the second marriage who remain. When

WASHINGTON'S RETIREMENT SCHEDULE

"I begin my diurnal course with the sun," Washington wrote to Secretary of War James McHenry on May 29, 1797. "If my hirelings are not in their places at that time I send them messages expressive of my sorrow for their indisposition." Washington, an exacting, demanding boss, found Mount Vernon had once again fallen into disrepair in his absence.[3]

MORNING	AFTERNOON	EVENING
Rides out at daybreak	Writes letters in the library	Tea or coffee
Visits all the farms	Dresses and dines	Reads or visits with
Returns for breakfast	between 2 and 3 p.m.	family and friends
	Social hour(s)	Retires at 9 p.m.,
	Writes more letters	no supper
	Tends to private affairs	

I shall be called upon to follow them, is known only to the giver of life. When the summons comes I shall endeavour to obey it with a good grace."[4] He had Martha write to Elizabeth Powel that "he has entered into an engagement with Mr Morris and several other Gentlemen not to quit the theatre of *this* world before the year 1800."[5] On a ride with another nephew, he pointed to the planned site of a new family mausoleum and said, "This change I shall make the first of all, for I may require it before the rest."[6]

Washington "Wash" Parke Custis, his step-grandson, was helping him get there. "Having heard nothing from you, or of you, since you left the Federal City, but hoping you got safe to Princeton, the sole intention of this letter is to cover the enclosed," he wrote to Wash, forwarding a letter from his sister, Eleanor "Nelly" Parke Custis, in May 1797.[7] Washington's note was four sentences long and somewhat unnecessary, considering that Wash and Nelly corresponded directly, so it seems written to convey his annoyance. Wash had indeed arrived in New Jersey, but by September he had been suspended "for various acts of meanness and irregularity."[8] Washington kept that part from Martha, who only knew he was switching colleges.

Wash wrote more often from the College of St. John, his new school in Annapolis, but it was never good news: He wanted to marry a merchant's daughter; he needed more money; he'd lost a friend's umbrella; most of all, he wanted to know if he could just quit school already. Seething over the question, Washington wrote in the summer of 1798 that it "really astonishes me! for it would seem as if *nothing* I could say to you made more than a *momentary* impression."[9] By August, he gave in to the reality that if Wash was going to complete his education, he would only do so by private tutor at home, where Martha could dote on him and Washington could watch him closely. ("Grandmamma always spoiled him," Nelly would later say of her brother.[10]) Tobias Lear, who lived in a house on the property with Fanny, stepped in.

James Monroe, whom Washington had recalled from France in 1796, helped raise his blood pressure even further the following year, when he published *A View of the Conduct of the Executive, in the Foreign Affairs of the United States,* a 473-page critique of Washington's administration and a defense of his own conduct. Washington, who rarely responded to criticism in writing, let loose in the margins of his copy, starting with the very first sentence. Monroe wrote: "In the Month of May, 1794, I was invited by the President of the United States, through the Secretary of State, to accept the office of the minister of plenipotentiary to the French Republic." To which Washington scrawled a tart rebuttal: "After several attempts had failed to obtain a more eligible character."[11]

Even without Monroe in Paris, the revolutionary committee that governed France continued to make its displeasure about the Jay Treaty

WASHINGTON UNBOUND

Washington could keep control of his anger in most situations, but he often left the impression that he was seething beneath it all. "His temper was naturally high toned," Jefferson recalled in January 1814. When "it broke its bonds, he was most tremendous in his wrath."[12] These marginalia offer some of the only firsthand evidence we have.

MONROE'S TEXT	WASHINGTON'S ANNOTATION
But it was my duty to answer this letter, which I did without a comment; for it was improper for me to censure and useless to advise.	When a rational answer and good reasons cannot be given, it is not unusual to be silent.
I shewed, it is true, no mark of undue condescension to that government.	Few will be of this opinion, who reads this Book.
Had France been conquered, to what objects that administration would have aspired, has fortunately, by her victories, been left a subject for conjecture only.	An insinuation as impudent, as unfounded.
I resolved, therefore, to stand firm at my post. . . .	Curious and laughable to hear a man under his circumstances talking seriously in this stile, when his recal was a second death to him.
The appearance of the treaty excited the general disgust of France against the American government, which was now diminished by the opposition which the American people made to the treaty.	Who were the contrivers of this disgust and for what purpose was it excited? Let the French Party in the U.S. and the British debtors therein answer the question.
But by this attack on me, a new topic has been raised for discussion, which has drawn the public attention from the conduct of the administration itself.	Self importance appears here.

. . . yet none of those acts or of the disposition which produced them were even glanced at in the president's address to congress, although it was to be inferred, such notice would have produced a good effect, and although it was then as just as it was politic to notice them.	What! declare to the world in a public speech that we were going to Treat with *this* and *that* Nation, and that France was to assist us! Insanity in the extreme!
Fourth, my appointment to the French republic with the circumstances attending it.	And an unfortunate one it was.[13]

known. The five members of the so-called Directory rejected John Adams's new ambassador to France and ordered that American trading ships be seized.

Adams, the first (and only) president who openly identified with the Federalists, wanted to muster an army in case hostilities broke out, and turned to sixty-six-year-old Washington, who had left the Continental Army fifteen years earlier, to lead it.[14] "We must have your Name, if you, in any case will permit Us to Use it," Adams pleaded in June 1798. "There will be more efficacy in it, than in many an Army."[15] Washington agreed, as long as he could remain at Mount Vernon until "the army is in a situation to require my presence, or it becomes indispensible by the urgency of circumstances."[16] He had no idea that Adams would promptly announce his appointment, followed by Alexander Hamilton and Charles C. Pinckney, as major general to assist in the organization of the Provisional Army, and that he would soon be bombarded with letters from men who wanted to serve under him.

By the end of the year, Washington did indeed travel farther than twenty-five miles. He rode to Philadelphia and spent five weeks advising Hamilton. Ultimately, though, Adams opted for a diplomatic solution.

The conflict became known as the Quasi-War, or the Half War, or the Undeclared War.

A year later, Jonathan Trumbull, Jr., the governor of Connecticut, urged Washington to resume another role: The presidential election of 1800 was near, and Adams was unpopular. Would he run on the Federalist ticket? Washington firmly declined. "It would be criminal therefore in me, although it should be the wish of my Countrymen," he wrote in protest in July 1799, sure "another would discharge with more ability." And besides, he'd become known as a Federalist partisan. "I should not draw a *single* vote from the Anti-federal side," he told Trumbull.[17]

Before leaving Philadelphia, he visited his old friend Robert Morris in debtors' prison; the financier who had once rented the Washingtons his own home was now without one. Washington was far from that fate, but he was also far from comfortable. "I shall not suffer false modesty to assert that my financies stand in no need of it," he wrote to Secretary of War James McHenry, declining a salary, out of pride, for the months he served as commander in chief. He should have taken it. Washington's crops had suffered from drought, and he was still owed monies from loans and rents. To stabilize his finances, he rented out his whiskey distillery and gristmill, and began making elaborate plans for his farms. He hoped to have it all sorted out by 1800, a year he would not live to see.

CHAPTER 20

"'Tis Well"

Washington's to-do list, by his estimate, was going to take three years to complete. He awoke on the morning of Thursday, December 12, 1799, to rain, hail, and snow, but wouldn't let the weather delay his agenda; he rode out to his farms and back, a journey of five hours. When Washington returned, he didn't change out of his wet clothes or warm himself by the fire; he had already kept Martha waiting long enough for dinner. Friday brought another snowy, windy day. By that point, according to Tobias Lear's diary, Washington had "taken cold (undoubtedly from being so much exposed the day before) and complained of a sore throat." But he remained set on accomplishing his next task—marking trees to be felled—and went out anyway.[1]

That evening, his voice was increasingly hoarse, but he wanted to stay up. Martha excused herself to check on Nelly upstairs; her granddaughter had given birth to a daughter, Francis Parke Lewis, in November.[2] Washington was in good spirits until Lear, who had been reading the papers in the parlor, shared the latest on the Virginia Assembly. Monroe had been elected governor, with Madison's backing, which left Washington "much affected." He "spoke with some asperity on the subject," Lear reported—probably a polite way to describe cursing.

Take some medicine, Lear suggested on the way out.

"You know I never take anything for a Cold," Washington replied. "Let it go as it came."

At 2 a.m., "he awoke Mrs. Washington." He could hardly speak. He had difficulty breathing. She wanted to send for help, but he protested. Martha had been sick, and he feared the early-morning air would cause her to relapse. Four excruciating hours later, Caroline, a household slave, came to light the fire in their room. Martha sent her to get Lear, and Lear sent a servant to get Dr. James Craik, who had attended to Washington since the French and Indian War; he had just been at the house to deliver Nelly's baby.

Washington asked for George Rawlins, an overseer who did a little bloodletting on the side. In the meantime, "a mixture of Molasses, Vinegar & butter was prepared to try its effects in the throat; but he could not swallow a drop; whenever he attempted it he appeared to be distressed, convulsed and almost suffocated." Christopher Sheels, who had replaced Billy Lee as Washington's enslaved manservant, propped Washington up by the fire. Caroline remained; she was soon joined by two other house slaves, Charlotte and Molly. Rawlins appeared after sunrise and nervously prepared to bleed him by cutting his arm.

"Don't be afraid," Lear heard Washington tell Rawlins, only to add that the cut was "not large enough." Others disagreed; Lear thought "the blood ran pretty freely" and Martha "begged that much might not be taken from him, lest it should be injurious." Lear was inclined to listen to her, and was about to untie the string that restricted the veins to promote blood flow, but "the General put up his hand to prevent it, and as soon as he could speak, said '*more, more!*'" By the time Craik arrived at 9 a.m., Washington had bled a pint of blood.

"'Tis very sore," he managed. He was still coughing, his breath short and shallow.

Craik had his own well-intentioned bad ideas. He produced a blister on his patient's throat with Spanish flies and gave him an enema and a vinegar and sage tea, which didn't go well. "[I]n attempting to use the gargle he was almost suffocated." At Craik's insistence, Washington tried to cough up phlegm, but couldn't. Around 3 p.m., two more doctors—Gustavus Richard Brown and Elisha Cullen Dick—arrived, and they spent the rest of the day coming in and out of the room, discussing options in the hallway. They administered an emetic to induce vomiting and evacuate his bowels, which left him dehydrated. Dick suggested a tracheotomy but, much to his regret, was overruled. Washington demanded to be bled again and again.

"The blood came very slow, was thick, and did not produce any symptoms of fainting," Lear observed in his diary. "He could only speak at intervals and with great difficulty," he wrote to Hamilton.[3]

"We were governed by the best light we had," Brown would later write to Craik. "We thought we were right; and so we were justified."[4] And by the medical standards of the day, and the information available to them, they were. But everything Craik, Brown, and Dick did made Washington's condition worse.

Around 4:30 p.m., Washington asked Lear to get Martha, who preferred to wait in another room.

He sent her to his study to get the wills. (He had two: The earlier one, possibly dated around June 1775, had been drawn by a lawyer friend; the other was more recent.[5]) As he neared death, Washington was still focused on what people around him were feeling, and what those left behind would remember about him.

☆ ☆ ☆

In the summer of 1799, Washington had written a new will. He had been an executor, administrator, and trustee for enough people to know that his last wishes needed to be clear. He filled twenty-nine water-marked pages with his neat, looping handwriting, endeavoring "to be plain, and explicit in all Devices."

The document, which includes a painstaking inventory of his worldly possessions, reveals him to be one of the richest men in America. He wasn't lying when he had claimed to be cash poor—though there always seemed to be money for finery, or to hire slave hunters to catch Hercules and Ona Judge—but he wasn't exactly telling the truth, either.

Washington was land rich, incredibly so, far past his own plantation. Washington owned 51,000 acres of land, mostly in what was then Virginia, but also Maryland, Pennsylvania, Kentucky, and what became Ohio, along with small tracts in various cities; that included properties in the City of Washington (now Washington, D.C., which is currently, for context, a total of 43,740 acres). Over the years, Washington had tried to sell some of it off, but he rarely succeeded; either there were no takers, or there were, but they didn't meet his criteria. Had he accepted the offers he received, he might have had enough money to do what he'd been talking about for two decades: emancipate the people he'd enslaved.

Instead, Washington failed to free a single slave during his lifetime. He was always waiting for something—a land deal, a law to compel him—but in the end, he always came back to the same problem: The fate of his slaves' families. Many of the people Washington enslaved had married the Custis slaves, who belonged to Martha's heirs, and it seems her family had no intention of freeing them.

But Washington wouldn't have to deal with any of those complications after he died. In his will he stipulated that his hundred and twenty-three slaves should be freed—after Martha had her use of them, and the income they would generate.

> Upon the decease of my wife, it is my Will & desire that all the Slaves which I hold in my *own right,* shall receive their freedom. To emancipate them during her life, would, tho' earnestly wished by me, be attended with such insuperable difficulties on account of their intermixture by Marriages with the dower Negroes, as to excite the most painful sensations, if not disagreeable consequences from the latter, while both descriptions are in the occupancy of the same Proprietor; it not being in my power, under the tenure by which the Dower Negroes are held, to manumit them.[6]

There were other provisions. His slaves should be "comfortably" clothed and fed; younger slaves, bound as servants until the age of twenty-five, should be taught to read and write and a trade; older or sick slaves should be provided with care after they were emancipated—whenever that happened. Martha might live for another ten years.

It is notable that Washington did not make all of his slaves wait until Martha's death. He singled out Billy Lee for special treatment:

> And to my Mulatto man William (calling himself William Lee) I give immediate freedom; or if he should prefer it (on account of the accidents which have befallen him, and which have rendered him incapable of walking or of any active employment) to remain in the situation he now is, it shall be optional in him to do so: In either case however, I allow him an annuity of thirty

dollars during his natural life, which shall be independent of the victuals and cloaths he has been accustomed to receive, if he chuses the last alternative; but in full, with his freedom, if he prefers the first; & this I give him as a testimony of my sense of his attachment to me, and for his faithful services during the Revolutionary War.

Washington had always seen Lee as exceptional. He did not free him sooner, though, because he truly believed, as he often said, that Lee was better off in his "care."

Martha brought her husband the two wills, and he made a decision. He chose the one drawn most recently that freed his slaves upon her death; that one, she put in her closet. The other one "he observed useless" and "desired her to burn it; which she did."

"I find I am going, my breath can not last long," he said to Lear, their hands intertwined. "I beleived from the first that the disorder would prove fatal." He asked that his longtime secretary see to his military letters and papers, his accounts and books, "as you know more about them than any one else." Washington's will gave Bushrod Washington, a favorite nephew and Supreme Court justice, control over his personal papers; after Martha died, he would inherit the mansion house, the surrounding farm, and much of the remaining estate.[7]

"Doctor, I die hard," Washington said when Craik appeared at his bedside around 5 p.m. "But I am not afraid to go." He thanked the rest of the doctors for their "attentions," but he would have no more. "Let me go quietly," he said, as all but Craik retired. "I cannot last long." They tried to make him comfortable, applying wheat bran to his legs and feet, then attempted another round of blistering. Eventually, though, all but

A MORE CONSERVATIVE NARRATIVE

Most modern accounts of Washington's will are fairly forgiving, even sometimes congratulatory. Mount Vernon, now a museum and presidential library, summarizes it thus: "At the end of his life Washington made the bold step to free all his slaves in his 1799 will—the only slave-holding Founding Father to do so."[8] The often repeated statement lacks crucial details and context: the slaves' manumission was not immediate and other slave-owning founders, including Benjamin Franklin, didn't emancipate their slaves in their wills because they had already done so while they were alive. After Franklin returned from France in 1785, he freed his slaves. In 1790, he petitioned Congress to abolish slavery—while Washington was president, three years before he signed the Fugitive Slave Law.

"If his countrymen in Washington's state of Virginia had followed his example in freeing their slaves as quickly as practicable," writes Ashley Bateman, a teacher, "who knows the impact it could have had on the South."[9] Bateman ignores that Virginians already had in-state models to follow. Prominent Virginian Robert Carter III (whom Washington may have known through his eldest half brother Lawrence) manumitted over four hundred and fifty slaves in his lifetime. Like Washington, Carter had hoped gradual emancipation would pass the Virginia legislature in his lifetime, but unlike Washington, when it seemed clear it would not, he began to do so himself in 1791.

Craik left "without a ray of hope." Over the next few hours, Washington rarely complained, though he often asked for the time. The bloodletting had continued, and by that point he had been drained of a few more pints of blood.

By 10 p.m., Washington finally showed fear. "Do not let my body be put into the Vault in less than three days after I am dead," he ordered

Lear, perhaps doubting that he, after surviving so much, would actually die. Lear reported that he "bowed assent, for I could not speak."

"Do you understand me?" Washington asked.

"Yes," Lear managed.

"'Tis well," Washington said, and his hands went limp. Craik closed his eyes. Martha, standing at the foot of the bed, asked if he was gone. Then, according to Lear, she repeated, "'Tis well."

Epilogue

A T 3 P.M. ON DECEMBER 18, 1799, FOUR DAYS AFTER WASHINGTON'S death, a schooner on the Potomac fired off a twenty-one-gun salute. On land, Virginia Cavalry led a funeral procession to the beating of drums; up at the front, two of the general's slaves, Cyrus and Wilson, led his riderless horse.

Washington received a military burial at home. Pallbearers, mostly Freemasons, carried his mahogany coffin from the mansion house, where it had been lying on the dining room table, down a footpath to the old burial vault. He died before a new one could be built. Family, friends, clergy, slaves, and staff stood quietly among the juniper and cypress trees as his coffin, draped in black velvet, was placed inside the communal tomb. (Patsy, his stepdaughter, and George Augustine, a nephew, were already there.) Eleven cannons fired, and Virginia infantry shot their muskets. It was a little more than he had wished in his will—"that my Corpse may be Interred in a private manner, without parade, or funeral Oration"—but less than most wanted. Across the country, elected officials, citizens, and military officers wore black.

His widow was noticeably absent from the funeral. Perhaps Martha was too overcome by the loss, or maybe she was just done being on display; those around her observed that she remained dry-eyed. "The world now appears to be no longer desireable to her and yet she yields not to the grief which would be softened by tears," Lear wrote to his mother.[1]

Martha seemed to believe that her career in public service, which she had never signed up for, was over. She did not travel to Philadelphia to attend the official congressional eulogy where General Henry Lee declared Washington "first in war, first in peace, and first in the hearts of his countrymen."[2] But she could not escape it all. When naval ships passed by Mount Vernon on the Potomac, they acknowledged, with a thirteen-gun salute, the man who had signed the department into law. Congress waived postage on letters and packages to her; she left most responses to Lear. When the seat of government moved to the City of Washington, she resigned herself to an ever-increasing number of visitors. Now that her husband was dead, paying their respects to his widow was the closest they could come to his approval.

Thomas Jefferson visited on June 1, 1800. "He must have known," Martha supposedly told Connecticut governor John Cotton Smith, a Federalist, "that we then had the evidence of his perfidy in the house."[3] She found his trip to Mount Vernon uniquely unpleasant; the leader of the Democratic-Republicans' treachery against Washington's administration was still fresh in her mind, from which she was not exempt. When he condemned their levees, dinners, and ceremonies as monarchical in newspapers, hiding behind pseudonyms, he was criticizing her; playing hostess was her chief role as the president's wife. Perhaps it was a coincidence that he visited six months after Washington's death, when he was running for president and would have benefitted from her support. Either way, she didn't give it, and he won anyway. When she found out, a guest recalled that "she spoke of the election of Mr. Jefferson as one of the most detestable of mankind, as the greatest misfortune our country has ever experienced."[4]

Martha finally shed tears, apparently, when she was reminded that her husband was not, even in death, fully hers; she had planned on her body being reunited with his in the vault upon her death, but Congress proposed a different plan. They wanted to erect a marble monument in the City of Washington and relocate his body there. She resigned herself to the news, having learned "never to oppose my private wishes to the public will," but wanted it to be known that "in doing this, I need not, I cannot, say what a sacrifice of individual feeling I make to a sense of public duty."[5] In the meantime, she frequently went to visit his grave, and kept private what she could, burning the letters she and Washington exchanged, missing just a few, stuck in the back of a drawer. (The plan to bury Washington under the Washington Monument did not materialize.)

She never returned to the bedroom in which her late husband had died, the one they shared for four decades, or to his study. She slept on the third floor, near Nelly, and down the hall from Wash. Did she ever notice that her grandson took a particular interest in several of the female slaves? The victims of these nonconsensual encounters were forced to bear his children. An article from 1865 suggests that Mary Anna Randolph Custis Lee, Wash's only legitimate daughter, knew that she had forty half siblings.[6] It would have been nothing new to Martha; her first husband had an emancipated half brother, Jack, whom their father acknowledged and provided for in his will.

Martha, it seems, was overcome by two emotions: She mourned the loss of her husband, and she was deathly afraid of his slaves.

Washington's will had been circulated in pamphlet form. Some of his slaves had decided to immediately emancipate themselves and fled Mount Vernon, while the rest watched her closely, knowing that her death meant their freedom. "She did not feel as tho her Life was safe in their Hands," Abigail Adams explained to her sister, Mary Adams.[7] At one point, Bushrod and Chief Justice John Marshall were called away from the Supreme Court because one or more of the slaves intended to burn down the mansion house.[8]

There is ample evidence to suggest that Martha was disinclined to free Washington's slaves before she had to, and may never have agreed to, or known about the plan to begin with. When she mentioned slaves in her letters, it was not uncommon for her to write things like "Blacks are so bad in thair nature that they have not the least Gratatude for the kindness that may be shewed to them."[9] In her own will, the slaves she controlled, whom she could have freed, she left to her family. It was not, then, morality that drove Martha to, on December 15, 1800, sign a deed of manumission, freeing all of her late husband's slaves. It was self-preservation.

In January 1801, one hundred and twenty-three people were free from bondage, but not, for many of them, heartbreak. When Martha died a little over a year later, on May 22, 1802, at the age of seventy, the hundred and fifty dower slaves who remained at Mount Vernon were divided among her four grandchildren. About twenty families were separated; many would never see each other again.

A FAMILY DIVIDED

Isaac and Kitty's family serves as one heartbreaking example of what the Washingtons' plan meant for their slaves. Isaac had been enslaved by Washington, and was the only free member of his family. Kitty, his wife, was a dower slave, and so were their nine daughters and seven grandchildren, who were divided among the Custis heirs. They went from living on one plantation to five different locations, far apart. There's no evidence they were ever reunited.[10]

CUSTIS HEIR	MEMBER OF KITTY'S FAMILY THEY CHOSE	SEPARATED FROM	MOVED TO
Eliza	Kitty (£50) and her two youngest daughters, Barbara (£40), aged thirteen, and Levina, aged nine (£5, flagged as an "invalid")	Kitty from Isaac and her other children and grandchildren; Barbara and Levina from Isaac, their sisters, nieces, and nephews	Washington, D.C.
Martha	Godfrey (£100); Lucy (£65), twenty-four, and her children Burwell (£25) and Hannah (£15); Letty (£70), twenty-four, and her daughter Tracy (£12), Nancy (£60), eighteen	Godfrey from his wife, Mima, and their children; Lucy from her parents, Isaac and Kitty, and her husband; Letty and Nancy from her parents, Isaac and Kitty, most of her sisters, and her nieces and nephews	Georgetown
Nelly	Sinah (£80), thirty, and her daughter, Nancy (£30), five, Mima (£65), twenty-eight, and her three young sons, John (£35), Randolph (£20), and Isaac (£6)	Sinah's husband, Ben, who had been owned by Washington Mima's husband, Godfrey	Woodlawn, on Mount Vernon land given to them by Washington
Wash	Grace (£60), twenty-two	From her husband, Juba, who was enslaved at Tobias Lear's farm; her parents Isaac and Kitty; her sisters, nieces, and nephews	Arlington, Virginia

☆ ☆ ☆

In 1831, Bushrod's nephew and heir, John Augustine Washington II, oversaw the completion of a new burial vault. The bodies of Washington, Martha, Bushrod, Fanny, and a few other family members were transferred to the exact verdant spot Washington had wanted, with small but significant deviations from what he'd envisioned. In 1837, his mahogany casket was enclosed in a marble sarcophagus bearing the Great Seal of the United States. During the Civil War, Confederate and Union soldiers carved their initials into the walls of the vault, a fitting addition to the resting place of the man whose fondest hope was for the nation to be unified. Both sides, the South and the North, the slave-owning and the free, viewed him as their inspiration. And both were right.

Since 2014, the woods near the vault have been undergoing excavation. The area is never mentioned in the thousands of documents Washington left behind. It is a cemetery for the people he enslaved, full of unmarked graves.

Acknowledgments

I am indebted to the documentary editors, archivists, and librarians at the University of Virginia and the Library of Congress. These are the people who transcribed and annotated George Washington's letters and uploaded them to the National Archives' Founders Online, a heavenly, free, easy-to-use website that allowed me to do the bulk of my research from my home. I cannot thank them enough.

A very special thank you to William M. Ferraro, the managing editor of the *Papers of George Washington* at UVA. I randomly emailed Bill a question a few years ago, and he's been stuck with me ever since. He graciously signed on to fact-check this book, and in the process he went far beyond the call of duty. He edited every chapter (several times) and talked me out of the fetal position (many times)—particularly in the final months. Thanks to Laura Ferraro for her support as well.

Over at Mount Vernon, Mary V. Thompson, the greatest living Washington scholar, was an absolute delight to correspond with, and a wonderful resource as well. I thank her and her colleagues for letting me wander the grounds during the week I spent there, and for all that they do; the symposiums, exhibitions, and catalogs they produce were vital resources. Thank you also to the Library of Congress, the Fraunces Tavern Museum, the New York Academy of Medicine Library, and the New York Historical Society. As always, I went straight to Sara Georgini at the Massachusetts Historical Society and John Overholt at the Houghton Library at Harvard. Thank you as well to Martha Saxton for the calls and emails about the much-maligned Mary Washington. Emily Schmitz took charge of the endnotes with unreasonably good cheer, for which I am eternally grateful.

It's an honor to be published by Viking. Thank you to my editor, Laura Tisdel, who picked up the project with much enthusiasm, and to Andrea Schulz, whose excitement never waned. I'm grateful to the entire team, including the many people who worked tirelessly behind the scenes: Christina Caruccio, Brianna Harden, Daniel Lagin, Brianna Linden, Lindsay Prevette, Amy Sun, Brian Tart, Melanie Tortoroli, and Eric Wechter. I had high hopes for an original George Washington portrait, and Alexis Franklin most certainly delivered!

Over the past eight years, Jay Mandel at WME has talked me out of my worst ideas and supported the hell out of my better ones. I'm grateful for the many reassuring calls and quick reads and sound advice. Thanks also to his former assistant Lauren Shonkoff and his current assistant, Sian-Ashleigh Edwards, for all their efforts, and to Bradley Singer, my WME television agent, for always looking out for me. While writing this book, Matthew Ginsburg and Tim Healy and the History Channel gave me the opportunity to consider Washington in a different medium. A special thanks to Doris Kearns Goodwin; it has been a great privilege to work with you.

Thank you to the friends who encouraged me along the way. You're too numerous to name here, but those who made the mistake of offering to read parts of the draft deserve a mention: Elizabeth Castoria, Daniel Jacobson, Laura Olin, Daniel Mallory Ortberg-Lavery, Aminatou Sow, and Avi Steinberg.

Fari, thank you for taking such good care of Poppy while I worked, and thanks to Emma, Jon, and Louisa for welcoming her into your home.

Thank you, most of all, to my husband, Anthony Lydgate, who kept me well fed and loved, and for his edits throughout this insane process. I do hope that, one day soon(ish), you achieve the George Washington-less life of your dreams. Poppy, I've never been so disrespected on a personal or professional level by anyone in my entire life! Thanks for making me slow down and be. You're the ideal tiny primate, and I love you and your dad more than anything.

Notes

I preserved the original spellings and syntax of the early American manuscripts I've quoted, all of which predate standardized dictionaries. The spelling was phonetic, the capitalization wild, monetary value inconsistent, and style and grammar varied greatly from person to person.* The letters and documents were meant to be read aloud back then, and I hope you will consume them that way, too. Consider, for instance, this brutally honest assessment from Jonathan Boucher, his stepson's tutor in Annapolis, and imagine Washington and Martha reading it in bed on December 18, 1770:

> I mean, his Love of Ease, & Love of Pleasure—Pleasure of a Kind exceedingly uncommon at his Years. I must confess to You I never did in my Life know a Youth so exceedingly indolent, or so surprizingly voluptuous.

* Money, which could mean coins, minted from copper, silver, and gold, is described in eighteenth-century units. There was also "money of account," which is what ledger sheets hold, and the back-and-forth between the tangible money and money described only on paper, in an account, introduces inconsistencies. Colonial currencies were especially fluid; when the Washingtons married in 1759, the Virginia pound fluctuated between 1.35 and 2.45 British Sterling.

LIST OF ABBREVIATIONS FOR ARCHIVES

DGW: Donald Jackson and Dorothy Twohig, eds. *The Diaries of George Washington*. 6 vols. Charlottesville: University Press of Virginia, 1976–1979.

JCC: Library of Congress. *Journals of the Continental Congress, 1774–1789*. 34 vols. Washington, D.C.: U.S. Government Printing Office, 1904–1937.

PAH: Harold C. Syrett and Jacob Cooke, eds. *Papers of Alexander Hamilton*. 27 vols. New York: Columbia University Press, 1961–1987.

PCC: *Papers of the Continental Congress, 1774–1789*. 204 rolls. Washington, D.C.: National Archives, National Archives and Records Service, General Services Administration, 1957–1959.

PGW, **Confederation:** W. W. Abbot et al., eds. *The Papers of George Washington: Confederation Series*. 6 vols. Charlottesville: University Press of Virginia, 1992–1997.

PGW, **CS:** W. W. Abbot et al., eds. *The Papers of George Washington: Colonial Series*. 10 vols. Charlottesville: University Press of Virginia, 1983.

PGW, **PS:** W. W. Abbot et al., eds. *The Papers of George Washington: Presidential Series*. 16 vols. Charlottesville: University Press of Virginia, 1987–.

PGW, **RWS:** W. W. Abbot et al., eds. *The Papers of George Washington: Revolutionary War Series*. 25 vols. Charlottesville: University Press of Virginia, 1985–.

PTJ: Julian P. Boyd, et al., eds. *The Papers of Thomas Jefferson*. 39 vols. Princeton, NJ: Princeton University Press, 1950–.

WGW: John Clement Fitzpatrick et al., eds. *The Writings of George Washington from the Original Manuscript Sources, 1745–1799*. 39 vols. Washington, D.C.: Government Printing Office, 1931–1944.

ALL THE PRESIDENT'S ANIMALS

1. "To George Washington from Frederick Kitt, 15 January 1798," *Founders Online*, National Archives, accessed April 11, 2019, https://founders.archives .gov/documents/Washington/06-02-02-0026.
2. "From George Washington to John Sinclair, 20 July 1794," *Founders Online*, National Archives, accessed April 11, 2019, https://founders.archives.gov /documents/Washington/05-16-02-0311.

PREFACE

1. I have plenty of books by women historians on Washington's wife, his marriage, his role as a slave owner, his title, or other focused approaches. In addition to Erica Dunbar's *Never Caught*, please see Patricia Brady's *Martha Washington*, Flora Fraser's *The Washingtons*, and Mary V. Thompson's *"The Only Unavoidable Subject of Regret."*

2. Women, such as Jeanne Heidler, coauthored books with their husbands, although in Heidler's case it is an excellent book on Washington's circle during his presidency, not a biography. Women have most often written about Washington's wife and marriage.

3. Annette Gordon-Reed's first book on Jefferson was published in 1997, but Pearl Graham began challenging Jefferson scholarship as early as the 1940s; significant scholarly contributions were also made by Fawn Brodie, Jan Lewis, Lucia Cinder Stanton, and Virginia Scharff.

4. I am referring to the journalist Noemie Emery, author of *Washington: A Biography*, and the travel writer Blair Niles, author of *Martha's Husband: An Informal Portrait of George Washington*. When I say "women historians," I think of women who identify as historians as well as women who are credentialed. There, the numbers get far worse. It may well be that we haven't seen one in a hundred years.

5. *The George Washington Financial Papers Project,* "Ledger B, 1772–1793," May 8, 1784, 179, http://financial.gwpapers.org/?q=content/ledger-b-1772-1793 -pg179.

6. I spoke about Weems as an itinerant minister on an Audible podcast I cohosted called "Presidents Are People Too!"

INTRODUCTION: THE THIGH MEN OF DAD HISTORY

1. Unger insists that Washington was also "human to the core: laughing, loving, and living life to the fullest." (Did he also dance like no one was watching?) Harlow G. Unger, *The Unexpected George Washington: His Private Life* (New York: Wiley, 2006), 1.

2. Of course, that very character trait is what stopped him from being as reckless as Hamilton or as power-hungry as Napoleon.

3. Richard Brookhiser, *Founding Father: Rediscovering George Washington* (New

York: Simon & Schuster, 1997), 4. Politicians have tried, too. Senator Henry Cabot Lodge, Supreme Court Chief Justice John Marshall, and President Woodrow Wilson all produced heavy books about America's first.

4. Joseph J. Ellis, *His Excellency: George Washington* (New York: Alfred A. Knopf, 2004), xiv.

5. John Ferling, who has authored several books on Washington, writes that he had "the striking look of what we would expect today in a gifted athlete." John Ferling, *The Ascent of George Washington: The Hidden Political Genius of an American Icon* (New York: Bloomsbury Publishing USA, 2010), 14.

6. Presidents' Day used to belong to Washington alone, but now, like much about his legacy, the particulars have been absorbed into a greater unifying symbol of national strength and heroism.

7. Alexis Coe, "What the Least Fun Founding Father Can Teach Us Now," *The New Yorker*, November 22, 2017, www.newyorker.com/books/page-turner /what-the-least-fun-founding-father-can-teach-us-now.

8. John K. Amory, "George Washington's Infertility: Why Was the Father of Our Country Never a Father?" *Fertility and Sterility* 81, no. 3 (March 2004): 495–99.

9. Ron Chernow, *Washington: A Life* (New York: Penguin Random House, 2010), 102.

10. Chernow, 80.

11. Chernow, 825.

12. "From George Washington to Robert Orme, 2 April 1755," *Founders Online*, National Archives, accessed November 9, 2017, https://founders.archives .gov/documents/Washington/02-01-02-0122.

13. Chernow, *Washington*, 53.

14. Chernow's exaggerations have gone unnoticed or unremarked upon. Gordon Wood, the well-known and respected historian of early American history, wrote that Chernow's "understanding of human nature is extraordinary and that is what makes his biography so powerful," and his book was "the best, most comprehensive, and most balanced single-volume biography of Washington ever written."

15. Chernow, *Washington*, 5, 6, 10, 11, 18, 54, 97, 98, 157, 432, 524, 525.

16. Paul Leicester Ford, *The True George Washington* (Philadelphia: J. B. Lippincott & Co., 1896), 17. Some of these historians have also made much of a lack of gravestone upon the spot where Mary is buried, which seems silly. She was

buried at home, not in a cemetery, and by the time Washington returned from Philadelphia, his sister had sold the land. The family no longer controlled the property. He may have intended to move it to the family vault during his retirement, but he died within a couple of years.

17. Carl Bode, "The First First Mother," *The Washington Post,* May 7, 1982, www.washingtonpost.com/archive/lifestyle/1982/05/07/the-first-first -mother/2aceb419-92ac-4df2-8cac-46d8bc3c3270/?utm_term=.864168 281093.

18. James Thomas Flexner, *Washington: The Indispensable Man* (New York: Little, Brown and Company, 1974).

19. Chernow, *Washington,* 11.

20. A. L. Bassett, "Reminiscences of Washington," *Scribner's Monthly* 14, no. 1 (May 1877): 78.

21. "Letter from Abigail Adams to John Adams, May 27, 1794," *Massachusetts Historical Society,* accessed October 14, 2017, www.masshist.org/digitaladams /archive/doc?id=L17940527aa.

22. Laura J. Galke, "The Mother of the Father of Our Country: Mary Ball Washington's Genteel Domestic Habits," *Northeast Historical Archaeology*: 38, no. 2 (2009).

23. "In her dealings with servants, she was strict," writes Douglas Southall Freeman. "They must follow definite round of work." Douglas Southall Freeman, *George Washington, A Biography, Vol. 5: Victory with the Help of France* (New York: Charles Scribner's Sons, 1952), 193.

24. "Court Case, 3 December 1751," *Founders Online,* National Archives, accessed February 2, 2017, https://founders.archives.gov/documents/Washington /02-01-02-0019.

25. "From George Washington to Betty Washington Lewis, 13 September 1789," *Founders Online,* National Archives, accessed April 2, 2017, https://founders .archives.gov/documents/Washington/05-04-02-0017.

CHAPTER 1: HIS MOTHER'S SON

1. The exact number is unknown to scholars.

2. David Hackett Fischer, *Albion's Seed: Four British Folkways in America* (New York: Oxford University Press, 1991), 11–22.

3. Archeologists have yet to excavate the slave quarters at Ferry Farm.

4. Charles Moore, ed., *George Washington's Rules of Civility and Decent Behaviour in Company and Conversation* (Boston: Houghton Mifflin Company, 1926), xi–xv.

5. "From George Washington to Lawrence Washington, 5 May 1749," *Founders Online,* National Archives, accessed April 9, 2017, https://founders.archives .gov/documents/Washington/02-01-02-0003.

6. As Chernow describes it, Lawrence and Colonel Fairfax came up with a plan to "spring fourteen-year-old George from his mother's domination." Ron Chernow, *Washington: A Life* (New York: Penguin Random House, 2011), 17.

7. Roland Pietsch, "Ships' Boys and Youth Culture in Eighteenth-Century Britain," *Northern Mariner* 14, no. 4 (October 2004): 11–24.

8. Edward G. Lengel, *General George Washington: A Military Life* (New York: Random House, 2005), 12.

9. Joseph Ball to Mary Washington, May 19, 1747, quoted in Marion Harland, *The Story of Mary Washington* (New York: Houghton, Mifflin & Co, 1893), 79–81.

10. David Humphreys, *Life of General Washington* (Athens: University of Georgia Press, 2006), 8. Mary and her son understood opportunity cost. The most obvious way to acquire wealth and prestige in early America wasn't through the Navy, nor was it, as Ball had suggested, to become an apprentice to a tinker, a vendor of household utensils. It was through land. And yet, Chernow spins this story as damning of Mary: "One can say with certainty," he writes, "that it was the first of many times she seemed to measure her son's worth not by what he might accomplish elsewhere but by what he could do for her, even if it meant thwarting his career." Chernow, *Washington*, 18.

11. "From George Washington to James Craik, 4 August 1788," *Founders Online,* National Archives, accessed May 30, 2017, https://founders.archives.gov /documents/Washington/04-06-02-0386.

12. Paula S. Felder, *Fielding Lewis and the Washington Family: A Chronicle of 18th Century Fredericksburg* (Fredericksburg, VA: The American History Company, 1998). Also see King George County Order Book, Book 2 (1735–1751). And proximity meant she would remain close to Mary, who would be present at the births of her grandchildren.

CHAPTER 2: "PLEASES MY TASTE"

1. Alicia K. Anderson and Lynn A. Price, eds., *George Washington's Barbados Diary, 1751–52* (Charlottesville: University of Virginia Press, 2018), 46.
2. Anderson and Price, 49.
3. Anderson and Price, 67.
4. George Washington to W. M. Fauntleroy, Sr., May 20, 1752, in *PGW*, CS, 1: 49–50.
5. "From George Washington to Robin, 1749–1750," *Founders Online*, National Archives, accessed January 17, 2017, https://founders.archives.gov/documents/Washington/02-01-02-0007.

CHAPTER 3: "THE WORLD ON FIRE"

1. The editors of Washington's papers at the University of Virginia discovered that, decades later, "he carefully scraped the original ink off the paper with a knife and then wrote his changes" to letter books from this time; overstrikes and insertions indicated conscious alterations. See "The Letter Book for the Braddock Campaign," *Founders Online*, National Archives, accessed May 2, 2017, https://founders.archives.gov/documents/Washington/02-01-02-0119.
2. "Instructions from Robert Dinwiddie, 30 October 1753," *Founders Online*, National Archives, accessed April 2, 2017, https://founders.archives.gov/documents/Washington/02-01-02-0029.
3. "From George Washington to John Stanwix, 10 April 1758," *Founders Online*, National Archives, accessed April 9, 2017, https://founders.archives.gov/documents/Washington/02-05-02-0087.
4. "Expedition to the Ohio, 1754: Narrative," *Founders Online*, National Archives, accessed June 2, 2017, https://founders.archives.gov/documents/Washington/01-01-02-0004-0002.
5. "From George Washington to Robert Dinwiddie, 29 May 1754," *Founders Online*, National Archives, accessed June 4, 2017, https://founders.archives.gov/documents/Washington/02-01-02-0054.
6. "From George Washington to John Augustine Washington, 31 May 1754," *Founders Online*, National Archives, accessed January 20, 2017, https://founders.archives.gov/documents/Washington/02-01-02-0058. [Original source:

PGW, CS, 1: 118–119.] Upon hearing this, King George reportedly said, "He would not say so, if he had been used to hear many." For more on that, see Horace Walpole, *Memoirs of the Reign of King George the Second,* vol. 1 (London: H. Colburn, 1847), 400.

7. "From George Washington to Robert Dinwiddie, 29 May 1754," *Founders Online,* National Archives, accessed March 1, 2017, https://founders.archives .gov/documents/Washington/02-01-02-0054. [Original source: *PGW,* CS, 1: 107–115.] For John Shaw's account, see William L. McDowell, Jr., ed., *Documents Relating to Indian Affairs,* 2 vols. (Columbia: University of South Carolina Press, 1958–1970).

8. "From George Washington to Robert Dinwiddie, 29 May 1754," *Founders Online,* National Archives, accessed April 9, 2017, https://founders.archives .gov/documents/Washington/02-01-02-0054.

9. George Washington to Augustine Washington, August 2, 1755, in *WGW,* 1: 156.

10. "From George Washington to Richard Corbin, February–March 1754," *Founders Online,* National Archives, accessed April 11, 2019, https://founders .archives.gov/documents/Washington/02-01-02-0034.

11. "From George Washington to Horatio Sharpe, 24 April 1754," *Founders Online,* National Archives, accessed August 7, 2017, https://founders.archives.gov /documents/Washington/02-01-02-0044.

12. "From George Washington to Robert Dinwiddie, 18 May 1754," *Founders Online,* National Archives, accessed February 11, 2017, https://founders .archives.gov/documents/Washington/02-01-02-0050.

CHAPTER 4: "BLOW OUT MY BRAINS"

1. *PGW,* CS, 1: 254–257.

2. Ron Chernow, *Washington: A Life* (New York: Penguin Random House, 2010), 55.

3. "From George Washington to Mary Ball Washington, 18 July 1755," *Founders Online,* National Archives, accessed November 15, 2017, https://founders .archives.gov/documents/Washington/02-01-02-0167.

4. On December 6, 1755, George Washington invoiced for "1 piece of Suitable Cambrick for Ruffles" and "2 pairs Men's Silk Stockings" among other goods.

"Invoice of Sundry Goods to be Ship'd for the Use of Geo. Washington at Mount Vernon, Potomac River Virginia," *WGW*, 1: 254.

5. "From George Washington to Robert Dinwiddie, 11–14 October 1755," *Founders Online,* National Archives, accessed December 4, 2017, https://founders.archives.gov/documents/Washington/02-02-02-0099.

CHAPTER 5: THE WIDOW CUSTIS

1. "From George Washington to George Augustine Washington, 25 October 1786," *Founders Online*, National Archives, accessed April 11, 2019, https://founders.archives.gov/documents/Washington/04-04-02-0279. [Original source: *PGW*, Confederation, 4: 307–310.]

2. "To George Washington from George Mercer, 17 August 1757," *Founders Online*, National Archives, accessed April 11, 2019, https://founders.archives .gov/documents/Washington/02-04-02-0242. [Original source: *PGW*, CS, 4: 370–375.]

3. "To George Washington from William La Péronie, 5 September 1754," *Founders Online*, National Archives, accessed April 11, 2019, https://founders.archives.gov/documents/Washington/02-01-02-0099. [Original source: PGW, CS, 1: 203–205.]

4. As Mary V. Thompson has often pointed out, any character-based arguments that can be made against this claim will inevitably sound an awful lot like the ones Thomas Jefferson's biographers made for decades before Fawn Brodie and Annette Gordon-Reed corrected them.

5. "From George Washington to Armand, 10 August 1786," *Founders Online*, National Archives, accessed December 12, 2017, https://founders.archives .gov/documents/Washington/04-04-02-0190.

6. George Washington to Eleanor Parke Custis, January 16, 1795, in *WGW*, 13: 27.

7. Washington to Custis, 28.

8. Washington to Custis, 27–28.

9. Washington to Custis, 28.

10. Washington to Custis, 28

11. *The George Washington Financial Papers Project,* "Ledger A, 1750–1772," May 4, 1758, 39, http://financial.gwpapers.org/?q=content/ledger-1750-1772-pg39.

12. Martha Custis to Robert Cary & Company, 1758, in Joseph E. Fields, ed., *"Worthy Partner": The Papers of Martha Washington* (Westport, CT: Greenwood Press, 1994), 25–26.

CHAPTER 6: "I CANNOT SPEAK PLAINER"

1. "From George Washington to Francis Halkett, 2 August 1758," *Founders Online*, National Archives, accessed May 5, 2017, https://founders.archives.gov/documents/Washington/02-05-02-0284.
2. "From George Washington to Sarah Cary Fairfax, 12 September 1758," *Founders Online*, National Archives, accessed September 21, 2017, https://founders.archives.gov/documents/Washington/02-06-02-0013.
3. "From George Washington to Sarah Cary Fairfax, 25 September 1758," *Founders Online*, National Archives, accessed September 25, 2017, https://founders.archives.gov/documents/Washington/02-06-02-0033.
4. "Sally Fairfax to a Sister-in-Law in Virginia, 1788," quoted in Wilson Miles Cary, *Sally Cary: A Long Hidden Romance of Washington's Life* (New York: The De Vinne Press, 1916), 45.
5. "From George Washington to William Fitzhugh, 15 November 1754," *Founders Online*, National Archives, accessed November 6, 2017, https://founders.archives.gov/documents/Washington/02-01-02-0114.

CHAPTER 7: "WHAT MANNER OF MAN I AM"

1. "From George Washington to Jonathan Boucher, 21 May 1772," *Founders Online*, National Archives, accessed November 12, 2017, https://founders.archives.gov/documents/Washington/02-09-02-0036, and "From George Washington to William Fitzhugh, 15 November 1754," *Founders Online*, National Archives, accessed November 6, 2017, https://founders.archives.gov/documents/Washington/02-01-02-0114.
2. "[Diary entry: 31 July 1770]," *Founders Online*, National Archives, accessed May 7, 2017, https://founders.archives.gov/documents/Washington/01-02-02-0005-0018-0031.
3. "From George Washington to Burwell Bassett, 20 June 1773," *Founders Online*, National Archives, accessed December 6, 2017, https://founders.archives.gov/documents/Washington/02-09-02-0185. [Original source:

PGW, CS, 9: 243–244.] Washington, worried that his wife, with Jack away at college in New York, would be too lonely, asks Bassett to see if he can compel Martha's mother to come and live with them: ". . . and that I was Master of Arguments powerful enough to prevail upon Mrs Dandridge to make this place entire, & absolute home. I should think, as she lives a lonesome life (Betcy being Married) it might suit her well, & be agreeable, both to herself & my wife, to me most assuredly it would."

4. George Washington to Reverend Jonathan Boucher, December 16, 1770, in *WGW,* 3: 35.

5. "To George Washington from Jonathan Boucher, 18 December 1770," *Founders Online,* National Archives, accessed October 26, 2017, https://founders .archives.gov/documents/Washington/02-08-02-0282.

6. "From George Washington to Robert Cary & Company, 28 September 1760," *Founders Online,* National Archives, accessed October 6, 2017, https://founders .archives.gov/documents/Washington/02-06-02-0266-0001.

7. "From George Washington to Robert Cary & Company."

8. Julian Ursyn Niemcewicz, *Under Their Vine and Fig Tree: Travels through America in 1797–1799, 1805 with Some Further Account of Life in New Jersey* (Elizabeth, NJ: The Grassman Publishing Company, Inc., 1965), 100. Of course, this was not a legal marriage. Perhaps a ceremony had taken place, and while Washington sought to keep families together—largely so they would pro-create, which increased his wealth—he did, on occasion, sell or separate them.

9. In the introduction to "The 1619 Project" at *The New York Times* (August 14, 2019), Nikole Hannah-Jones describes Thomas Jefferson's Monticello as a "forced-labor camp."

10. "To George Washington from Anthony Whitting, 16 January 1793," *Founders Online,* National Archives, accessed April 11, 2019, https://founders.archives .gov/documents/Washington/05-12-02-0005. "From George Washington to Anthony Whitting, 20 January 1793," *Founders Online,* National Archives, accessed April 11, 2019, https://founders.archives.gov/documents/Wash ington/05-12-02-0013.

11. Mary V. Thompson, *"The Only Unavoidable Subject of Regret": George Wash-ington, Slavery, and the Enslaved Community at Mount Vernon* (Charlottes-ville: University of Virginia Press, 2019), 247–258. Thompson is the foremost living George Washington scholar, and has published several books and many essays on him and Mount Vernon, where she has worked for decades. This

book is her most recent, and the most exhaustive study of Washington and slavery in existence.

12. At one point, he described plans to drain the Dismal Swamp south of the Chesapeake and use the Potomac canal for commerce, all in an effort to ship produce farther west.

13. "From George Washington to George Mason, 5 April 1769," *Founders Online,* National Archives, accessed February 8, 2017, https://founders.archives.gov /documents/Washington/02-08-02-0132.

14. James MacGregor Burns and Susan Dunn, *George Washington* (New York: Henry Holt & Co., 2004), 17.

15. "From George Washington to Robert Cary & Company, 20 August 1770," *Founders Online,* National Archives, accessed April 26, 2017, https://found ers.archives.gov/documents/Washington/02-08-02-0248-0001.

16. "From George Washington to Bryan Fairfax, 20 July 1774," *Founders Online,* National Archives, accessed March 2, 2017, https://founders.archives.gov /documents/Washington/02-10-02-0081.

CHAPTER 8: "THE SHACKLES OF SLAVERY"

1. "From George Washington to Bryan Fairfax, 20 July 1774," *Founders Online,* National Archives, accessed March 2, 2017, https://founders.archives.gov /documents/Washington/02-10-02-0081.

2. James MacGregor Burns and Susan Dunn, *George Washington* (New York: Henry Holt & Co., 2004), 22.

3. "From George Washington to George William Fairfax, 10–15 June 1774," *Founders Online,* National Archives, accessed June 7, 2017, https://founders .archives.gov/documents/Washington/02-10-02-0067.

4. *The Works of Samuel Johnson,* (Troy, NY: Pafraets & Company, 1913) vol. 14, 93–144.

5. "Letter from John Adams to Abigail Adams, 29 May 1775," Massachusetts Historical Society, accessed October 8, 2017, www.masshist.org/digitaladams /archive/doc?id=L17750529ja&bc=%2Fdigitaladams%2Farchive%2Fbrowse %2Fletters_1774_1777.php.

6. Thomas Cushing to James Bowdoin, 21 June 1775, in *Bowdoin and Temple Papers* in *Massachusetts Historical Society Collections,* 6th ser., 9: 384–385.

7. Noemie Emery, *Washington: A Biography* (London: Cassell, 1977), 179.

8. "From George Washington to George William Fairfax, 31 May 1775," *Founders Online,* National Archives, accessed April 5, 2017, https://founders.archives.gov /documents/Washington/02-10-02-0281.

9. "From George Washington to Martha Washington, 18 June 1775," *Founders Online,* National Archives, accessed August 6, 2017, https://founders.archives .gov/documents/Washington/03-01-02-0003.

PART II: GENERAL GEORGE WASHINGTON'S AMERICAN REVOLUTION

1. James MacGregor Burns and Susan Dunn, *George Washington* (New York: Henry Holt & Co., 2004), 27.

2. Joseph J. Ellis, *His Excellency: George Washington* (New York: Alfred A. Knopf, 2004), 74.

CHAPTER 9: HARDBALL WITH THE HOWE BROTHERS

1. Mark Mayo Boatner III, *Encyclopedia of the American Revolution* (New York: David McKay Co., Inc., 1966), 798.

2. Andrew Jackson O'Shaughnessy, *The Men Who Lost America* (New Haven, CT: Yale University Press, 2013), 98.

3. George F. Scheer and Hugh F. Rankin, eds., *Rebels & Redcoats: The American Revolution Through the Eyes of Those Who Fought and Lived It* (New York: Da Capo Press, Inc., 1987), 156. Also see Sir John Barrow, *The Life of Richard Earl Howe, K.G.* (London: John Murray, 1838).

4. "From George Washington to John Hancock, 9 February 1776," *Founders Online,* National Archives, accessed April 10, 2017, https://founders.archives .gov/documents/Washington/03-03-02-0201.

5. The patriots got muskets and wool from privateering, capturing supplies (like at Fort Ticonderoga), and trading with the French and other European nations. Food and provisions were readily available to the patriots, especially early in the war. For the most part, the British were waiting on these basic necessities to ship from England.

6. Boatner, *Encyclopedia of the American Revolution*, 846.

7. Ambrose Serle, July 14, 1776, quoted in Edward H. Tatum, Jr., ed., *The American Journal of Ambrose Serle, Secretary to Lord Howe, 1776–1778* (San Marino, CA: The Huntington Library, 1940), 33.

8. "General Orders, 11 March 1776," *Founders Online*, National Archives, accessed June 13, 2018, https://founders.archives.gov/documents/Washington/03-03-02-0326.

9. Carlos E. Godfrey, *The Commander-in-Chief's Guard: Revolutionary War* (Washington, D.C.: Stevenson-Smith Company, 1904), 20.

10. Henry Knox to Lucy Knox, July 22, 1776, in Scheer and Rankin, *Rebels & Redcoats*, 157.

11. Scheer and Rankin, *Rebels & Redcoats*, 158.

12. "From George Washington to John Hancock, 14 July 1776," *Founders Online*, National Archives, accessed March 21, 2017, https://founders.archives.gov/documents/Washington/03-05-02-0218.

13. "From Alexander Hamilton to John Jay, 2 June 1777," *Founders Online*, National Archives, accessed June 16, 2017, https://founders.archives.gov/documents/Hamilton/01-01-02-0174.

14. For more, see Holger Hoock, *Scars of Independence: America's Violent Birth* (New York: Crown Publishers, 2017), 152.

15. Large-scale exchanges of prisoners would later become impossible, and both sides would be stuck with a constant swell of prisoners. The British would break first, however, at least in the local ranks, when officers on the ground negotiated release without ever mentioning the crown—an expedient way to maintain their government's official position while still decreasing the number of prisoners under their guard.

16. Hoock, 168. As Hoock notes, "America's commander in chief was framing his version of the war while he was fighting it."

17. The ongoing conflict in Afghanistan is the longest.

CHAPTER 10: THE COURT OF PUBLIC OPINION

1. Palmer testimony can be found in *PCC*, 53: "Papers and Affidavits Related to the Plunderings, Burnings, and Ravages Committed by the British, 1775–84," fol. 29–40, NARA M247.

2. I interviewed Holger Hoock about Abigail Palmer for *Lenny*. Alexis Coe, "How Rape Was Used as a Weapon During the Revolutionary War," *Lenny*,

July 25, 2017, www.lennyletter.com/story/how-rape-was-used-as-a-weapon
-during-the-revolutionary-war.

3. Francis, Lord Rawdon to his uncle Francis Hastings, 10th Earl of Hunting-don, August 4, 1776, in Francis Bickley, ed., *Report on the Manuscripts of the Late Reginald Rawdon Hastings* (London: Historical Manuscripts Commission, 1934), 179.

4. "From George Washington to William Livingston, 3 March 1777," *Founders Online,* National Archives, accessed February 19, 2017, https://founders.archives.gov/documents/Washington/03-08-02-0524.

5. *PCC,* 53: "Papers and Affidavits Related to the Plunderings, Burnings, and Ravages Committed by the British, 1775–84," fol. 29–40, NARA M247.

6. "Reporting on the Revolutionary War," *George Washington's Mount Vernon,* accessed April 9, 2017, www.mountvernon.org/george-washington/the
-revolutionary-war/reporting-the-revolutionary-war-an-interview-with
-todd-andrlik/.

7. Washington Irving, *The Life and Times of Washington* (New York: G.P. Putnam & Sons, 1876), 219. The poem's publication did them both a service. Along with the benefits it provided Washington, it revived Wheatley's fame and fortune for a while, which had waned. (Her fame lasted until she married John Peters, an improvident, slackard freeman, and dropped into obscurity.)

8. "From George Washington to Major General John Sullivan, 31 May 1779," *Founders Online,* National Archives, accessed February 20, 2017, https://founders.archives.gov/documents/Washington/03-20-02-0661.

9. David Hackett Fisher, *Washington's Crossing* (New York: Oxford University Press, 2006), 438. At the time, the thirteen figures in the boat were a show of diversity: The man in the Balmoral bonnet may have been a Scottish immigrant; the man in the big hat, a farmer from Pennsylvania. The soldier, Lieutenant James Monroe, carried the American flag while Washington—his solid legs spread confidently, his sword prominently placed—kept his eyes on the Jersey Shore.

CHAPTER 11: GEORGE WASHINGTON, AGENT 711

1. "To George Washington from John Jay, 19 November 1778," *Founders Online,* National Archives, accessed August 19, 2017, https://founders.archives.gov/documents/Washington/03-18-02-0218.

2. "From George Washington to Elias Boudinot, 3 May 1779," *Founders Online,* National Archives, last modified June 13, 2018, http://founders.archives .gov/documents/Washington/03-20-02-0267.

3. It was likely made of tannic acid. See Alexander Rose, *Washington's Spies: The Story of America's First Spy Ring* (New York: Bantam Books, 2006), 106–111, 310–312.

4. "From George Washington to Major General William Heath, 5 September 1776," *Founders Online,* National Archives, accessed August 11, 2017, https:// founders.archives.gov/documents/Washington/03-06-02-0181.

5. On any other day, Hale may have been given some kind of performative trial, but the British needed a patriot to publicly pay for the Great New York Fire of 1776, when Trinity Church and nearly six hundred houses had been burned to the ground. Hale had nothing to do with it, but not long after Robert Rogers (a master tracker and hunter who had been serving the British since the French and Indian War) delivered him as the fall man, he had a noose fixed around his neck. Hale's hasty execution and utter failure as a spy should have guaranteed his obscurity in favor of so many other heroes and martyrs, but his alleged last words are still well-known today: "I only regret that I have but one life to give for my country."

6. "From George Washington to Robert Morris, 30 December 1776," *Founders Online,* National Archives, accessed July 10, 2017, https://founders.archives .gov/documents/Washington/03-07-02-0382.

7. Our knowledge of what followed should be far less, but Washington was a poor spymaster in at least one regard: He didn't always destroy the evidence. His staff made copies of most of his letters, and at the end of the war those letters were boxed up with the rest of his papers and sent to the Library of Congress. Any researcher can request the hundreds of letters, written under aliases.

8. For more information, see Benjamin Quarles, *The Negro in the American Revolution* (New York: W. W. Norton & Company, 1961).

9. "Lafayette's Testimonial to James Armistead Lafayette," *George Washington's Mount Vernon,* accessed February 20, 2018, www.mountvernon.org /george-washington/the-revolutionary-war/spying-and-espionage/american -spies-of-the-revolution/lafayettes-testimonial-to-james-armistead -lafayette/.

10. "From George Washington to Elias Boudinot, 3 May 1779," *Founders Online,*

National Archives, accessed November 3, 2017, https://founders.archives
.gov/documents/Washington/03-20-02-0267. They would not have called
themselves "occupied," since it was a British territory, for some time. Tallmadge's older brother, William, was taken prisoner in the Battle of Long
Island in 1776 and was "literally starved to death." If the war hadn't been personal as much as political before then, it certainly was after.

11. Though Tallmadge viewed the whole raid, thwarted by weather, as a failure,
Washington encouraged him, writing, "Tho' you have not met with that success you deserved & probably would have obtained had the Enterprize proceeded, yet I cannot but think your whole conduct in the affair was such as
ought to entitle you still more to my confidence & esteem. . . . Another time
you will have less opposition from the Winds & Weather; & success will amply
compensate you for this little disappointment." "From George Washington to
Benjamin Tallmadge, 10 December 1782," *Founders Online,* National Archives,
accessed July 12, 2017, https://founders.archives.gov/documents/Washington
/99-01-02-10171. [This is an Early Access document from *PGW.* It is not an
authoritative final version.]

12. James Rivington, an editor at the *Royal Gazette,* is also believed to have passed
on vital information contributing to Cornwallis's surrender at Yorktown.

13. "Culper Spy Ring Code," *George Washington's Mount Vernon,* accessed February 22, 2018, www.mountvernon.org/education/primary-sources-2/article
/culper-spy-ring-code/. [Original source: *George Washington Papers at the
Library of Congress, 1741–1799,* Library of Congress, Series 4: General Correspondence, 1697–1799.]

14. "General George Washington Issues Orders to the Famed Culper Spy Ring
Through His Spy Master," *Raab Collection,* accessed January 15, 2017, www
.raabcollection.com/presidential-autographs/washington-spy.

15. Washington had been relying on misinformation since the beginning, scar-
ing Loyalist neighbors and redcoats alike with massive exaggerations of
patriot forces, their movements, numbers, and even attacks. He learned that
lesson early on, when he took command in Cambridge at the outset of the war
and discovered that the three hundred barrels of gunpowder in reserve there
had been sent to Bunker Hill. Only thirty-two barrels remained—nine
rounds per soldier. Supposedly too stunned to speak for half an hour, Washington then sent men to Boston to spread rumors that they had more than
eighteen hundred barrels.

16. Washington was willing to try almost anything, so long as it was honorable, and that included relying on women for intelligence. One of them was Lydia Darragh, a Quaker midwife in Philadelphia. The Tories considered her innocuous enough that they used her house as a "council chamber," never suspecting that she spent hours lying on the floor above eavesdropping through the wooden boards as they discussed their battle plans. Darragh's husband would write out her dispatches in shorthand notes, which they then hid in large, cloth-covered buttons sewn onto her fourteen-year-old son's clothes. He would be relieved of them the next time he visited his brother, a lieutenant in the Continental Army. That's how Washington's army came to ambush the British at Valley Forge. They showed up shortly before Christmas 1777, assuming the tired and hungry colonists would be easy prey, and there were Washington's men, lying in wait with cannons loaded and muskets at the ready. Darragh escaped without suspicion. An interrogator told her he wouldn't bother to ask her when she went to bed, "because I know you retire each night exactly at nine." Thomas Fleming, "George Washington, Spymaster," *American Heritage,* February/March 2000, www.americanheritage.com /george-washington-spymaster.

17. An earlier version of this appeared in *The Washington Post.* Alexis Coe, "What Drove Benedict Arnold to Give Up the Patriot Cause and Turn Treasonous?" *The Washington Post,* July 13, 2018, www.washingtonpost.com/outlook/what-drove -benedict-arnold-to-give-up-the-patriot-cause-and-turn-treasonous/2018 /07/13/0dbb97c6-6b47-11e8-bea7-c8eb28bc52b1_story.html?noredirect =on&utm_term=.30cf5974b0db.

18. Washington receives much sympathy from historians over the loss of his father and how it deprived him of a carefree boyhood, yet Arnold's early tale of woe—he was yanked out of boarding school when his alcoholic father's business collapsed and forced to give up his education for an apprenticeship— has more often been cited as the origin of his personal bitterness. Perhaps it's a fair point. Arnold bragged about his beautiful wife's prowess in bed and complained constantly about everything else, calling his doctors in Albany "ignorant pretenders" and politicians far worse.

19. "General Orders, 6 April 1780," *Founders Online,* National Archives, accessed April 11, 2019, https://founders.archives.gov/documents/Washington /99-01-02-01375. [This is an Early Access document from *PGW*. It is not an authoritative final version.]

20. "From George Washington to William Heath, 21 March 1781," *Founders Online,* National Archives, accessed April 8, 2017, https://founders.archives .gov/documents/Washington/99-01-02-05145. [This is an Early Access document from *PGW.* It is not an authoritative final version.]

21. Quoted in James Thomas Flexner, *The Traitor and the Spy: Benedict Arnold and John André* (Syracuse, NY: Syracuse University Press, 1991), 304.

22. Washington put Townsend and others on furlough for a few months, just in case, but all ultimately returned to their posts. They were never caught. Sam Roberts, "War of Secrets; Spy History 101: America's Intelligence Quotient," *The New York Times,* September 8, 2002, www.nytimes.com/2002 /09/08/weekinreview/war-of-secrets-spy-history-101-america-s-intelligence -quotient.html.

23. Quoted in James Kirby Martin, *Benedict Arnold, Revolutionary Hero: An American Warrior Reconsidered* (New York: New York University Press, 1997), 428. See also Peter Force, *American Archives: Consisting of a Collection of Authentick Records, State Papers, Debates, and Letters and Other Notices of Publick Affairs, the Whole Forming a Documentary History of the Origin and Progress of the North American Colonies; of the Causes and Accomplishment of the American Revolution; and of the Constitution of Government for the United States, to the Final Ratification Thereof,* Library of Congress, vol. 5: 1273.

CHAPTER 12: EIGHT YEARS AWAY

1. "From George Washington to Lund Washington, 20 August 1775," *Founders Online,* National Archives, accessed May 10, 2017, https://founders.archives.gov /documents/Washington/03-01-02-0234.

2. "To George Washington from Lund Washington, 5 October 1775," *Founders Online,* National Archives, accessed June 20, 2017, https://founders.archives .gov/documents/Washington/03-02-02-0105.

3. "Lord Dunmore's Proclamation," *The Gilder Lehrman Institute of American History,* accessed June 7, 2017, www.gilderlehrman.org/content/lord-dunmore %E2%80%99s-proclamation-1775.

4. Marquis de Lafayette to George Washington, April 23, 1781, in Stanley J. Idzerda et al., eds., *Lafayette in the Age of the American Revolution: Selected Letters and Papers, 1776–1790* (Ithaca, NY: Cornell University Press, 1981), 4: 60–61. George Washington to Lund Washington, April 30, 1781, in *WGW,* vol. 22: 14.

5. Lund Washington, "List of Runaways, April 1781," *WGW*, 22: 14. This list and others are unfortunately scant on biographical detail.

6. *PGW*, CS, 10: 137.

7. *Mount Vernon Commemorative Guidebook 1999: George Washington Bicentennial Edition* (Mount Vernon, VA: Mount Vernon Ladies' Association, 1998), 28.

8. George Washington to Lund Washington, December 18, 1778, *WGW*, 13: 428–429.

9. "From George Washington to John Augustine Washington, 29 April 1776," *Founders Online,* National Archives, accessed August 9, 2017, https://founders.archives.gov/documents/Washington/03-04-02-0139.

10. "From George Washington to Jonathan Boucher, 20 April 1771," *Founders Online,* National Archives, accessed February 2, 2017, https://founders.archives.gov/documents/Washington/02-08-02-0309.

11. "From George Washington to Major General Horatio Gates, 28 January 1777," *Founders Online,* National Archives, accessed April 4, 2017, https://founders.archives.gov/documents/Washington/03-08-02-0180.

12. "From George Washington to John Hancock, 21 July 1775," *Founders Online,* National Archives, accessed April 11, 2019, https://founders.archives.gov/documents/Washington/03-01-02-0085.

13. "To George Washington from John Hancock, 21 May 1776," *Founders Online,* National Archives, accessed March 11, 2017, https://founders.archives.gov/documents/Washington/03-04-02-0290.

14. "From George Washington to Burwell Bassett, 4 June 1776," *Founders Online,* National Archives, accessed January 21, 2017, https://founders.archives.gov/documents/Washington/03-04-02-0347.

15. George Washington, "Cash Accounts," May 3, 1768, *PGW*, CS, 8: 82–83. Also see Worthington C. Ford, *Washington as an Employer and Importer of Labor* (Brooklyn, NY: Privately printed, 1889), 8–9. Washington often refers to Billy Lee as a "mulatto." Frank would serve as a waiter and butler at Mount Vernon.

16. "To George Washington from Lund Washington, 30 December 1775," *Founders Online,* National Archives, accessed May 3, 2019, https://founders.archives.gov/documents/Washington/03-02-02-0577. [Original source: *PGW*, RWS, 2: 620–621.]

17. Paula S. Felder, *Fielding Lewis and the Washington Family: A Chronicle of 18th*

Century Fredericksburg (Fredericksburg, VA: The American History Company, 1998), 301.

18. Mary Ball Washington to Lund Washington, December 19, 1778, *PGW,* RWS, 19: 459. [Original source: Historical Society of Pennsylvania, https://digitallibrary.hsp.org/index.php/Detail/objects/14378#.] The price of corn had shot up from ten shillings a barrel to six pounds during the war.

19. "From George Washington to John Augustine Washington, 16 January 1783," *Founders Online,* National Archives, accessed December 2, 2017, https://founders.archives.gov/documents/Washington/99-01-02-10433. [This is an Early Access document from *PGW*. It is not an authoritative final version.]

20. "To George Washington from Mary Ball Washington, 13 March 1782," *Founders Online,* National Archives, accessed September 2, 2019, https://founders.archives.gov/documents/Washington/99-01-02-07962. [This is an Early Access document from *PGW*. It is not an authoritative final version.]

21. Some historians have claimed, without evidence, that Mary formally requested relief from the state.

22. "From George Washington to Benjamin Harrison, Sr., 21 March 1781," *Founders Online,* National Archives, accessed April 11, 2019, https://founders.archives.gov/documents/Washington/99-01-02-05144. [This is an Early Access document from *PGW*. It is not an authoritative final version.]

23. "From George Washington to John Augustine Washington, 15 June 1783," *Founders Online,* National Archives, accessed October 1, 2017, https://founders.archives.gov/documents/Washington/99-01-02-11462. [This is an Early Access document from *PGW*. It is not an authoritative final version.]

24. Felder, *Fielding Lewis and the Washington Family,* 310.

25. Paul Leicester Ford, *The True George Washington* (Philadelphia: J. B. Lippincott & Co., 1896), 301. [Original source: *WGW,* 13: 408.]

26. Eliza Parke Custis Law, "Self-Portrait: Eliza Custis, 1808," ed. William D. Hoyt, Jr., *Virginia Magazine of History and Biography* 53, no. 2 (April 1945): 97.

27. "Knox, Henry (1750–1806) to Clement Biddle," *The Gilder Lehrman Institute of American History,* accessed June 3, 2017, www.gilderlehrman.org/collection/glc0243701287?back=/mweb/search%3Fneedle%3DFirst%2520Lady%253B%2526fields%3D_t301001410.

28. "To George Washington from John Parke Custis, 10 June 1776," *Founders Online,* National Archives, accessed April 11, 2019, https://founders.archives .gov/documents/Washington/03-04-02-0380. [Original source: *The Papers of George Washington,* Revolutionary War Series, vol. 4, *1 April 1776–15 June 1776,* ed. Philander D. Chase (Charlottesville: University Press of Virginia, 1991), 484–486.]

29. "[Diary entry: 5 November 1781]," *Founders Online,* National Archives, accessed February 1, 2017, https://founders.archives.gov/documents/Wash ington/01-03-02-0007-0007-0001. [Original source: *DGW,* 3: 437.]

30. "From George Washington to Jonathan Trumbull, Jr., 6 November 1781," *Founders Online,* National Archives, accessed April 11, 2019, https://founders .archives.gov/documents/Washington/99-01-02-07391. [This is an Early Access document from *PGW.* It is not an authoritative final version.]

31. George Washington to Marquis de Lafayette, October 20, 1782, *WGW,* 25: 278–281. Colonel John Laurens, a former Washington aide, died at the Battle of the Combahee River. The news was most devastating to Alexander Hamilton, who was so fond of Laurens that biographers have wondered as to the nature of their relationship. According to Chernow, "Hamilton did not form friendships easily and never again revealed his interior life to another man as he had to Laurens." After Laurens's death, he goes on, "Hamilton shut off some compartment of his emotions and never reopened it."

32. Washington's brother Charles was a drunkard, and his other brother John Augustine had too many children of his own to take on the ones Samuel left behind. His widow, Susannah Perrin, had been left destitute with a baby and four children from Samuel's previous marriages; before her, he had buried four wives. Ferdinand, the eldest of Samuel's children, would stay with the widow and help support her, but four-year-old Harriot, six-year-old Lawrence Augustine Washington, and eight-year-old George Steptoe Washington would be their uncle's responsibilities.

33. George Washington to Lund Washington, June 11, 1783, *WGW,* 27: 1.

CHAPTER 13: "FROM WHENCE NO TRAVELLER RETURNS"

1. "From George Washington to George William Fairfax, 10 July 1783," *Founders Online,* National Archives, accessed January 17, 2017, https://founders

.archives.gov/documents/Washington/99-01-02-11584. [This is an Early Access document from *PGW*. It is not an authoritative final version.]

2. "From George Washington to Joseph Jones, 14 December 1782," *Founders Online,* National Archives, accessed April 11, 2019, https://founders.archives.gov/documents/Washington/99-01-02-10202. [This is an Early Access document from *PGW*. It is not an authoritative final version.]

3. Douglas Southall Freeman, *George Washington, a Biography, Vol. 5: Victory with the Help of France* (New York: Charles Scribner's Sons, 1952), 434–435.

4. "From George Washington to James Craik, 8 September 1789," *Founders Online,* National Archives, accessed August 19, 2017, https://founders.archives.gov/documents/Washington/05-04-02-0001.

5. "From George Washington to Thomas Mifflin, 20 December 1783," *Founders Online,* National Archives, accessed April 11, 2019, https://founders.archives.gov/documents/Washington/99-01-02-12212. [This is an Early Access document from *PGW*. It is not an authoritative final version.]

6. George Washington, "To the Burgesses and Common Council of the Borough of Wilmington, December 16, 1783," *WGW,* 27: 276–277.

7. "From George Washington to Friedrich Wilhelm Ludolf Gerhard Augustin, Baron [von] Steuben, 23 December 1783," *Founders Online,* National Archives, accessed April 11, 2019, https://founders.archives.gov/documents/Washington/99-01-02-12226. [This is an Early Access document from *PGW*. It is not an authoritative final version.]

8. "I. Report of a Committee on Arrangements for the Public Audience, [22 December 1783]," *Founders Online,* National Archives, accessed April 4, 2017, https://founders.archives.gov/documents/Jefferson/01-06-02-0319-0002.

9. "III. Washington's Address to Congress Resigning His Commission, [23 December 1783]," *Founders Online,* National Archives, accessed August 6, 2017, https://founders.archives.gov/documents/Jefferson/01-06-02-0319-0004.

10. "Editorial Note: George Washington's Resignation as Commander-in-Chief," *Founders Online,* National Archives, accessed April 1, 2017, https://founders.archives.gov/documents/Jefferson/01-06-02-0319-0001. [Original source: *The Papers of Thomas Jefferson,* vol. 6, *21 May 1781–1 March 1784,* ed. Julian P. Boyd (Princeton, NJ: Princeton University Press, 1952), 402–409.] See also *PGW,* Confederation, 1: 71–72.

11. "James McHenry to Margaret Caldwell, 23 December 1783," in Paul A.

Smith, ed., *Letters of Delegates to Congress, 1774–1789* (Washington, D.C.: Library of Congress, 1976–2000), 21: 222–223. Jefferson, suffering from what must have been a migraine, had tried to leave much of the Congressional response to McHenry, but McHenry had not heard from his intended, the beautiful Margaret Caldwell, and declared himself "becoming mad" on "a rack of suspense." His contributions were likely minimal in planning and in crafting a response, as were Gerry's, though we cannot know for certain, as the original draft was lost.

12. Editorial Note: George Washington's Resignation as Commander-in-Chief," Founders Online, National Archives, accessed September 29, 2019, https://founders.archives.gov/documents/Jefferson/01-06-02-0319-0001.

13. Benjamin West to Rufus King, May 3, 1797, in Robert E. Spiller et al., *Literary History of the United States* (New York: MacMillan, 1963), 200. Also see Benjamin West quoted in Garry Wills, *Cincinnatus: George Washington and the Enlightenment* (New York: Doubleday & Company, Inc., 1984), 13.

PART III: MR. PRESIDENT

1. John Adams, *The Works of John Adams*, vol. 9 (Boston: Little, Brown and Co., 1856), 300.

2. "From John Adams to Benjamin Rush, 22 April 1812," *Founders Online*, National Archives, accessed April 11, 2019, https://founders.archives.gov/documents/Adams/99-02-02-5777. [This is an Early Access document from The Adams Papers. It is not an authoritative final version.]

3. Thomas Jefferson, *Notes on the State of Virginia* (Boston: Wells and Lilly, 1829), 68.

4. "Thomas Jefferson to Walter Jones, 2 January 1814," *Founders Online*, National Archives, accessed April 11, 2019, https://founders.archives.gov/documents/Jefferson/03-07-02-0052.

5. Philip S. Foner, ed., *The Writings of Thomas Paine*, vol. 2 (New York: Citadel Press, 1945), 1167.

6. Thomas Paine to George Washington, July 30, 1796, quoted in Thomas Paine, *The Political Works of Thomas Paine: In Two Volumes*, vol. 2 (London: W.T. Sherwin, 1819), 36.

7. "From James Madison to Edmund Randolph, 18 March 1783," *Founders Online*, National Archives, accessed April 11, 2019, https://founders.archives.gov/documents/Madison/01-06-02-0117.

8. "From James Madison to Thomas Jefferson, 4 April 1796," *Founders Online,* National Archives, accessed April 11, 2019, https://founders.archives.gov /documents/Madison/01-16-02-0191.

9. "To Thomas Jefferson from James Monroe, 12 July 1788," *Founders Online,* National Archives, accessed April 11, 2019, https://founders.archives.gov /documents/Jefferson/01-13-02-0256.

10. Unsent draft letter, Gratz Collection, Historical Society of Pennsylvania.

CHAPTER 14: UNRETIREMENT

1. Martha Washington, "Letter, Martha Washington to Elizabeth Powel, January 18, 1788," in Martha Washington, Item #33, accessed April 4, 2018, http://marthawashington.us/items/show/33.

2. "To George Washington from Thomas Jefferson, 10 December 1784," *Founders Online,* National Archives, accessed August 11, 2018, https:// founders.archives.gov/documents/Washington/04-02-02-0142.

3. "From George Washington to Bushrod Washington, 13 April 1786," *Founders Online,* National Archives, accessed May 2, 2017, https://founders.archives .gov/documents/Washington/04-04-02-0020. [Original source: *PGW,* Confederation, 4: 18.]

4. "From George Washington to John Hoomes, 17 February 1791," *Founders Online,* National Archives, accessed April 11, 2019, https://founders.archives .gov/documents/Washington/05-07-02-0216.

5. "From George Washington to Gilbert Simpson, 13 February 1784," *Founders Online,* National Archives, accessed February 4, 2018, https://founders .archives.gov/documents/Washington/04-01-02-0084.

6. "From George Washington to Richard Henry Lee, 8 February 1785," *Founders Online,* National Archives, accessed April 11, 2019, https://founders .archives.gov/documents/Washington/04-02-02-0240.

7. Le Marquis de Lafayette to Adrienne de Lafayette, August 20, 1784, quoted in Stanley J. Idzerda and Rover Rhodes Crout, eds., *Lafayette in the Age of the American Revolution: Selected Letters and Papers, 1776–1790,* 5 vols. (Ithaca, NY: Cornell University Press, 1983), 5: 403–404. Nelly, Jack Custis's widow, remarried David Stuart, a doctor in Alexandria; she seemed content to raise her two eldest children with him, and leave her two youngest with the Washingtons. The Stuarts stayed at Mount Vernon on numerous occasions.

8. James R. Gaines, *For Liberty and Glory: Washington, Lafayette, and Their Revolutions* (New York: W.W. Norton & Company, 2007), 199.

9. Elkanah Watson, *Men and Times of the Revolution* (New York: Dana & Co., 1856), 119.

10. *PGW,* Confederation, 5: 33–37.

11. "From George Washington to John Jay, 18 May 1786," *Founders Online,* National Archives, accessed April 11, 2019, https://founders.archives.gov /documents/Washington/04-04-02-0063.

12. "To George Washington from John Jay, 27 June 1786," *Founders Online,* National Archives, accessed April 11, 2019, https://founders.archives.gov /documents/Washington/04-04-02-0129.

13. "From George Washington to James Madison, 30 November 1785," *Founders Online,* National Archives, accessed April 11, 2019, https://founders.archives .gov/documents/Washington/04-03-02-0357.

14. "To George Washington from Henry Knox, 9 April 1787," *Founders Online,* National Archives, accessed April 11, 2019, https://founders.archives.gov /documents/Washington/04-05-02-0129.

15. "George Washington to Robert Morris, May 5, 1787," Library of Congress, accessed February 17, 2019, www.loc.gov/resource/mgw2.014/?sp=100.

16. May 14–September 17, 1787, in *Diaries* 5:156–185.

17. "To Thomas Jefferson from James Monroe, 12 July 1788," *Founders Online,* National Archives, accessed April 11, 2019, https://founders.archives.gov /documents/Jefferson/01-13-02-0256.

18. "To George Washington from Alexander Hamilton, September 1788," *Founders Online,* National Archives, accessed April 11, 2019, https://founders.archives .gov/documents/Washington/05-01-02-0011.

19. Gouverneur Morris to George Washington, December 6, 1788, quoted in Bruce Chadwick, *George Washington's War: The Forging of a Revolutionary Leader and the American Presidency* (Naperville, IL: Sourcebooks, 2004), 463.

20. Neither Mary nor Washington left a record of the visit, but George Washington Parke Custis did.

21. Martha Washington to Fanny Bassett Washington, February 25, 1788, quoted in Joseph E. Fields, ed., *"Worthy Partner": The Papers of Martha Washington* (Westport, CT: Greenwood Press, 1994), 205–206.

CHAPTER 15: THE PRESIDENCY; OR, "THE PLACE OF HIS EXECUTION"

1. "From Thomas Jefferson to James Madison, 29 July 1789," *Founders Online,* National Archives, accessed April 11, 2019, https://founders.archives.gov /documents/Jefferson/01-15-02-0307. The italics indicate that Jefferson wrote in code, not that he intended emphasis.
2. "John Adams to Abigail Adams, 19 December 1793," *Founders Online,* National Archives, accessed April 11, 2019, https://founders.archives.gov /documents/Adams/04-09-02-0278.
3. "From George Washington to Henry Knox, 1 April 1789," *Founders Online,* National Archives, accessed April 11, 2019, https://founders.archives.gov /documents/Washington/05-02-02-0003.
4. "From George Washington to Henry Knox, 1 April 1789," *Founders Online,* National Archives, accessed April 11, 2019, https://founders.archives.gov /documents/Washington/05-02-02-0003.
5. "Address by Charles Thomson, 14 April 1789," *Founders Online,* National Archives, accessed April 11, 2019, https://founders.archives.gov/documents /Washington/05-02-02-0056.
6. "[April 1789]," *Founders Online,* National Archives, accessed April 11, 2019, https://founders.archives.gov/documents/Washington/01-05-02-0005-0001.
7. Martha Washington to John Dandridge, April 20, 1789, quoted in Joseph E. Fields, ed., *"Worthy Partner": The Papers of Martha Washington* (Westport, CT: Greenwood Press, 1994), 213–214.
8. Martha Saxton, *The Widow Washington: The Life of Mary Washington* (New York: Farrar, Straus and Giroux, 2019). This is the best book on Washington's mother; unfortunately, it was published too close to this book's publication to cite extensively, but Saxton and I spoke on the phone and exchanged emails on the subject in 2018.
9. "From George Washington to Clement Biddle, 28 July 1784," *Founders Online,* National Archives, accessed April 11, 2019, https://founders.archives .gov/documents/Washington/04-02-02-0014.
10. "From George Washington to the Ladies of Trenton, 21 April 1789," *Founders Online,* National Archives, accessed April 11, 2019, https://founders.archives .gov/documents/Washington/05-02-02-0095.

11. "From George Washington to Bushrod Washington, 27 July 1789," *Founders Online*, National Archives, accessed April 11, 2019, https://founders.archives .gov/documents/Washington/05-03-02-0189.

12. "Abigail Adams to Mary Smith Cranch, 12 July 1789," *Founders Online*, National Archives, accessed April 11, 2019, https://founders.archives.gov /documents/Adams/04-08-02-0210.

13. For the Conway loan, see "From George Washington to Richard Conway, 4 March 1789," *Founders Online*, National Archives, accessed April 11, 2019, https://founders.archives.gov/documents/Washington/05-01-02-0272, and "From George Washington to Richard Conway, 6 March 1789," *Founders Online*, National Archives, accessed April 11, 2019, https://founders.archives .gov/documents/Washington/05-01-02-0279.

14. On November 4, 1752, Washington paid the Fredericksburg Masonic Lodge two pounds and three shillings to join, and by the next year, he had reached the highest degree of membership: Master Mason. We don't know what, if any, hazing his brothers subjected him to, or what was discussed at the meetings he attended at various lodges throughout his life. We can't even pinpoint the origins of Freemasonry, a secretive fraternal organization also known as "the Craft." All we know is that it originated in Scotland, and that the benefits to a joiner with higher aspirations, like Washington, were obvious. Quite a few Founding Fathers were members, including Benjamin Franklin and Paul Revere. For more information, see Ronald E. Heaton and James R. Case, *The Lodge at Fredericksburgh: A Digest of the Early Records* (Norristown, PA: Ronald E. Heaton, 1975), and J. Travis Walker, *A History of Fredericksburg Lodge No. 4, A.F. & A.M., 1752–2002* (Fredericksburg, VA: Sheridan Books Inc., 2002).

15. "To George Washington from Betty Lewis, 24 July 1789," *Founders Online*, National Archives, accessed April 11, 2019, https://founders.archives.gov /documents/Washington/05-03-02-0167.

16. John McVickar, *A Domestic Narrative of the Life of Samuel Bard* (Carlisle, MA: Applewood Books, 2010), 136–137.

17. Martha Washington to Mercy Otis Warren, June 12, 1790, quoted in Fields, *Worthy Partner*, 226.

18. Fisher Ames to George Richards Minot, May 3, 1789, quoted in Fisher Ames and John Thornton Kirkland, *Works of Fisher Ames: With a Selection*

from His Speeches and Correspondence, vol. 1 (Boston: Little, Brown and Co., 1854), 34.

19. For more, see *PGW*, PS, 4: 56, 102, 132.

CHAPTER 16: INFANT NATION

1. Kenneth R. Bowling and Helen E. Veit, eds., *The Diary of William Maclay and Other Notes on Senate Debates* (Baltimore, MD: Johns Hopkins University Press, 1988), description between 128–130.

2. "To George Washington from Henry Knox, 7 July 1789," *Founders Online*, National Archives, accessed April 11, 2019, https://founders.archives.gov /documents/Washington/05-03-02-0067. [Original source: *PGW*, PS, 3: 134–141.]

3. Bowling and Veit, *The Diary of William Maclay*, description between 128–129.

4. "From George Washington to Lafayette, 3 June 1790," *Founders Online*, National Archives, accessed April 11, 2019, https://founders.archives.gov /documents/Washington/05-05-02-0292.

5. When Washington received mail addressed to "The President and Members of the American Congress," he sent it to Congress, unopened, for legislators to decide which branch of government should have at it first. He even consulted his attorney general when, in the face of a yellow fever outbreak, it seemed as though an emergency session might have to be called: Would an alternative location, removed from disease, be acceptable?

6. "To James Madison from George Washington, 5 May 1789," *Founders Online*, National Archives, accessed April 11, 2019, https://founders.archives.gov /documents/Madison/01-12-02-0082.

7. Martha Washington to Mercy Otis Warren, December 26, 1789, quoted in Joseph E. Fields, ed., *"Worthy Partner": The Papers of Martha Washington* (Westport, CT: Greenwood Press, 1994), 223–224.

8. Martha Washington to Fanny Bassett Washington, October 23, 1789, quoted in Fields, 219–220.

9. "From George Washington to Tobias Lear, 9 September 1790," *Founders Online*, National Archives, accessed April 11, 2019, https://founders.archives .gov/documents/Washington/05-06-02-0195.

10. "From George Washington to Tobias Lear, 3 April 1791," *Founders Online,* National Archives, accessed April 11, 2019, https://founders.archives.gov /documents/Washington/05-08-02-0035.

11. "To George Washington from Tobias Lear, 24 April 1791," *Founders Online,* National Archives, last modified June 13, 2018, http://founders.archives .gov/documents/Washington/05-08-02-0099.

12. George Washington Parke Custis and Mary Randolph Custis Lee, *Recollections and Private Memoirs of Washington* (New York: Derby & Jackson, 1860), 422–424.

13. "To George Washington from Tobias Lear, 24 April 1791," *Founders Online,* National Archives, last modified June 13, 2018, http://founders.archives .gov/documents/Washington/05-08-02-0099.

14. "To George Washington from Tobias Lear, 5 June 1791," *Founders Online,* National Archives, accessed April 11, 2019, https://founders.archives.gov /documents/Washington/05-08-02-0172.

15. "From George Washington to Tobias Lear, 22 November 1790," *Founders Online,* National Archives, accessed April 11, 2019, https://founders.archives .gov/documents/Washington/05-06-02-0331.

16. While we have no idea what "business plan" that baker operated under, his return policy, at least for Washington, was likely a way to separate himself from other caterers who left the trouble and expense of managing leftovers to the purchaser—a real hassle before refrigeration.

17. "From George Washington to Tobias Lear, 12 April 1791," *Founders Online,* National Archives, accessed April 11, 2019, https://founders.archives.gov /documents/Washington/05-08-02-0062.

18. "From George Washington to Thomas Jefferson, 26 November 1791," *Founders Online,* National Archives, accessed April 11, 2019, https://founders.archives .gov/documents/Washington/05-09-02-0131.

19. There is not a single confident explanation of the derivation of the word "cabinet" for the president's councilors. In his Thomas Jefferson biography, Dumas Malone notes that Jefferson preferred the term "executive council," with no comment on how "cabinet" became the common appellation. The word was used in foreign languages, but the OED offers nothing on its transfer to a United States context.

20. "Thomas Jefferson to Walter Jones, 5 March 1810," *Founders Online,* National

Archives, accessed April 11, 2019, https://founders.archives.gov/documents
/Jefferson/03-02-02-0223.

21. Fenno ascribed his financial backing generally to Federalists. Many biographers, without citation, name Hamilton alone.

22. "From Alexander Hamilton to Edward Carrington, 26 May 1792," *Founders Online,* National Archives, accessed April 11, 2019, https://founders.archives .gov/documents/Hamilton/01-11-02-0349. [Original source: *PAH,* 11: 426–445.] Hamilton, Jefferson, Madison, and Monroe frequently wrote politically sensitive portions of their letters in code; in no small part because of the aggressively partisan press and fears of letters being read by opponents.

23. "From George Washington to Thomas Jefferson, 23 August 1792," *Founders Online,* National Archives, accessed April 11, 2019, https://founders .archives.gov/documents/Washington/05-11-02-0009.

24. "From George Washington to Alexander Hamilton, 26 August 1792," *Founders Online,* National Archives, accessed April 11, 2019, https://founders .archives.gov/documents/Washington/05-11-02-0015.

25. "From Alexander Hamilton to George Washington, 9 September 1792," *Founders Online,* National Archives, accessed April 11, 2019, https://found ers.archives.gov/documents/Hamilton/01-12-02-0267.

26. "To George Washington from Thomas Jefferson, 9 September 1792," *Founders Online,* National Archives, accessed April 11, 2019, https://founders.archives .gov/documents/Washington/05-11-02-0049. Jefferson sent his formal resignation on December 31, 1793.

27. "From Thomas Jefferson to George Washington, 23 May 1792," *Founders Online,* National Archives, accessed April 11, 2019, https://founders.archives .gov/documents/Jefferson/01-23-02-0491.

28. "To George Washington from Elizabeth Willing Powel, 17 November 1792," *Founders Online,* National Archives, accessed April 11, 2019, https://founders .archives.gov/documents/Washington/05-11-02-0225.

29. "To Thomas Jefferson from James Madison, 30 June 1789," *Founders Online,* National Archives, accessed April 11, 2019, https://founders.archives.gov /documents/Jefferson/01-15-02-0221.

30. The nature of the army and navy was still evolving. Troops were called into federal service from state militias for specific expeditions or purposes.

31. In a letter to his wife, Abigail, the following month, Adams vowed to make

better use of the vice presidency this time around: "I am determined in the meantime to be no longer the Dupe, and run into Debt to Support a vain Post which has answered no other End than to make me unpopular," he wrote. Letter from John Adams to Abigail Adams, 28 December 1792 [electronic edition], *Adams Family Papers: An Electronic Archive*, Massachusetts Historical Society, www.masshist.org/digitaladams/.

CHAPTER 17: "POLITICAL SUICIDE"

1. See Minutes of a Cabinet Meeting, April 19 1793, *PGW*, PS 12: 459–460.
2. "Thomas Jefferson's Notes on a Cabinet Meeting, 6 May 1793," *Founders Online*, National Archives, accessed April 11, 2019, https://founders.archives .gov/documents/Washington/05-12-02-0426. Jefferson's notes were from the April 19, 1793, meeting.
3. "Enclosure: [Proclamation by George Washington], [April 1793]," *Founders Online*, National Archives, accessed April 11, 2019, https://founders.archives .gov/documents/Hamilton/01-14-02-0200-0002. It explains authorship and distribution.
4. "From George Washington to George Cabot, 7 September 1795," *Founders Online*, National Archives, accessed April 11, 2019, https://founders.archives .gov/documents/Washington/05-18-02-0425.
5. Benjamin H. Latrobe, July 16, 1796, quoted in *WGW*, 35: 141.
6. Gilbert Chinard, ed., *George Washington as the French Knew Him* (New York: Greenwood Press, 1940), 105.
7. *PGW*, PS, 13: 19.
8. "John Adams to Thomas Jefferson, 30 June 1813," *Founders Online*, National Archives, accessed April 11, 2019, https://founders.archives.gov/documents /Jefferson/03-06-02-0216. Jefferson submitted his official resignation in July, but Washington made a special trip to Monticello to once again compel him to stay; he agreed to another extension. He had some relief from Hamilton, who, along with Eliza, his wife, came down with yellow fever in late summer. (Most of the government raced out of the city; Philadelphia governor Samuel Powel, Elizabeth's husband, refused to leave, and he, along with four thousand others, died.)
9. "Thomas Jefferson to James Madison, 9 June 1793," *Founders Online*, National

Archives, accessed April 11, 2019, https://founders.archives.gov/documents /Jefferson/03-06-02-0216. In the end, Genêt didn't go home. It seems he was set to stand trial for crimes against the revolution, a sure death sentence. Washington granted him asylum, and Genêt spent the rest of his life in upstate New York, eventually marrying Governor George Clinton's daughter Cornelia. From there, he lived a quiet life, but his legacy took shape in Democratic-Republican Societies popping up all over the country.

10. Distilling grain was better economically because the product—whiskey—commanded a higher price than raw grain. Excise taxes increased costs at every stage and cut into profits.

11. "To George Washington from Alexander Hamilton, 5 August 1794," *Founders Online*, National Archives, accessed April 11, 2019, https://founders.archives .gov/documents/Washington/05-16-02-0357.

12. See PGW, PS 16: 470, which is Henry Knox to GW, same date, n. 4. The writ eventually led to a proclamation on September 25, 1794. See *PGW*, PS, 16: 725–727.

13. "From Alexander Hamilton to James McHenry, 18 March 1799," *Founders Online*, National Archives, accessed April 11, 2019, https://founders.archives .gov/documents/Hamilton/01-22-02-0344.

14. "From George Washington to Henry Knox, 9 October 1794," *Founders Online*, National Archives, accessed April 11, 2019, https://founders.archives.gov/doc uments/Washington/05-17-02-0027.

15. "From George Washington to Cherokee Nation, 29 August 1796," *Founders Online*, National Archives, accessed April 11, 2019, https://founders.archives .gov/documents/Washington/99-01-02-00897. [This is an Early Access document from *PGW*. It is not an authoritative final version.]

16. "From Thomas Jefferson to James Monroe, 26 May 1795," *Founders Online*, National Archives, accessed April 11, 2019, https://founders.archives.gov /documents/Jefferson/01-28-02-0275.

17. "From George Washington to the U.S. Senate and House of Representatives, 19 November 1794," *Founders Online*, National Archives, accessed April 11, 2019, https://founders.archives.gov/documents/Washington/05-17-02-0125.

18. "From James Madison to James Monroe, 4 December 1794," *Founders Online*, National Archives, accessed April 11, 2019, https://founders.archives.gov /documents/Madison/01-15-02-0306.

19. "From Alexander Hamilton to George Washington, 1 December 1794," *Founders Online*, National Archives, accessed April 11, 2019, https://founders.archives .gov/documents/Hamilton/01-17-02-0392. [Original source: *PAH,* 17: 413.] And "To George Washington from Henry Knox, 28 December 1794," *Founders Online*, National Archives, accessed April 11, 2019, https://founders.archives .gov/documents/Washington/05-17-02-0221.

20. Robert R. Rankin, *The University of California Chronicle,* vol. 9, no. 2 (Berkeley, CA: The University Press, 1907), 30.

21. "To George Washington from John Jay, 25 February 1795," *Founders Online*, National Archives, accessed April 11, 2019, https://founders.archives.gov /documents/Washington/05-17-02-0388.

22. "To George Washington from Petersburg, Va., Citizens, 1 August 1795," *Founders Online*, National Archives, accessed April 11, 2019, https://founders .archives.gov/documents/Washington/05-18-02-0327.

23. "From George Washington to Alexander Hamilton, 29 July 1795," *Founders Online*, National Archives, accessed April 11, 2019, https://founders .archives.gov/documents/Washington/05-18-02-0311.

24. "To George Washington from Edmund Randolph, 19 August 1795," *Founders Online*, National Archives, accessed April 11, 2019, https://founders.archives .gov/documents/Washington/05-18-02-0368.

25. George Washington to Alexander Hamilton, December 22, 1795, *WGW,* 13: 146, and Alexander Hamilton to George Washington, December 24, 1795, *WGW,* 13: 147.

26. Madison, who opposed the treaty, would ultimately suffer the most. It was among the chief causes of the War of 1812, which occurred during his presidency and resulted in several embarrassments.

27. William Cobbett, *Beauties of Cobbett* (London: Cobbett's Register Office, 1836), 50.

28. "From George Washington to Timothy Pickering, 27 September 1795," *Founders Online*, National Archives, accessed April 11, 2019, https://founders .archives.gov/documents/Washington/05-18-02-0482.

29. *Annals of Congress,* 4th Cong., 1st Sess., 355. *Annals of Congress* can be found most easily online at *The Century of American Lawmaking,* a Library of Congress website: https://memory.loc.gov/ammem/amlaw/.

CHAPTER 18: FAREWELL TO "CUNNING, AMBITIOUS, AND UNPRINCIPLED MEN"

1. George Washington to Thomas Law, February 10, 1796, *PGW, PS,* 19: 446.
2. For more on Ona Judge's story, see Erica Armstrong Dunbar, *Never Caught* (New York: Simon & Schuster, 2017).
3. S. Decatur and T. Lear, *Private Affairs of George Washington: From the Records and Accounts of Tobias Lear, Esquire, His Secretary* (Boston: Houghton Mifflin Company, 1993), 268.
4. Rev. T. H. Adams, "Article Reporting Interview with Ona Judge Staines, Granite Freeman, May 22, 1845," in Martha Washington, Item #4, http://martha washington.us/items/show/4 (accessed September 1, 2019). All quotes from Ona Judge Staines come from this source.
5. "To Thomas Jefferson from George Washington, 6 July 1796," *Founders Online,* National Archives, accessed April 11, 2019, https://founders.archives.gov /documents/Jefferson/01-29-02-0107.
6. "To Thomas Jefferson from George Washington, 28 August 1796," *Founders Online,* National Archives, accessed April 11, 2019, https://founders.archives .gov/documents/Jefferson/01-29-02-0136.
7. Moncure Daniel Conway, ed., *The Writings of Thomas Paine,* vol. 3 (New York: G.P. Putnam's Sons, 1895), 215, 217, 243.
8. Paul M. Zall, ed., *Washington on Washington* (Lexington: University Press of Kentucky, 2003), 129.
9. "From Alexander Hamilton to George Washington, 30 July 1796," *Founders Online,* National Archives, accessed April 11, 2019, https://founders.archives .gov/documents/Hamilton/01-20-02-0181-0001. Hamilton reframed Washington's idea for a national university that would allow students (meaning men) from all over the country to observe congressional debates and find common ground; Hamilton, who had gone to Columbia, considered the plan influenced by Washington's military education.
10. George Washington, "Farewell Address to the People of the United States," September 17, 1796, *WGW,* 35: 214–238.
11. Thomas Jefferson to James Madison, January 8, 1797, quoted in *Thomas Jefferson, The Republic of Letters: The Correspondence between Thomas Jefferson and James Madison,* vol. 2 (New York: W. W. Norton & Company, 1995), 955.

12. "From George Washington to William Pearce, 14 November 1796," *Founders Online*, National Archives, accessed April 11, 2019, https://founders.archives .gov/documents/Washington/99-01-02-00003. [This is an Early Access document from *PGW*. It is not an authoritative final version.]

13. From George Washington to Joseph Whipple, 28, November 1796," Founders Online, National Archives, accessed September 29, 2019, https://founders .archives.gov/documents/Washington/99-01-02-00037; "From George Washington to Oliver Wolcott, Jr., 1 September 1796," *Founders Online*, National Archives, accessed April 11, 2019, https://founders.archives.gov /documents/Washington/99-01-02-00910. [This is an Early Access document from *PGW*. It is not an authoritative final version.]

14. "From George Washington to Frederick Kitt, 29 January 1798," *Founders Online*, National Archives, accessed April 11, 2019, https://founders.archives.gov/doc uments/Washington/06-02-02-0053.

15. "From George Washington to Joseph Whipple, 28 November 1796," *Founders Online*, National Archives, accessed April 11, 2019, https://founders.archives .gov/documents/Washington/99-01-02-00037.

16. "From George Washington to John Francis Mercer, 9 September 1786," *Founders Online*, National Archives, accessed April 11, 2019, https://founders .archives.gov/documents/Washington/04-04-02-0232.

17. "From George Washington to Alexander Spotswood, 23 November 1794," *Founders Online*, National Archives, accessed April 11, 2019, https://founders .archives.gov/documents/Washington/05-17-02-0136.

18. "From George Washington to Joseph Thompson, 2 July 1766," *Founders Online*, National Archives, accessed April 11, 2019, https://founders.archives .gov/documents/Washington/02-07-02-0300.

19. "An Act to Authorize the Manumission of Slaves (1782)," *Encyclopedia Virginia*, accessed May 6, 2019, www.encyclopediavirginia.org/An_act_to_authorize _the_manumission_of_slaves_1782.

20. "From George Washington to Lund Washington, 7 May 1787," *Founders Online*, National Archives, accessed April 11, 2019, https://founders.archives .gov/documents/Washington/04-05-02-0161. The best resource on this is Mary V. Thompson. Please see her most recent book, *"The Only Unavoidable Subject of Regret": George Washington, Slavery, and the Enslaved Community at Mount Vernon* (Charlottesville: University of Virginia Press, 2019).

21. "John Adams to Abigail Adams, 5 March 1797," *Founders Online*, National

Archives, accessed April 11, 2019, https://founders.archives.gov/documents
/Adams/04-12-02-0005, and "John Adams to Abigail Adams, 9 March 1797,"
Founders Online, National Archives, accessed April 11, 2019, https://founders
.archives.gov/documents/Adams/04-12-02-0009.

CHAPTER 19: FINAL RETIREMENT

1. "From George Washington to Lawrence Augustine Washington, 3 September 1797," *Founders Online,* National Archives, accessed April 11, 2019, https://founders.archives.gov/documents/Washington/06-01-02-0302.

2. "From George Washington to James Anderson (of Scotland), 7 April 1797," *Founders Online,* National Archives, accessed April 11, 2019, https://founders .archives.gov/documents/Washington/06-01-02-0059.

3. "From George Washington to James McHenry, 29 May 1797," *Founders Online,* National Archives, accessed April 11, 2019, https://founders.archives .gov/documents/Washington/06-01-02-0128.

4. "From George Washington to Burgess Ball, 22 September 1799," *Founders Online,* National Archives, accessed April 11, 2019, https://founders.archives.gov/docu ments/Washington/06-04-02-0266.

5. "Martha Washington to Elizabeth Willing Powel, 17 December 1797," *Founders Online,* National Archives, accessed April 11, 2019, https://founders.archives .gov/documents/Washington/06-01-02-0462.

6. Washington Irving, *The Life of George Washington,* vol. 5 (New York: G.P. Putnam & Sons, 1859), 138.

7. "From George Washington to George Washington Parke Custis, 22 May 1797," *Founders Online,* National Archives, last modified June 13, 2018, http://founders.archives.gov/documents/Washington/06-01-02-0121.

8. Virginia Kays Creesy, "George Washington as a Princeton Parent," *Princeton Alumni Weekly,* July 4, 1976.

9. "From George Washington to George Washington Parke Custis, 24 July 1798," *Founders Online,* National Archives, accessed April 11, 2019, https:// founders.archives.gov/documents/Washington/06-02-02-0354.

10. George Washington Parke Custis and Mary Randolph Custis Lee, *Recollections and Private Memoirs of Washington* (New York: Derby & Jackson, 1860), 38.

11. "Comments on Monroe's *A View of the Conduct of the Executive of the United*

States, March 1798," *Founders Online*, National Archives, accessed April 11, 2019, https://founders.archives.gov/documents/Washington/06-02-02-0146. Washington's copy ended up at Harvard's Houghton Library because his nephew, Bushrod Washington, gave it to his fellow Supreme Court Justice, Joseph Story. Story taught at Harvard Law School and donated the book.

12. "Thomas Jefferson to Walter Jones, 2 January 1814," *Founders Online,* National Archives, accessed April 11, 2019, https://founders.archives.gov/documents /Jefferson/03-07-02-0052.

13. *PGW,* RS, 2: 169–217.

14. The United States still had no meaningful standing army. It was not until after the founding of West Point and the near disaster of the War of 1812 that such a force came into existence. An army was raised by nationalizing state militia regiments.

15. John Adams to George Washington, June 22, 1798, *PGW,* RS, 2: 351–352.

16. "From George Washington to John Adams, 13 July 1798," *Founders Online,* National Archives, accessed April 11, 2019, https://founders.archives.gov /documents/Washington/06-02-02-0314.

17. "From George Washington to Jonathan Trumbull, Jr., 21 July 1799," *Founders Online,* National Archives, accessed April 11, 2019, https://founders.archives .gov/documents/Washington/06-04-02-0165.

CHAPTER 20: "'TIS WELL"

1. Unless otherwise noted, all quotations come from Tobias Lear's *Narrative Accounts of the Death of George Washington.* "II, 14 December 1799," *Founders Online,* National Archives, accessed April 11, 2019, https://founders.archives .gov/documents/Washington/06-04-02-0406-0002.

He officially died, according to Craik and Dick, of "cynanche trachealis," an inflamed upper windpipe. But most historians, consulting with physicians, have argued it was acute epiglottitis caused by virulent bacteria, which partially obstructed his airway, and his symptoms are consistent with that diagnosis. When the epiglottis is inflamed, it can be very sore and painful, sometimes swelling to the size of a golf ball. As it grows, it obstructs the larynx, making breathing and swallowing extremely painful. Although later accounts would describe Washington experiencing "with so little pain" during his "beautiful death," he more than likely spent much of that last day feeling as if he was being smothered.

2. Nelly had married Lawrence Lewis, the late Betty Washington Lewis's son.

3. Tobias Lear to Alexander Hamilton, January 16, 1800, *PAH,* 24: 199.

4. Gustavus Richard Brown to James Craik, *WGW,* 14: 257.

5. "From George Washington to Martha Washington, 18 June 1775," *Founders Online,* National Archives, accessed April 11, 2019, https://founders.archives .gov/documents/Washington/03-01-02-0003.

6. "George Washington's Last Will and Testament, 9 July 1799," *Founders Online,* National Archives, accessed April 11, 2019, https://founders.archives.gov/doc uments/Washington/06-04-02-0404-0001.

7. Bushrod Washington did a poor job of keeping the documents, handing them out as mementos to friends and colleagues. He also allowed great liberties to John Marshall, George Washington's first biographer, and Jared Sparks, George Washington's first editor, that led to further dispersal of the collection.

8. "10 Facts About Washington and Slavery," *George Washington's Mount Vernon,* accessed May 13, 2019, www.mountvernon.org/george-washington /slavery/ten-facts-about-washington-slavery/.

9. Ashley Bateman, "George Washington's Anti-Slavery Legacy," *The Federalist,* accessed May 16, 2019, https://thefederalist.com/2016/02/22/george -washingtons-anti-slavery-legacy/.

EPILOGUE

1. *Annual Report* (Mount Vernon, VA: The Mount Vernon Ladies' Association of the Union, 1936), 54.

2. Henry Lee, *Funeral Oration on the Death of General Washington* (Boston: Printed for Joseph Nancrede and Manning & Loring, 1800), 10.

3. John Cotton Smith, *The Correspondence and Miscellanies of the Hon. John Cotton Smith with an Eulogy Pronounced before the Connecticut Historical Society at New Haven, May 27th, 1846. By the Rev. William W. Andrews* (New York: Harper & Brothers, 1847), 224–225. Smith's account, published years after the reported event in an extremely critical essay of Thomas Jefferson, was most likely somewhat exaggerated.

4. William P. Cutler and Julia P. Cutler, *Life, Journals, and Correspondence of Rev. Manasseh Cutler, LL.D.*, vol. 2 (Cincinnati, OH: R. Clarke & Co., 1888), 56–57.

5. Martha Washington, December 31, 1799, quoted in John Adams, *The Works of John Adams*, vol. 9 (Boston: Little, Brown and Co., 1856), 92.

6. "Virginia F. F's.," *Cleveland Daily Leader*, September 26, 1865.

7. Abigail Adams to Mary Adams, December 21, 1800, in Fritz Hirschfeld, *George Washington and Slavery: A Documentary Portrayal* (Columbia: University of Missouri Press, 1997), 214.

8. Horace Binney, *Bushrod Washington* (Philadelphia: C. Sherman & Son, 1858), 25–26.

9. "Letter, Martha Washington to Fanny Bassett Washington, May 24, 1795," *George Washington's Mount Vernon*, accessed May 21, 2019, www.mountvernon.org/education/primary-sources-2/article/letter-martha-washington-to-fanny-bassett-washington-may-24-1795/.

10. Information about enslaved people has been drawn from Washington's 1786 and 1799 slave lists: George Washington, Diary, February 18, 1786, and "Washington's Slave List," 1799, *PGW*; "List of the Different Drafts of Negros," ca. 1802, in scrapbook, box 34, Peter Family Archives, Washington Library.

Index